CHALLENGES BEFORE BUSINESS EDUCATION IN INDIA

CHALLENGES BEFORE BUSINESS EDUCATION IN INDIA

Chief Editor
S.S. HUGAR

Associate Editors
S.G. HUNDEKAR ★ R.L. HYDERABAD
M.R. SHOLLAPUR

ATLANTIC

ATLANTIC PUBLISHERS AND DISTRIBUTORS

Published by
ATLANTIC PUBLISHERS AND DISTRIBUTORS
B-2, Vishal Enclave, Opp. Rajouri Garden, New Delhi-110027
Phones : 5413460, 5429987

Sales Office
4215/1, Ansari Road, Darya Ganj, New Delhi-110 002
Phones : 3273880, 3285873, 3280451
Fax : 91-11-3285873
e-mail : info@atlanticbooks.com
web : www.atlanticbooks.com

ISBN 81-269-0043-1

Typeset at
APD Computer Graphics, Delhi
Printed in India at
Mehra Offset Press, Delhi

PREFACE

The New Economic Policy has brought about a sea change in the Indian Economy. The LPG (Liberalisation, Privatisation and Globalisation) process has drastically changed the situation in the business world. Of course, changes are very common in the business world as this field is highly sensitive to various variations. This ever changing phenomenon of business world has posed varieties of challenges to Business Education. The main task of Business Education is, therefore, to make students fit to face the challenges of ever changing business environment. This warrants a dynamic approach on the part of all concerned serving in different areas of Business Education. With this background, a 'National Seminar on Business Education in India — Backward and Forward Linkages' was organised during March 1998, so as to pool the ideas of academicians, institutions engaged in imparting Business Education and business world.

This National Seminar happily coincided with the Golden Jubilee of country's Independence and 40th anniversary of our Postgraduate Department of Studies in Commerce. Hence, it is a matter of jubilation for all of us to associate ourselves in this academic endeavour. The P.G. Department of Studies in Commerce of our University is the oldest Department in the State of Karnataka.

We are immensely thankful to our beloved Vice-Chancellor Dr. A.M. Pathan who has been kind enough in extending his moral and material support to this venture. Similarly, our thanks are due to all the authorities of the University who have helped in materialising this programme.

We extend our profound sense of gratitude to Prof. C.M. Kotturashettar, Dr. K.S. Daniel and Shri K. Nagendra Babu for their constant inspiration, encouragement and co-operation throughout these days. We express our gratitude to all the contributors who have timely responded to our invitation. We will be failing in our duty if we don't acknowledge with high sense of gratitude to all our patrons who have come forward generously to support us. Last but not the least, we are indebted to M/s Atlantic Publishers and Distributors, New Delhi for their kind response in bringing out this volume neatly and attractively.

—Editors

CONTENTS

Preface v

1. Business Education — An Integrated Approach 1
   —*R.M. Chidambaram*
2. Business Education — Forward Linkages 5
   —*H.R. Appannaiah*
3. Globalisation and Rethinking of Business Education in India 13
   —*Parimal Vyas* and *Sandip Bhatt*
4. Business Education in India — Challenges and Opportunities 25
   —*Nafees Baig*
5. Role of Business Education in India 30
   —*T. Aranganathan*
6. Perspectives of Entrepreneurship Education and Training 39
   —*D. Nagayya* and *P.B. Appa Rao*
7. Reviving Commerce Education — Need for a Radical Approach 51
   —*G. Kotrappa*
8. Business Education for Rural/Semi-Urban Youth 54
   —*S. Narasing Rao*
9. Business and Education : Interlinkage and Emerging Challenges 62
   —*M.R. Patil* and *T.M. Popker*
10. Management Education — Strategic Issues 70
    —*M.C. Poornima*
11. Business Education Through Information Technology : Virtual-Classroom and Resource Sharing 81
    —*H.K. Shubhangi*

12. Case Study Approach as an Effective Tool for Teaching Business Studies : A Model Building — 87
—M.R. Shollapur

13. Innovations in Management Education — Some Structural Issues — 99
—A.H. Chachadi

14. Progress and Problems of Business Education in India Since Independence — 112
—Z.U. Kahrioowala, Rais Ahmad Khan and *M.S.M. Al-Shaikh*

15. Computer Based Business Simulation Games — A Method of Teaching — 118
—M. Manickam

16. Computer Application in Business Education — A Forward Linkage — 126
—C.S. Rayudu and *S.B. Nageswara Rao*

17. Current Issues in Commerce Education — 131
—S.S. Hugar and *S.G. Hundekar*

18. Training the Trainers in Business Education — Impact of Refresher Courses in Commerce and Economics — 136
—M.R. Chandawarkar

19. Progress and Problems of Business Education During 50 Years of Post-Independence Period — 151
—K.K. Kuriakose

20. Business Education : A Manifesto for Rethinking — 155
—Shreedhar Shetty and *Manjunath Kotian*

21. Challenges Before Business Education in India in Open Regime — 162
—C. Kishan Rao

22. Towards Restructuring Business Education — 171
—P.S. Yadapadithaya and *M.P. Hrishikesh*

23. Challenges Before Business Education in India — 176
—A.B. Kalkundrikar

24. Skill-Building : A Key to Curriculum Development in Commerce Education 183
—S.G. Hundekar and *M.R. Shollapur*

25. Challenges Before Business Education 188
—M.R. Hegde

26. Business Education in India — Forward and Backward Linkages 193
—A.C. Bhawsar and *M.K. Rakibe*

27. Business Education Needs Change 198
—B. Vijaya and *Bheemanagouda*

28. TQM in Management Education : Restructuring Paradigm 205
—A.P. Kalkundri

29. Emerging Trends in Business Education : A Critical Review 215
—A.G. Prasad and *M.R. Chandawarkar*

30. Business Education in India — Backward and Forward Linkages 226
—Y. Vrushabhendrappa

31. New Dimensions of Business Education in India 232
—E.B. Brahmankar

32. The Role of Academicians and Practising Managers in Today's Business Education 237
—Sandeep Shandilya

33. Challenges Before Commerce Education in India 246
—G.Y. Shitole

34. Commerce Education in Indian Universities : A Study of Students Enrolment 256
—S.S. Ainapur and *C.S. Basavaraj*

35. Action Plan for 21st Century Business Education 264
—P.N. Udayachandra

36. Case Approach for Management Education 270
—K. Swamy

37. Progress and Problems of Business Education During 50 Years of Post-Independence Period 276
—S.H. Tekkannavar

38. Challenges Before Business Education 283
—V.M. Bhandari

39. Challenges Before Business Education 290
—S.G. Kulkarni

40. The Challenges Before Business Education in India 295
—G.A. Hegde

41. Business Education : Problems and Solutions 300
—P.G. Dandin

42. Business Education for Posterity 305
—R.V. Ganachari

43. Business Education in India : Renaissance — Need of the Hour 308
—G.L. Narayanappa, D. Pradeep Kumar and *V. Mallikarjuna*

44. Challenges Before Business Education in India in Open Regime 313
—B.L. Pawar

45. Business Education in Retrospect and Prospect 320
—J.G. Naik

46. University-Industry Interface in Business Education 326
—M.R. Shollapur

47. Management of University B-Schools 335
—R.L. Hyderabad

48. Re-Designing of Commerce Education in India in the Context of Changing Business Environment 344
—D. Obul Reddy

49. Impact of E-Commerce and Internet on Accounting Education, Profession and Practice 358
—P.B. Appa Rao

List of Contributors 370

1 Business Education — An Integrated Approach

—R.M. CHIDAMBARAM

Business education programmes assume greater significance today due to the following reasons :

1. Entrepreneurial cult makes youngsters to learn the intricacies of business.
2. Business houses prefer people with qualifications in business education.
3. Better employment prospects motivate many to aspire degrees/diplomas in business education.
4. Business education programmes offer a good scope for self-employment ventures.
5. The policy of Liberalisation aims at removing the shackles to business development. Better business prospects make universities to launch a number of need-based business education programmes.
6. Variety requirements and wide markets are the outcome of globalisation. This necessitates learners to acquire knowledge in foreign exchange, import and export procedure, etc.
7. In a vast country like India where population is ever increasing, consumption is inevitable. As consumption is very closely associated with marketing, the need for marketing personnel is ever growing. Demand-Supply mismatch motivates many to register themselves for business education programmes.
8. In a growing economy, business complexities are common. Courses on business law thrive much as those

qualified in law have good opportunities to wade away such complexities.

Indian universities offer a number of business education progarmmes both at the graduate and postgraduate levels. B.A. (Economics), B. Com., B. Coop. (Bachelor of Cooperation), B.B.A. (Bachelor of Business Administration), B.B.M. (Bachelor of Bank Management), B.C.S. (Bachelor of Corporate Secretaryship), B.L. M.A. (Business Economics), M. Com., M. Coop., M.B.A., M.B.M., M.C.S. and M.L. are to name a few.

Institutes like IIMs, Institute of Company Secretaries of India, Indian Institute of Foreign Trade, Institute of Chartered Accountants of India, Indian Institute of Bankers, Insurance Institute of India, and Institute of Cost and Works Accountants of India offer business education in the chosen area.

Universities also offer courses in business education through distance education mode. In fact, instruction through distance education mode is instrumental for the popularity of business education in India.

While appreciating the development of business education in India in the recent past, educationists have to come across certain valid criticisms. Few such criticisms are narrated below :

1. Business education programmes are not comprehensive in the sense Management courses lack accounting thrust, commerce students lack knowledge in functional management areas, Bank Management students lack awareness in general commercial laws and students of Corporate Secretaryship lack the required knowledge in banking practice.
2. The training component is either inadequate or ineffective in most of the programmes offered by Indian universities. As the Distance Education Directorates handle numerous students simultaneously, the extent of the casualty is very much.
3. Industry-University interaction is yet to be a reality in the Indian scene especially in the case of business education programmes.

Suggestions given below can be thought of by universities to make business education programmes value-added and need-based :

1. Any business education programme is complete only when it has the components of functional management areas, accounting concepts, business laws, corporate administration, banking law and practice, life and general insurance, basic mathematical concepts, quantitative techniques, entrepreneurial culture and development, business economics, monetary management, import and export procedures, business communication and Computer Operations. It is impossible to incorporate all these aspects either in a 3-year graduate programme or a 2-year postgraduate programme. As such business education programmes offered by universities are not comprehensive. It is suggested to launch an integrated programme for 5-year duration in order to give a comprehensive coverage of all aspects of business education. Though the programme is for 5-year duration, an option may be given for learners to withdraw on the successful completion of 3-year study.

2. Business education programmes sans practical training have no relevance. Functional Managers, Chartered Accountants, Bankers, Insurers, Export Houses, Corporates, Cooperative Institutions and Lawyers can give better practical exposure in the chosen areas. As training is sandwiched in between two years of study, the scope for intensive and extensive training is more in a 5-year integrated business education programme. Observation training should not be encouraged throughout the training period. Hands-on experience is essential. In order to make practical training a rewarding exercise, universities have to interact with industrial houses as a regular feature.

3. Academic bodies have to identify the requirements of business and industry. Similarly industrial houses have to pinpoint their requirements to academics. This is possible only when there is effective interaction between

universities and industries. While designing the course content for business education programmes, associating the concerned business/industrial houses will be a boon in the sense that those successfully completing such programmes find better placements.

4. Associating with academics, offering suggestions for curriculum revision, and engaging learners as trainees are some of the responsibilities to be undertaken by business/industrial houses as social obligations for mutual benefit and development.

To include, an integrated approach is essential for business education programmes not only to design a comprehensive curriculum for a duration of 5 years, but also to integrate the well established theoretical concepts to the practicalities of business and to ensure interaction between universities and industries as an ongoing process for ever.

2 Business Education — Forward Linkages

—H.R. APPANNAIAH

For the past eight years, Indian economy has undergone several changes. With the introduction of New Economic Policy in 1991, "Market Economy" concept has been given full scope. This looked like a better change for first five years. Annual growth rate of the economy was increased (Today 7.2%), due to liberal economic and financial policies. Structural changes like scaling down the role of PSUs, encouraging private sector, attracting MNCs to participate in Indian business, adopting voluntary retirement schemes, closure of sick units, large scale automation in business operations have made the educational sector to restructure its operations. Structural changes in the economy have a greater impact on business education in India.

"Business education", as it is called today, has to be given a new look and has to become more effective to cater to the needs of the changing economic scenario of the country. "Commerce education", as it was called before, was identified as a professional course by the central and state governments, specialised educational promoters like U.G.C. and Universities. Though the "Professional" status was given, the operations and curriculum were general in character and this segment of education was allowed to grow only in general stream. In the process, professional concept is missing in commerce education. This was the main cause as to why the business houses did not and are not accepting our graduates for carrying out their business operations. There was a mismatch between the expectations of business houses of the commerce graduates and the university curriculum in commerce education. Commerce education which originally started as a diploma course, gradually assumed the status of degree in the universities of the country with more of pure economics subjects. The course content was more of knowledge based and was generic. Aptitudes and skills required for business operations were missing. Only recently, new dimensions were added to the course content. Accounting, finance, statistics, secretaryship studies, and management subjects were brought into the curriculum business education is now crystalising.

TOMORROW'S NEEDS

Change is a must and it should be a continuous activity for growth. This applies to every business enterprise. Tomorrow's business enterprises will have the following features :

— Tomorrow's business house will be a changing enterprise moving with changes in the economy.

— Human resources at work in business houses will consist primarily of highly skilled and knowledgable workers.

— Team spirit becomes the order of the business enterprise.

— The business houses become flatter and thinner due to the introduction of automation in business operations like internet, multi-media, and other host of automatic equipment. It will have a global character.

— Employees, though agitate in the initial stages for such changes, gradually adjust to these changes. They have to work in multi-cultural environment.

— As the policies and strategies of business will be changing, the human element will be a learning element.

— Business operations need more of skills. Production will shift to products with small amounts of material but with larger components of human intelligence and skill.

— More technology flows in, from domestic and foreign sources and it will be at a greater speed. Life cycle of methods, procedure and strategies becomes shorter. Fast flow of technology makes the product related strategies to change. This demands greater flexibility in business operations and in workers.

This is the broad scenario of future business enterprises. The current day commerce education is nowhere catering to the needs of these business operations. We are aware as to what sort of business graduates we are producing. The current curriculum is not encouraging independent thinking and behaviour. It is not instilling self-confidence in those who seek business education. Business enterprises need visionary leaders. The course content should contain communication skill development programmes to develop these visionaries. Curriculum should help the students to learn the business process on their own, utilising the available infrastructural facilities like learned guides (teachers), Library, information systems, sports, studying the life styles of contemporary successful entrepreneurs, exposure to business operations, etc. The course should direct the learners to develop team spirit, tolerance, entrepreneurship, negotiation skills, scholarship and problem finding (forecasting) skills. Hence the change. The concept of "Business Education" is replacing "Commerce Education". The new concept is yet to be properly defined to cover industry, trade, farm and service sectors. The learning process has to be restructured. Turn around activity has to take place to give a practical look to the business education.

THE TRACK (PATH WAY)

As said earlier, the business operations will be ever changing as "change" is an essential aspect of growth. The business educators should understand this. The business environment should be analysed before developing the curriculum. As on today, "Service Sector" is growing at a faster rate in the Indian economy. Manufacturing and farm activities are also assuming the new dimension of "Specialisation". Business educators should also forecast the direction of growth of the economy. Spot the sectors likely to boom in future and design the curriculum accordingly. It should also be noted that annual examination should not only be the parameter to judge the capacity of business graduates to take up positions in business houses. "Skill development" should occupy the prime place in business education. Communication skills, understanding and analysing work culture in business houses, decision making skills, leadership skills, crisis management skills, conflict management skills have to be developed in the students. These can be achieved only through the interaction with business houses. But there is an apprehension that business houses do not interact with educational institutions and university bodies. This is not true. Without making an attempt we come to the conclusion.

Business houses are also badly in need of quality human resources to run their show. They have also realised the importance of "Quality" in their business operations. They are having regular training programmes for their workers. Training and development of human resources according to the needs of business houses have become a common feature. Business educationists should realise this and design the educational programme in such a way that these trained people can comfortably occupy positions in business houses, thus bringing down the cost of training in business houses. Business houses are also interested in having interaction with university departments and business colleges. Attempts are already on here and there. But only a beginning has to be made to bring together these two — business educationists and business houses.

The track-Forecasting the business operations, restructuring the course, interaction with business houses, training the trainers is rugged. Where there is will there is way. It can be achieved with an "Action Plan" and the sincere efforts of all concerned.

ACTION PLAN

Restructuring of business education can take place in two levels : 1. Graduate level and 2. Postgraduate level.

Level-1 : In the first level emphasis should be given to develop basic knowledge of business and specialisation in one area of business.

Nearly ninety per cent of students dropout at degree level. They should fit into either self-employment or paid-employment with the basic business knowledge and skill they acquire during these three years of their study.

The course content at this level should be as follows :

The first two years should have the core subjects with practical component in each subject and three should be examination for both theory and practicals.

The practical component in each subject should contain group study, role play, simulation exercises, communication skills, interaction with specialists in the field in the form of guest lectures and discussion. Audio-visual aids should be profusely used to impart knowledge and skill. Field surveys on local business and economic problems can be conducted on a smaller scale which gives more knowledge about business operations.

In the third year, one area of business has to be specialised. The thrust should be on skill development. Business areas for specialisation can be : (i) Marketing, (ii) Finance, (iii) Human resource management, (iv) Production management, (v) One of the areas in service sector like tourism, hospitality management, health care services, personal care services, educational services, (vi) Accounting, (vii) Secretaryship studies, (viii) Entrepreneurship development. Field work and interaction with industries, service and farm sectors should take place in third year. Students have to be exposed to business world.

FACULTY

Faculty have a greater role to pay. They should come out of the existing method of teaching and dictating notes. Teachers should acquire the role of "mentors". They should not only teach, but also involve themselves in developing skills amongst the students. The classroom teaching technique should be changed. The classroom should be equipped with audio-visual aids to make teaching more interesting. Notes dictating should be fully stopped. Colour charts, diagrams, transparencies, should be profusely used to explain the concepts and topic material. At the end of each chapter, cyclostyled chapter synopsis has to be given. Four to six assignments on each subject of study should be given and they are to be corrected by teachers. Every teacher should undergo periodical training to equip oneself with development in business operations. They should have continuous interaction with business houses and professional bodies, to acquire first hand information about the areas of their teaching. "Trainers training" should be continuous activity in every business education institution. Every teacher should be made to subscribe individually atleast for two business magazines of their choice.

Level-2 : At the second level — postgraduate level, business education faculty should possess all the business branches like

Marketing, Finance, HRM, Production, Secretaryship Studies, Accounting, Entrepreneurship development, International marketing, Business Services, etc. These departments, under business education faculty, (existing commerce faculty) should have focus on research and development. Each department should have interaction with business houses and should take up consultancy for business houses in their field of specialisation. The graduates who take up masters courses in these branches should be made to participate in field studies and research work taken by the business houses. It is possible only with continuous interaction with business houses. Postgraduate departments in business education should become virtually the consultancy service centres for business houses. The initiative and drive is a must from the P.G. Centres in converting these centres into research and consultancy wings of business houses. The vision and creativity of these centres and the resources, both human and technical, should be used to develop students at the grass-roots level *i.e.* Graduate level.

Finally, these two levels have to work in an integrated manner, to achieve quality and professionalism in business education. Discussing the possibilities of improving the quality of business education in seminars and conferences can provide solution to the problems faced by this educational system. These meets definitely create awareness. An action plan be prepared in this direction by involving the following organisations :

1. Postgraduate centres of business education of each University of Karnataka.
2. Federation of Karnataka Chambers of Commerce and Industry and their affiliated organs throughout the state.
3. Federation of Teachers Councils of Commerce and Management in Karnataka and their affiliated Forums of each University of Karnataka.
4. Interested business educationists and business houses.
5. The local chapters of professional institutes like, ACA, IC&WA, Chartered Secretary Institute, etc.

The organisers of this seminar can take lead in this direction and form "Business Education Council of Karnataka" — BECK.

FUNDING

Finance looks to be a major constraint. But this can be solved, if we can give an insight into this problem. It is only in the initial stages of restructuring, substantial money is required. This has to be borne by the beneficiaries.

Level-1

At the first level, colleges have to provide necessary infrastructure like fully equipped classrooms (classrooms fixed with audio-visual aids), a quality library, cassette library, (provision for playing cassettes on the respective subjects), faculty development programmes and personality development programmes for students. This is the area where huge money is required. The college managements should be made to provide these facilities at their cost, obtaining funds from UGC, wherever possible. If these conditions are incorporated in the course content, it becomes mandatory for managements to provide these facilities. This solves major financial problem.

It is also essential that members of faculty should equip themselves by spending atleast one per cent of their earnings. This spending makes them to identify more with the course and profession. The spending will be in the form of subscribing to the quality business periodicals, participation in seminars and conferences and designing and developing teaching aids, contribution for programmes on training.

The concerted effort of managements, teachers and local business houses can solve the funding problem to a greater extent. The state will also participate in its own way by sanctioning some grants.

Level-2

At the second level — P.G. Level — the funds can be obtained in four forms : (i) The University funds (from development schemes), (ii) Consultancy and service charges from the business houses, (iii) Direct grants from the funding agencies like UGC, ICSR, Philanthropic business houses and (iv) By taking up government and private projects on business activities. The funds collected from these sources will be sufficient to take up research programmes and consultancy services.

ANNEXURE

RESTRUCTURED MODEL FOR A COLLEGE

At the first level, which is the basic level, firm foundation should be laid. The following "Model" or "Action Plan" can be adopted to restructure the business education at first level :

— Review the existing situation of the college in the light of restructuring the system. Identify the strengths and weakness.

— Spell out the "Focus" and "Positioning" ideas as a part of restructuring the system, keeping in view a time frame of five years. Management, teachers and interested parents have to be involved in this process.

— Design a promotional plan for the college in the backdrop of restructured system.

— Develop faculty improvement programmes to convert teachers as mentors.

— Identify and provide necessary equipped classrooms, library and laboratory.

— Develop alliances with local business houses, to develop joint projects, student training programmes during vacation, drawing faculty from these enterprises to teach in the college. Mous, if possible, can be entered into.

— Conduct personality development programmes, availing expertise from outside.

— Set up a review panel including management, teachers and industry mentors to get feedback and to adopt corrective measures.

3 Globalisation and Rethinking of Business Education in India

—PARIMAL VYAS AND SANDIP BHATT

Globalisation can be defined as "The degree of openness in most countries".

Globalisation refers to "A process of increasing economic integration and growing economic interdependence between countries in the World economy".

Globalisation is associated not only with an increasing cross-boundary movement of goods, services, capital, technology, information and people but also with an organisation of economic activities which straddles national boundaries. However, more significant than globalisation of trade and commerce is the globalisation of business education resultant into globalisation of knowledge.

An attempt has been made to review and evaluate the emerging business education scenario in India as on now and strategies that the country's business schools need to follow for ensuring a high degree of self-reliance and, hence, national development.

In the introduction part possible objectives of business education are listed. The part I brings out significant developments that have taken place in India and the world economy in context of ongoing winds of globalisation. The part II provides a brief sketch on initiation of offering of business education in India and also other crucial issues relating to business education like courses, technology, language, structure, course coverage and offerings, study inputs, teaching methodology, inexperienced participants, teaching standards, and so on.

The part III throws light on certain broad-based generalisations with regard to offering of business education in India as perceived, reflected and expressed by researchers, academicians, industry experts, bureaucrats and management consultants from time to time. The paper is concluded at the end.

To sum up, business education needs to become qualitative, customised contingent, pragmatic and purposive. It needs to be focussed on specialised areas of applications and also for not-for-profit organisations. It calls for maintaining standards both from faculties and participants with techno-cum-tool based teaching and study inputs with the help of networking of schools to result into common norms at an entry level and also for infrastructure, support services and evaluation for the beneficiaries and business schools. It should consider public policy, build in definite core spiritual human values, and also advocate for business ethics with strong socio-economic orientation among those who offer and also for the participants. To the end, it is needless to say that those business schools which will set up new social contacts and integrated competitive strategy in order to improve performance, competitiveness and adaptiveness will only survive whereas others will deservedly close down.

BACKGROUND

The cutting edge for excellence at the national, corporate, group or individual level will be provided by the professional excellence of human resources. Excellence of human resources requires a thrust in quality professional education, which is in apparent conflict with the national implementation of the concept of equity.

Management Education (or) Business Education referred as synonymous in this article. It has become prestigious in India with increasing complexities and uncertainties due to changing business environmental conditions, upward moving awareness about social accountability and rising social expectations to result into improved performance standards and decent living to all.

INTRODUCTION

It is indeed commendable on the part of the Powers that be Government, Business, University — to have realised the need and significance of business education in developing a cadre of competent, trained, skilled managerial human resources to meet the emerging challenges of our economy. It is evident that business education in India is here to stay and flourish. Not everything is very fine with business education in India. There are quite a few specific issues such as poor physical facilities, dearth of competent faculty, problem of teaching techniques, inadequate library, and laboratory facilities facing business education in our country which have to be met squarely and overcome successfully.

Knowledge is universal and must be applied to resolve problems of people either in business place or at society. Cross cultural co-operation of business education which must be time specific and location specific.

The aims of business schools alike business institutions, universities and Postgraduate departments offering business education may be outlined as follows :

- To turn out postgraduate in management adequately equipped to make an effective start in their development as management trainee.
- To bring out management researchers for teaching or research positions.
- To serve as repositories of management knowledge through the acquisition of an up-to-date library of management and allied literature.
- To undertake both basic and applied research in the field of management.
- To bring both new and existing management knowledge to industry, trade and commerce, Government and other users of such knowledge for the benefit of society in general.
- To organise supervisory and executive management development programmes both to develop existing, practicing managerial personnel and also to maintain

contact with latest frontiers of management knowledge and practices.

Now, what kind of business education is being imparted? Do the business schools satisfy all the requirements in real sense as specified in detail and elaborated by the AICTE, New Delhi? What are the emerging trends and their influences on business education in India? How are business schools needs to re-orient, update and improve their academic offerings in the wake of sweeping globalisation.

An attempt has been made to review and evaluate the emerging business education scenario in India as on now and strategies that the country's business education institutions need to follow for ensuring a high degree of self-reliance and, hence, national development. The paper is concluded at the end.

The late nineteenth century and early twentieth century period also witnessed globalisation.

Globalisation can be defined as "The degree of openness in most countries".

Globalisation refers to "A process of increasing economic integration and growing economic interdependence between countries in the World economy".

Globalisation is associated not only with an increasing cross-boundary movement of goods, services, capital, technology, information and people but also with an organisation of economic activities which straddles national boundaries, However, more significant than globalisation of trade and commerce is the globalisation of business education resultant into globalisation of knowledge.

PART-I

GLOBALISATION : INDIA AND THE WORLD ECONOMY

The logical way to start would be to foresee the likely socio-economic and other macroenvironmental changes and make an attempt to predict about what kind of shifts would be likely to come and also needed in the forthcoming years so that what would be needed on the part of the business schools to bring about and shape up "The whole person" in form of professional, positive, creative and committed Indian Manager as a mission objective along with academic objectives, moral and spiritual values and social sensibilities through social, intellectual and physical activities and induced performance standards.

Each economy has distinctive social profile, economic history and political structure with varying values system, customs and differing traditions of the given society. In India, our efforts at structural adjustment which began in the midst of the unprecedented financial and fiscal crisis in 1991 was based on the tenet that our objective of self-reliant growth and social justice called for a change in attitude towards and the form of microeconomic management both in respect of current problems and basic economic structure. The policies of liberalisation, marketisation, privatisation, and above all globalisation initiated were aimed at improving the competitiveness of Indian economy.

In India, we find increasing mobility, cultural homogenization, self-awareness about health, training and development and improving computer literacy in the recent past. The sizable growth of the infrastructure sector, emergence of the service sector, strategic focus on the small scale, rural and unorganised sector, rise of knowledge industry and lastly emergence of the middle class of country as the biggest consumption community are few significant happenings in India.

At this juncture, one cannot ignore global happenings, changes and trends in the much globalised world economy. To be brief, the world economy has witnessed emergence of black South Africa, collapse of communism, reunification of Europe, emergence of several regional trading blocs, World Trade Organisation (WTO) and formation of Trade Agreements like General Agreement on Trade and Tariff (GATT), the acceptance of product patents and intellectual property rights, awareness about human rights, ISO 9000, the microprocessor technological revolution and the end of the dominance of an American economy are some of the key highlights of the global developments in the near past.

PART-II

ISSUES RELATING TO GLOBALISATION AND BUSINESS EDUCATION IN INDIA

In a wide and more liberal vision of the world, business education is undergoing fundamental changes in its quality, content and approach. The move towards free market economy, efficiency and effectiveness due to transformation of regulated to liberalised and an open economy has opened the doors for globalisation of Indian industries.

The early sixties saw the emergence of evolution of premier management institutions *i.e.* IIMs, XLRI and we have around 1500 business schools with approximately 8000 seats in 1995 compared to just 6 business schools with 200 seats of 1962. We have several central and state universities with management faculties, Post-graduate departments imparting business education via offering of degrees, diplomas, certificate courses with the help of residential, full-time, part-time and/or via distance education or correspondence courses. We have specialised business schools like National Institute of Construction Management and Research, National Institute of Port Management, National Institute of Transport Management, National Institute of Bank Management, National Institute of Coal Management, National Institute of Plantation Management and others as well as management development centres and developed by the corporate sectors to meet the specific needs of the concerned industrial sectors. However, the success story of this impressive growth sounds hollow when the question of quality is raised.

To support, buttress and further strengthen recent developments in the world economy, Indian business schools face a tough task of developing the country's most crucial human resource to meet the emerging challenges. Globalisation calls for internationalisation and multinationalisation of business education in India. Globalisation of business education is also influenced by global business environment, interactions among Government, professional organisations, companies and business schools. It focuses on courses, technology, language, study inputs and course coverage, skills and strategies that will suit business schools in near future. It reveals following picture to us :

Courses

Professional business education started in India around 1960's earlier emphasised on learning by doing and on the basis of trial and error. We need to upgrade the quality of business education to exploit the emerging opportunities in the wake of globalisation, Bench-marking, TQM, Re-engineering, Strategic Alliances and so on in the global business. Indian business schools find it tough to offer world class business education because of inward-looking, anti-business and misperceived concept of self-sufficiency which has taken them away from major knowhow knowledge agreements. Any country which is of the view that it can develop without outside help cannot find a better recipe for committing suicide. The economy has no choice but to follow the path of liberalisation and globalisation.

Indian business schools need to develop a structure that puts emphasis on on-the-job training, updated knowledge on specialisation, and on "Global markets, strategic alliances, global competitiveness, new world economic order, joint ventures, objective benchmarking, global business linkages, and corporate work culture" with the accessibility and use of high information technology and communication medias in near future. The future managers of the country should be provided with indepth knowledge on global business, global economic environment, global marketing, and such other global developments in production, finance, business policy, organisation and strategic management.

Technology

Technology has also influenced managerial style, managerial decision-making, structure, system and services which in turn has also influenced offering of business education in the form of instructions, evaluations and interactions. Technology management has also emerged as key area and one needs to develop awareness among participants about changes and environmental impacts of science and technology on human lives. The rapid changes in the form of information technology in areas of computers, microprocessors, electronics and telecommunication revolutions have stimulated need to focus on increased use of multi-point conferencing across national boundaries, networking, multi-media use, virtual school and upper education, software packages and operating system in near future. The country should not build a wall against emerging innovative technologies in the name of self-reliance. Globalisation calls for developing international technology-orientation through appropriate course-adaptation in subjects like selection, negotiation and innovation in technology management to prepare the future managers for managing technology of the near future.

Language

There is no doubt about emergence of English language as the key language of the whole world. In the wake of the globalisation, one will be required to go beyond local, regional and national languages. As companies go global, understanding of value system, culture and traditions plays significant role in global markets. As it has been observed, we need to equip participants with atleast one or two courses of foreign language. We, therefore, come across a number of business schools to have tie-ups with foreign universities, faculty exchange programme and arrangement of overseas studies and training for students studying in India.

Structure

Business schools abroad are modifying their curriculum and syllabus to introduce necessary changes in courses. Indian business schools have a long way to go if they have to remain relevant in an ever-changing business environment with increased emphasis on cost-reduction, productivty, quality, customer-service and innovative product offerings to meet the challenges of modernisation and competitiveness. Some of the important weaknesses of business schools can be put forward as follows :

Course Coverage and Offerings

Most of the business schools offer a large number of variety of business courses to cover almost all areas of management. Taking available time-frame and duration of variety of business courses and considering its nature of offering like full-time, part-time Degree, Diploma, Certificate and correspondence courses by a large number of schools, they hardly manage to provide reasonable working knowledge that too in selected topics of basic areas of management like production, HRD, finance and marketing and because of such fragmented approach these basic courses turn into time-bound capsules which fail to create an interest, insight and research-orientation among the participants. At the end, these schools just manage to teach only compulsory courses in a brief way.

Study Inputs

The Indian business schools have long depended upon case-studies and study-materials from business schools of abroad, and little attempt has been made to develop indigenous study inputs.

Teaching Methodology

The teaching methodology mainly consists of lectures, group-discussions and case-studies. It is high time that business schools inevitably decide to offer techno-cum-tool based instruction by preparing suitable mixture of available sophisticated teaching aids and study inputs to participants in near future.

Inexperienced Participants

One the problems confronting business schools is inexperienced students. These factors must be borne in mind while designing courses and curriculum.

Teaching Standards

Teaching standards have deteriorated generally because teaching has emerged as an unattractive profession in India on one hand and the mushroom growth of business schools in all kinds of places with or without potentiality and basic facilities to tap the emerging business opportunities on the other hand. The quality of those who teach with and without academic vigour, experience and exposure to industry also needs crucial consideration.

To Conclude

The majority of business schools which consists of premier institutions, university departments, deemed universities, colleges and other institutions offer courses in a seller's market as they manage to produce around 6000 management students against expected requirement of 15000 management students each year and there is an increasing demand for management Postgraduates in the near future. This attributes towards slower improvement in performance and qualitative offerings of business education in India.

PART-III

The business schools need to provide qualitative, contingent, pragmatic and purposive business education in the wake of the information explosion, reform era and technological developments taking place in our country.

As on now, it makes one to offer following broad-based generalisations with regard to offering of business education in India as perceived, reflected and expressed by researchers, academicians, industry experts, bureaucrats and management consultants as well as educators from time to time.

Business education has to address itself in a big way to not-for-profit organisations like educational institutions, schools, colleges, universities, hospitals, government departments offering public utilities and other service institutions where the primary objective is to provide the basic infrastructure to any business or industry.

We need to develop customised courses as most of the participant view business education as an instrument to earn Degree/Diploma/ Certificate and to advance career prospects. Most of the business schools offer specialisation in core areas like Finance, Marketing, Production, HRD and so on. They need to focus on relatively neglected customised areas which calls for application of management education namely Technology Management, Service Management, Health-care Management, Energey Management, Tourism Management, Transportation Management, Water Management and Soil and Forest Management in order to exploit available vast reservoir of natural and human resources of our country.

In matter of maintaining a minimum standard and some sort of uniformity of courses, evaluation, instruction, interaction, participation and admission, we witness huge differences among premier business schools, reputed management institutions and university departments of different qualities and/or grades and till date we feel strong absence of a statutory body which may look into academic, administrative and accredition norms to rationalise, regulate and also promote purposive business education in India.

The business education should focus on developing entrepreneurial initiative, leadership qualities, long-term perspective and achievement motivation.

The business education should increasingly become participatory.

We need a networking of business schools which should go beyond a forum for increasing cooperation and collaboration among them.

It shall conduct admission test for each of the business schools at the national level with the help of a professional agency to ensure just and fair admission to business programmes. It can also make integrative efforts to prepare business professionals alike Chartered Accountants through homogeneous offerings in instruction, study inputs and evaluation.

At the end, the business schools should also emphasise on "Development" rather than merely training.

Conclusion

The basic objective of business education is to promote, provide and ensure optimum use of scarce resources of the economy to meet rising social expectations through improved performance standards to offer decent living to all. There exists urgent need to expand the frontiers of business education in under-managed or neglected customised areas of management to tap available opportunities and resources of our economy. It is high time that business education focuses on "Public Policy" issue in imparting instruction and training to future managerial resource of the country. It should offer a sound business education with definite values as well as ability to analyse, evaluate, interpret and understand present socio-economic issues and business challenges facing the country.

The process of globalisation has posed many threats and challenges to companies, business schools and the country. If we will not reorient business schools it will create problems relating to commitment, creativity, innovativeness and thrust areas of application to improve standard of living. The government and business schools would have to rethink, reconsider and suitably alter their roles to face the challenges of education. To the end, those business schools which will set up new social contacts and integrated competitive strategy in order to improve performance and adaptiveness will survive whereas others will deservedly close down.

4 Business Education in India — Challenges and Opportunities

—NAFEES BAIG

In India, the growth of business education is directly linked to the process of economic development. The concept that commerce, trade and industry, etc. do not require any formal education and training does not hold good now. It is firmly believed that for any successful pursuit of business, education and training in the principles and concepts of business are essential. There is a need for education and training of a new generation of businessmen with fresh outlook and dynamic approach to the present day business problems. This is more so when we require talented young men and women to man the five year plans initiated to usher in socio-economic growth and development in our society.

IS BUSINESS EDUCATION LIBERAL, PROFESSIONAL OR TECHNICAL?

There is a long-standing controversy as to whether business should be treated as liberal, academic-oriented and broad-based or it should be taken as professional or technical education. There is some degree of uncertainty and anomaly in this regard. Those who hold the view that business discipline should be treated just like other University disciplines, argue that Universities should produce generally and liberally educated people and not technicians and professionals. Universities have to educate and not to train and thus business graduates should be given in-service training and not pre-service training in the Universities[1]. On the other hand, in most, of the University manuals and handbooks, business courses are mentioned as professional courses. While it is generally correct that the business courses are and should be liberal, broad-based and academic-oriented in the sense that our products are not prepared for direct placement in the jobs in trade, commerce and industry, at the same time, we should teach to our students the basics of business and industry so that they may tackle the day-to-day problems of business. They are provided with basic tools to handle any business situation in the practical sense of the term. It implies that the business graduates enter the broad market of industry, trade and commerce with certain fundamental or basic business principles and general knowledge but without specific or special skills. The V.K.R.V. Rao Committee (1961) has also observed that commerce or bustness education is a University discipline and must fulfil the broad liberal requirements of University Education[2].

NEED AND OBJECTIVE

With the start of planning in India in 1951, there has been tremendous demand for human resource to man the economic plan for our socio-economic advancement. As a natural corollary to this, the demand for business education has also risen. It has now grown from a subject to a full-fledged faculty in most of the Universities. In addition to this, non-University institutions and institutes of professional and technical nature like the Indian Institute of Bankers, the Indian Institute of Company Secretaries, the Institute of Chartered Accountants of India, the Institute of Cost and Works Accountants of India, etc. and various courses on business run by the central and state Govts., and Council of Technical Education, Govt. of India bear testimony to the popularity of business education and its growth in the country in recent years.

OBJECTIVES

The Radhakrishnan Committee Report on University education gave its verdict that commerce or Business education and courses offered in commerce or business by the Universities were not clear. The V.K.R.V. Rao Committee on commerce education laid down the following objectives of commerce education[3] :

1. The primary object of commerce education must be imparting liberal education of the same kind as is available to graduates in other subjects.

2. Commerce education has to give a graduate some special aptitudes which is not likely to accompany the imparting of education in other fields.
3. Specialized knowledge in commerce subjects should be imparted at postgraduate level rather than at the undergraduate level.
4. Specialization should be preceded by basic liberal education and grounding in the tool subjects of language, accounts, law and economics.

In view of recent developments and advancements in the industrial arena of the country it may be spelled out that the following may be taken as the broad objectives of business education in the country :

(i) Giving general grounding to the students in the tool subjects of Economics, Statistics and Mathematics, etc.
(ii) Imparting professional education in the field of accounting, Audit, Secretarial work, Banking, Commercial and Industrial laws, etc.
(iii) Developing expertise among students in tackling business problems at macro and micro levels.
(iv) Inculcating entrepreneurial talents for promoting industrial and business activity.
(v) Creating skills in the student for self-employment.

In view of these objectives, the business education in the country needs structural and academic reforms in the field of curriculum, syllabi, examination system, teaching methodology, evaluation, assessment, and other related matters like faculty development, orientation, refresher courses, etc. It, thus, becomes now imperative that a meaningful linkage should be established between the business education and the socio-economic milieu obtaining in the country. This calls for drastic changes, reforms and improvements in the present state of affairs in regard to course contents, teaching and research methodology, teacher improvement plans, structural and academic changes in the management of business education in the country, etc.

There is a general complaint against business graduates that they are not given enough practical training. In some countries a degree/diploma is not granted till a student undergoes a training programme in some office, industrial establishment, social organisation, club or association, etc. We may also introduce similar system of training to our graduates so that they become proficient in the skill of analytical ability and problem solving. Attendance by students in seminars, symposia, discussion, debates, paper reading, quiz programmes, G.K. Competitions, dialogues elocution contests, and participation of students in social service programme, etc. should become the order of the day. Likewise, educational tours, excursions, visits to manufacturing establishments, and continuous interaction with managers, etc. of business and industry should form an important ingredient of the educational curricula. Writing of project reports and sessionals/papers should also form part of the syllabi of business courses. The various Departments/Faculties should undertake writing of book projects keeping in view the needs and objectives of business education. Audio-visual aids should be utilized for making the course-contents interesting. In these days of explosion of electronic media, the role of T.Vs, radios, projectors, video cassettes, etc. cannot be over-emphasized. Due advantage should be taken to improve and streamline business education through these media.

The most important allegation against business education is that of its aloofness and isolation from the realities of the business world. There is a need, therefore, to have liaison and cooperation between the business community and the business education. The education imparted should be linked to the industry situation while the industry should cooperate with educational authorities in the preparation of syllabi, training programme, etc. for the benefit of business graduates. There should then be greater interaction between the two worlds — the academic and the business world.

RESTRICTED INTAKE

There has been a mushroom growth of business institutes in recent years. The time has come when we should restrict the intake of students in business stream. Quality would be preferred to the quality and there must be a meaningful restriction on the admission to Business Courses.

DISTANCE EDUCATION IN BUSINESS

The concepts of "Open University", "distance education" and "correspondence courses" are emerging as new dimensions in the field of education. As a corollary to the restrictions of admission in regular courses, these new vistas will meet the pressure on enrolment by opening up of opportunities for higher education in Business.

TEACHERS' TRAINING AND IMPROVEMENT PROGRAMMES

It has become now essential to provide to teachers some sort of training for their development at regular intervals. The establishment of Academic Staff Colleges in various Universities by the U.G.C. is a welcome step in this direction.

RESEARCH

In the field of research in business, there is a problem of developing "research culture" in our University departments. To develop this culture, we should avail ourselves of the opportunities thrown open by the U.G.C., I.C.S.S.R. and other bodies.

LIAISON WITH OTHER INSTITUTES AND INDUSTRIES

There is a need to bridge the gulf between the Universities, colleges, and Institutes on one side and the industry on the other. Meaningful dialogues and interactions like the present seminar can do a lot in this regard. The era of doubts, apprehensions, fear and suspicion should go and a fresh era of further goodwill and cooperation should emerge.

REFERENCES

1. Farooqi, Q.H., *Commerce and Management Education in India and Abroad*, AMU, Aligarh, p. 1.
2. *V.K.R.V. Rao Committee Report*, pp. 20-21.
3. *Radhakrishnan Committee Report on University Education*.

5 Role of Business Education in India

—T. ARANAGANATHAN

INTRODUCTION

The commerce discipline was considered as a part of the economics discipline and there was no separate Commerce faculty in most of the Indian universities in 60's. With the rapid professionalisation in industry, trade, banking, insurance and Government undertakings, commerce education has also established its own strength and intensity both in the academic and business world. Business education in India is composed of commerce education, professional education and management education[1].

OBJECTIVES OF THE STUDY

1. Business Education in India since Independence in general.
2. Business Education in India with special reference to Annamalai University since 1960.
3. To find out the significant role and growth of Business Education in the department of Economics, Commerce and School of Business Management in Annamalai University.
4. Impact of Information Technology in Business Education.

METHODOLOGY

A survey of faculty-wise enrolment of students and course-wise (both regular and Correspondence) enrolment of students in the Department of Economics, Commerce and Business Administration has been carried out for the study. The existing situation the technological advancement in the business world and the infrastructure have been discussed. The research and development in the above departments has been analysed.

BUSINESS EDUCATION IN GENERAL

Business education is an essential part of the preparation of people for running any business effectively and efficiently, since business is dynamic. The factors which affect the development of business are curriculum trends, rapid industrialisation and urbanisation, economic forces — both national and international, new methodologies in classrooms, etc.

BUSINESS EDUCATION IN INDIA SINCE INDEPENDENCE

The first commercial school was started by 1886 by the Pachiappa's Charities, in 1913 the Sydenham College of Commerce and Economics was established by the Government in Bombay. In 1955 an Institute was started for cost accounting. But by 1960's there were about 35 universities offering commerce courses along with 15 secondary education boards dealing with commerce education at school level. Now nearly 80% of the Universities have included the commerce subjects[2]. The growth rate and the enrolment of students in commerce education in India for selected years have been exhibited in Table 1.

TABLE 1

Faculty-wise Students Enrolment in India (1950-1982)

Subjects	1950-51	1966-67	1970-71	1976-77	1980-81	1981-82
Arts	65,783	4,74,874	8,19,550	10,50,637	11,14,417	11,90,117
Science	35,483	3,36,459	5,08,396	4,34,954	5,33,859	5,78,766
Commerce	17,915	1,23,119	2,51,985	4,25,459	5,54,253	6,28,031
All	1,65,381	11,55,548	19,07,272	23,59,670	27,52,437	29,52,066

Source : Annual report of the UGC.

The above table reveals that during the five year period 1977-78 to 1981-82, the percentage of the enrolment of students in commerce rose from 18.1% to 21.3%. It is also inferred that there is a tremendous increase in commerce between the years 50's and 80's.

The following table illustrates the enrolment of students in commerce and the level of percentage to the total enrolment. It is understood that there was a gradual increase in the 70's, and it maintains the same level of percentage in 80's and 90's.

TABLE 2

Enrolment of Students in Commerce (1972-92)

Sl. No.	Year	Enrolment in Commerce	Total Enrolment	Percentage share
1.	1972-73	3,18,888	21,68,107	14.7
2.	1977-78	4,63,957	25,64,972	17.0
3.	1982-83	6,69,813	31,33,093	21.4
4.	1987-88	8,57,971	39,10,828	21.9
5.	1991-92	10,09,832	46,11,107	21.9

Source : UGC reports.

Top Ten Best Colleges in India

The National Assessment and Accreditation Council set up in 1994 examined and selected 10 colleges (Table 3) as the top ten in India by considering the criteria like, goals and objectives, curriculum design, teaching-learning assessment, research and publications, etc. The ranking was done by taking 145 colleges in 10 major cities *viz*., Mumbai, Delhi, Calcutta, Chennai, Bangalore, Hyderabad, Ahmedabad, Pune, Lucknow and Patna. From Table 3 it is interesting to note that the commerce education course dominates in most of the colleges in India which shows that the business concerns need skilled and qualified people to look after global business activities. Today the largest higher education systems in the world is about 203 universities, 9,278 colleges with more than 55 lakhs of students.

BUSINESS EDUCATION IN ANNAMALAI UNIVERSITY SINCE INDEPENDENCE

The growth in the department of commerce, economics, business administration is found to be insignificant during the period 1978. The study period taken for consideration is twenty years (1978-97). The trends in the students enrolment in A.U. from 1961-97 have

TABLE 3

Top ten best colleges in India

Sl. No.	Name of the College	Place	Year of Establish-ment	No. of Seats	Subjects		Best Course
1.	St. Stephen's College	Delhi	1881	350	Arts-75%	Eco-87%	B.A.-Eco
2.	Presidency	Calcutta	1855	500	Arts-60%	Science-65%	BSc.-Eco
3.	Lady Shri Ram	Delhi	1956	600	Arts-74%	B. Com-87.25%	BA.-Psycho
4.	St. Xavier's	Mumbai	1869	600	Arts-75%	Science-84%	BSc.-Maths
5.	Loyola	Chennai	1925	1000	B.Com-95%	Science-95%	B.Com
6.	Sri Ram College of Commerce	Delhi	1926	400	B.Com-7.5%	Eco-86.75%	B.Com
7.	St. Xavier's	Calcutta	1860	1400	Arts-65%	Science-95%	B.Com
8.	Stella Maris	Chennai	1947	600	B.Com-95%	Maths-98%	B.Com
9.	Hindu College	Delhi	1899	400	B.Com-85%	Eco-86%	B.A.-Eco
10.	Vivekananda	Chennai	1946	655	B.Com-7.5%	Science 93%	BSc.-Maths

Source : *India Today*, June 23, 1997, pp. 50-54.

been analysed in Table 4 by computing compound growth rates with reference to different faculties which have been existing since 1961. Among the faculties, the students enrolment in Engineering and Technology has been increasing more significantly at the rate of 5.36% during the past three decades. Next to E & T, Education stands second in which the students enrolment has been increasing at the rate of 4.91% followed by the Faculty of Agriculture (3.69%) and the Faculty of fine arts (1.83%). But in the faculties of Arts, Science, and Indian Languages, the students enrolment showed negative trends *viz.*, –1.65%, –1.35%, and –5.97% and the R^2 values comparatively lower for the regression estimates in the case of Arts and Science faculties, which indicates that the influence of time has had no effects on the students enrolment. Hence it could be concluded that the students' enrolment in the professional courses has been significantly increasing since 1961. But in Arts and Science, which included a number of business degree courses, the students' enrolment under the regular scheme has been stagnant and decreasing during the period 1961-97.

TABLE 4

Trends in the Students' Enrolment in Annamalai University (model : Log y = a + bt)

Faculties	Regression Coefficients a	Regression Coefficients b	R^2	Compound Growth Rate
Arts	7.470	-0.0166* (-2.50)	0.1511	-1.65
Science	7.331	-0.0136* (-4.03)	0.3165	-1.35
Indian Languages	5.819	-0.0616* (-5.19)	0.4348	-5.97
Engineering & Technology	6.544	0.0522* (16.72)	0.8887	5.36
Education	5.126	0.0479* (8.38)	0.6676	4.91
Fine arts	4.257	0.0181* (3.58)	0.2675	1.83
Agriculture	5.359	.03620* (15.74)	0.8825	3.69

Source : Annual report : AU.

The variations occurred in the students' enrolment during this period have been exhibited in Table 5.

It is found from the table that the enrolment in arts faculty has increased to the maximum of 40.17% during 1971-75, whereas the corresponding increase in the science faculty is 23.33% in 1976-80, it is understood that there is an increasing trend in this period and there is a gradual decline in the later period since 1981-85 in these faculties. But in the case of professional courses like Engineering & Technology, Agriculture, Medicine, etc., there is an increasing trend from 1961. This increase is steady but not sudden as in the case of Arts & Science. It is obvious that these courses provide

TABLE 5

Faculty-wise Students' Enrolment in Annamalai University (1961-97)

S.No.	Faculty	1961-65	1966-70	1971-75	1976-80	1981-85	1986-90	1991-95	1996-97
1	2	3	4	5	6	7	8	9	10
1.	Arts	4321 (23.06)	9708 (33.30)	9879 (40.17)	11537 (34.27)	6877 (22.36)	4432 (12.11)	4213 (9.48)	1536 (9.13)
2.	Science	5439 (29.03)	8581 (29.44)	3565 (14.50)	7853 (23.33)	5746 (18.68)	4692 (12.83)	4691 (10.56)	951 (5.66)
3.	Indian Languages	939 (5.01)	1773 (6.08)	1507 (6.13)	932 (2.77)	117 (0.38)	288 (0.79)	309 (0.70)	151 (0.90)
4.	Engineering & Technology	6032 (32.19)	5750 (19.73)	5084 (20.67)	7682 (22.82)	11993 (38.99)	17215 (47.06)	21663 (48.76)	8629 (51.32)
5.	Education	667 (3.56)	1332 (4.57)	2619 (10.65)	2841 (8.44)	2059 (6.69)	2914 (7.97)	3880 (8.73)	2057 (12.23)
6.	Fine arts	503 (2.68)	472 (1.62)	302 (1.23)	404 (1.20)	525 (1.72)	655 (1.79)	716 (1.64)	348 (2.07)
7.	Agriculture	835 (4.46)	1532 (5.26)	1639 (46.65)	1766 (5.25)	2090 (6.79)	3334 (9.11)	3926 (8.82)	1487 (8.84)
8.	Legal Studies	—	—	—	615 (1.81)	333 (1.03)	—	—	—
9.	Medicine	—	—	—	36 (0.11)	1019 (3.31)	1647 (4.50)	3503 (7.87)	1072 (6.37)
10.	Dentistry	—	—	—	—	—	1402 (3.84)	1529 (3.44)	585 (3.48)
	Total	18736 (100)	29148 (100)	24595 (100)	33666 (100)	30759 (100)	36584 (100)	44430 (100)	16816 (100)

Source : Annual Reports.
Note : Figures in parenthesis indicate the percentage share.

employment & self-employment opportunities. Some of these faculties have arranged for the campus interview which may also be the reason for the attraction of students.

Among the courses in Arts faculty, business education accounts more number of students in spite of the tight employment market. In this context it would be relevant to mention the distance education courses offered by various Indian Universities. To highlight this aspect Table 6 has been presented and it is obvious that the business education courses account more number of students in

TABLE 6

Course-wise Enrolment of Students in Business Education in AU (1978-97)

Courses	Regular	Corres.	Open	Total	Percentage
B.Com.	3103	8111	11458	95672	43.74
M.Com.	4219	54205	—	58424	26.70
B.A. (Eco)	653	10538	3637	14828	6.77
M.A. (Eco)	2454	12730	6701	21885	10.0
BBA	—	21985	—	21985	10.0
MBA (Full & Part time)	3132	2814	—	5946	2.70
Total	13561 (6.20)	183383 (83.84)	21796 (9.96)	218740 (100)	100.00

Source : Annual reports : AU.

distance education than the regular courses. Specifically, B.Com. & M.Com. Degree courses have more number of students' enrolment which is to be modified in regular stream in order to retain its position and to attract more students such as professional and distance education courses.

TABLE 7

Department-wise (Commerce, Eco. & Bus. Admn.) Enrolment of Research Students in AU (1978-97)

Course	1978-82	1983-87	1988-92	1993-97	Total	Percentage
M. Phil.						
Commerce	27	135	93	33	288	41.98
Economics	51	136	56	40	283	41.26
Bus. Admn.	7	11	—	—	18	2.63
Ph. D.						
Commerce	4	7	10	20	41	5.98
Economics	6	17	11	16	50	7.28
Bus. Admn.	—	2	—	4	6	0.87
Total	95 (13.84)	308 (44.89)	170 (24.78)	113 (16.47)	686 (100)	100

Source : Annual Reports : AU.

Table 7 reveals the potentialities of the research activities in the field of business education at Annamalai University. It is understood from the table that the peak level of enrolment for M.Phil. course is during 1983-87, and there is a declining trend during the later period, whereas the Ph.D., enrolment has shown a steady increase. To meet out the emerging trend in new techo-economic world, the research areas should be given more importance with the changing environment in the business education.

IMPACT OF INFORMATION TECHNOLOGY ON BUSINESS EDUCATION

Technology causes significant changes in the business education and the modes of such advanced Information Technologies are : (a) Teleconferencing or Video conferencing, (b) Electronic Mailing system (E.Mail), (c) Fixed Wireless system and (d) Internet.

Teleconferencing : Through this method the worldwide company's officers could meet by sitting on their own place with the help of facsimile devices, electronic blackboards (which have the impressions that they are watching the TV at home) and other electronic media. The Pondicherry University Community College has utilised this opportunity and communicating with the US Community College people.

E-Mail (Electronic Mailing) : This exactly acts as postal letters. But the advantage with respect to the business education is that any type of doubts in the management or with the subject content could be cleared on the spot if we contact the particular person or any institution throughout the world. With high speed, relevant problems could be solved with moderate cost. The "chat box" is one of the examples for such business discussion. It is possible to organize remote or distance education and to set up virtual classroom with global reach through the web.

Fixed Wireless Service : The radio is the best example and we know very well that many educational institutions broadcast the courses thro' radio. Ex : MKU, Madurai.

Internet : It is possible to learn and get degree through on-line basis. The US has announced recently for a course for the Information Technology professionals. One more example is Exen's site for Online Management Education. The site address for this Executive Education Network is (www.exen.com). This is an emerging business in on-line education, especially in teacher-student deficit market such as in India. The exen company brings the best course modules in management from top US business schools to executives' offices via internet and electronic mail. The distance education technology has prompted business schools and institutions to design the educational packages for on-line studies[4].

Conclusion

If the commerce education is strengthened, it will be useful for business, commercial, and industrial enterprises. It is necessary to give priority in practice when it is attempted at the PG and Research level. In the context of privatisation, liberalisation and globalisation of Indian economy, it has become imperative on the part of business academicians to cater to the need of the market by imparting business education in all levels. The business education in the regular stream at Annamalai University has been improved to some extent by providing the internet services and some other advanced technologies to the academic community.[5]

REFERENCES

1. Commerce & Societal Needs, *The Hindu*, Nov. 8th, 1994.
2. *Commerce Education in India* by Dave's Bhorali.
3. *India Today*, June 23, 1997.
4. "Education on Demand", *The Economic Times*, 19th Jan. 1998.
5. *Business Today*, Aug. 22 — Sept. 6, 1996.

6 Perspectives of Entrepreneurship Education and Training

—D. NAGAYYA AND P.B. APPA RAO

Entrepreneurship development programme was initiated in the context of small enterprise promotion through training and counselling interventions, with necessary research support. It has since been extended to entrepreneurial education and cultural aspects for entrepreneurising the society. A good beginning has been made in some parts of the country. This needs to be spread to many other regions as well.

The paper deals with entrepreneurial initiatives of various national and state level institutions. It advocates effective networking among institutions for producing better results at a faster pace. Interesting examples of training and education imparted by various institutions in Maharashtra and Karnataka are cited. Distance learning programme is another direction which has been pursued in the last few years in a few states. With this background, the paper pinpoints directions for the future in the field of entrepreneurship development in the small enterprise sector to face the challenges of the competitive environment.

INTRODUCTION

Entrepreneurship development (ED) as a process and programme with focus on promotion of small enterprises started in the country in the mid-sixties through research and training with initial experiments carried out at the Small Industry Extension Training Institute (SIET Institute), later renamed as National Institute of Small Industry Extension Training (NISIET), Hyderabad. The work initiated by the SIET Institute in collaboration with Dr. David C. McClelland of Harvard University in East Godavari District of Andhra Pradesh and North Arcot District of Tamil Nadu (Rajahmundry, Kakinada and Vellore towns) established that entrepreneurship can be developed among adults through training and follow-up intervention. These are well documented in the 1967 publication authored by David C. McClelland and David G. Winter titled *Motivating Economic Achievement*. Since then the programme has undergone many phases and is utilized extensively in the context of a number of programmes with diverse objectives. The core of the programme continues to be creation of new enterprises and development of existing enterprises.

Entrepreneurship process for new enterprise creation is now used extensively for various self-employment avenues in the field of small enterprises for different categories of persons who evince interest in setting up new enterprises. Apart from enterprises in the small scale sector at higher investment level, enterprises with low and very low investment levels are also covered under this programme at present. In poverty alleviation programmes, setting up of industries, services and businesses through enterprise promotion effort has received wide popularity. For different target groups such as persons with science and technology background, women, weaker sections such as scheduled castes/scheduled tribes and other special categories to whom special attention needs to be paid, entrepreneurship development programmes (EDPs) covering training and counselling are being extensively administered. Success rate in these programmes has been improved through more of research, counselling and follow-up efforts.

Entrepreneurising the society by catching the students young and inculcating entrepreneurial spirit in them is a recent development. In the education curricula, enterprising qualities and entrepreneurial outlook are being incorporated in different courses. At an appropriate higher level of education, entrepreneurship as a career in a chosen line is being emphasized. A beginning has been made in entrepreneurship education and creation of mass awareness, apart from well-planned and well-directed training programmes for various target groups of prospective entrepreneurs.

CENTRAL AND STATE LEVEL INSTITUTIONAL FRAMEWORK

ED institutions at central, state and district levels can be categorised as follows :

(i) Training, research and consultancy organisations exclusively engaged in *Entrepreneurship* development training or as part of managerial programmes.

(ii) Sponsoring institutions which initiate the programme with necessary policy orientation and funding support.

(iii) Agencies implementing small enterprises programme which provide the overall backup support for stimulatory, support and sustenance role which is vital for new enterprise creation and for the sustainability of enterprises created earlier.

For overseeing the work relating to ED at the national level, two apex boards set up are : National Entrepreneurship Development Board under the Ministry of Industry, and the National Science and Technology Entrepreneurship Development Board under the Ministry of Science and Technology. Under the Ministry of Human Resource Development, education institutions dealing with science and technology, professional institutions dealing with engineering and other branches of technology, and certain departments of various universities and other educational institutions coming under their purview contribute to entrepreneurship education and training. Organizations which are sponsoring/encouraging training, escort, monitoring and evaluatory studies are : Development Commissioner (Small Scale Industries), Development Commissioners associated with various categories of village industries. Department of Science and Technology, All India Council for Technical Education, Industrial Development Bank of India (IDBI), Small Industries Development Bank of India (SIDBI) and National Bank for Agriculture and Rural Development (NABARD). NABARD's special interest has been in rural EDPs and involvement of NGOs in conducting these programmes. Apex organizations associated with the welfare of weaker sections such as National Scheduled Castes and Scheduled Tribes Finance and Development Corporation, National Backward Classes Finance and Development Corporation,

National Minorities Finance and Development Corporation and Central Social Welfare Board, have been supporting EDPs initiated by their state level counterparts by providing part-funding. They would like the state level Corporations and other specialized bodies to be involved in the conducting of the programmes in various states by sharing the costs.

Major All India training and research institutions providing the widespread spectrum and direction for conducting EDPs through their programmes of training and research are : Entrepreneurship Development Institute of India (EDII), Ahmedabad, National Institute for Entrepreneurship and Small Business Development (NIESBUD), New Delhi, National Institute of Small Industry Extension Training (NISIET), Hyderabad, and Indian Institute of Entrepreneurship (IIE), Guwahati serving primarily the North-Eastern region of the country. These institutions work closely with the relevant all India sponsoring and funding organizations and evolve new strategies for ED.

At the state level, industrial and technical consultancy organisations (TCOs) established with the support of financial institutions and state level corporations operating in 18 locations have been undertaking the training and follow-up function of entrepreneurship development in various states. In recent years, state level institutions/centres for entrepreneurship development have been established in 12 states. The states covered are : Bihar, Goa, Gujarat, Himachal Pradesh, Jammu and Kashmir, Karnataka, Kerala, Madhya Pradesh, Maharashtra, Orissa, Tamil Nadu and Uttar Pradesh. The CEDs/IEDs have drawn manpower initially from TCOs. In states where these centres are not yet opened, the TCOs continue to perform the function. In all the states, Small Industries Service Institutes (SISIs) coming under the Union Ministry of Industry, office of Development Commissioner (Small Scale Industries), play a leading role in conducting EDPs and also in offering skill-oriented technical courses at state and district levels. State Productivity councils and a few leading voluntary organisations are also associated with ED efforts. Popularising the ED movement extensively among school children, in vocational and technical training, and other educational institutions has been pursued vigorously by state level CEDs.

ENTREPRENEURIAL CULTURE AND EDUCATION

Entrepreneurial culture is something which needs to be stimulated or nurtured from early childhood in the families, schools and colleges so that continuous supply of entrepreneurs is built into the system. The entrepreneurial education in the school curriculum is not aimed directly at stimulating entrepreneurship but to develop enterprising qualities in people, and in particular, to inculcate the inclination towards self-reliance, creativity, perseverance, persuasiveness, resourcefulness, negotiating skills, motivation and commitment to achieving through the process of learning. It is to develop in young people a perception, insight and motivation towards entrepreneurship without directly addressing the issues of self-employment or indeed conventional business skills and knowledge. The experiences that the children gain at the young age have a significant impact on their frame of mind and life goals, apart from development of their personality while skills and experiences can be built up later, entrepreneurial spirit can be developed preferably at an early age.

EXPERIENCES OF MCED

In this context, work carried out by the Maharashtra Centre for ED (MCED), Aurangabad (Maharashtra) deserves special mention. It adopted the policy of entrepreneurising the society, *i.e.*, it started appealing to the masses rather than just train selected batches of candidates. As a result of the mass efforts at entrepreneurising the society through novel methods, MCED has been able to get a continuous flow of potential entrepreneurs for its training programmes.

Some of the key activities pursued by it are recalled here :

(i) While carrying out mass programmes of one day or even half-a-day, MCED started charging nominal fees and was successful in cultivating the habit of paying fee for training programmes.

(ii) MCED launched a Marathi monthly magazine to reach the masses of Maharashtra. In fact this magazine served as a continuous EDP which kept on motivating the masses to embrace entrepreneurial culture.

(iii) MCED joined hands with other agencies to launch mass education programmes like Udyog Sadhana on All India Radio. This has also helped in creating an awareness about entrepreneurship movement.

(iv) MCED also organized short-duration self-employment oriented programmes called development programme for self-employment — rural EDPs. MCED has also helped a number of colleges in Maharashtra to promote entrepreneurship development cells in the respective colleges.

(v) MCED conducted a number of trainers' training programmes and teacher training programmes to motivate teachers, trainers with different backgrounds to propagate the concept of ED.

(vi) MCED also launched the vocational training based entrepreneurship development programmes. In these programmes there has been a good blend of skill development training and entrepreneurship development training.

(vii) In the context of self-employment programmes such as PMRY (Prime Minister's Rozgar Yojana), bankers workshops are being organized apart from training programmes for beneficiaries.

(viii) Training of trainers is another healthy direction initiated by MCED. Workshops are organized annually for trainers to share their experiences and evolve new strategies. All India Trainers' Association has been formed for ED with secretariat as MCED. It is planned to give awards to the best of trainers' and non-trainers associated with EDP and related activities. Evolving new models to cope up with the emerging challenges is the undercurrent of all these initiatives.

EXPERIENCES OF OTHER INSTITUTIONS

In the curriculum of the engineering colleges for B. Tech course and in MBA offered by a number of institutions, *entrepreneurship and small business management* has been introduced as a special paper. Some universities are also offering a Post Graduate Diploma of one year duration on *Entrepreneurship and Small Business Management*. In Tamil Nadu, at Madurai, the Centre for Entrepreneurship Development (CED) is organizing programmes in collaboration with the Department of Entrepreneurship Studies of Madurai Kamaraj University, and also in association with an industrial unit at Coimbatore, namely K-Soft Systems Ltd. The two-year programme is on M.S. in information technology and management. KSOFT and CED plan to open regional centres in a few locations in the southern states for offering educational and training programmes on information technology and ED. A number of engineering colleges and University Departments are organizing entrepreneurship awareness programmes of short duration and EDPs of 6 to 8 weeks duration. Indian Institutes of Management and Indian Institutes of Technology are also involved in offering educational programmes on ED at the postgraduate level and also in pursuing advanced research for doctoral programme and in undertaking special projects on ED.

By involving industry association, EDPs and related specialized trade oriented courses are being organized in few states.

INSTITUTIONS IN KARNATAKA

In Karnataka, apart from CEDOK (Centre for Entrepreneurship Development of Karnataka) located at Dharwad, with the support of Canara Bank and local voluntary organizations, and with the overall support from NABARD, a number of rural development and self-employment training institutions (RUDSET Institutes) have been set up. RUDSET Institutions focus on skill oriented training and entrepreneurship training. In view of this, their programmes are of a longer duration of nearly six months for persons with traditional skills or no skills or with low level of education. CEDOK also has district level representatives who organize training programmes in individual districts. Technical Consultancy Organization of Karnataka (TECSOK) was associated with this function earlier and currently it provides technical services to entrepreneurs.

Small Industries Service Institute (SISI) organizes product and process EDPs, apart from EDPs for various categories of beneficiaries such as Science & Technology persons, women, SC &

ST, etc. Some of the products in which SISIs at Bangalore and Hubli have been conducting EDPs for educated unemployed youth are :

1. PCB design, fabrication and assembly
2. Computer maintenance and service
3. Desk Top Publishing
4. Leather/rexine utility articles
5. Computer aided design
6. Business Management
7. Decoration of glass and ceramic ware
8. Readymade garments for exports
9. Repair and servicing of electrical appliances

EDPs among women are conducted in the following areas :

1. Hosiery knitting
2. Leather utility articles
3. Floriculture
4. Bakery products

Besides conducting product-cum-process EDPs on their own SISIs at Bangalore and Hubli have also been actively assisting NGOs in conducting EDPs by providing the infrastructural support, faculty and laboratory facilities wherever required. Complementary role of leading Central organizations located at the state level is thus important to spread the message of new enterprise creation in different parts of the state.

For providing necessary support for ED, a Science and Technology Entrepreneurs Park (STEP) has been functioning at Mysore promoted by the local Engineering College. Similarly at the regional engineering college, Mangalore and in few other engineering colleges, entrepreneurship development cells have been operating for conducting EDPs on a regular basis for organizing industry-institution interface periodically. STEPs and EDCs are supported by Department of Science and Technology, New Delhi.

DISTANCE LEARNING PROGRAMMES

Another direction of contribution is from Development Education (International) Society in Pune, established in 1987. This institute has been popularising entrepreneurship training through mass media such as radio/television/video and audio programmes. They have successfully carried out media education for ED in the states of Madhya Pradesh, Maharashtra, Orissa and Uttar Pradesh. Response from the listeners and viewers has been quite positive. It is catching up fast. Distance learning is thus an important direction. Mass media gave information on the following aspects for the benefit of aspiring entrepreneurs : Achievement motivation, opportunities for new enterprises creation, resource mobilisation, managing an enterprise and opportunities in various specialized fields in different parts of the state. They have produced a number of video cassettes and audio lessons in Hindi. They plan to do them in other languages as well. In distance/open learning for ED, EDII, with the support of Friedrich Naumann Stiftung and the Department of Science and Technology introduced in 1995 a certificate course of nine months duration in new enterprise creation and management through correspondence and personal counselling. Optionals given for the medium of instruction at present are Gujarati, Marathi, Hindi or English, Facility for admission is four times a year (in March, June, September and December). Two months' post training guidance is also offered as part of the package. At the state level, EDII associates the institute working in the field of ED for providing necessary guidance to the candidates enrolled under the programme. With trainers training programmes and specialized programmes in various aspects of ED being organized on a regular basis, there are opportunities for state level ED institutions and Universities to get faculty trained in these accreditation programmes for pursuing research and training interests.

DIRECTIONS FOR THE FUTURE

Canvas of small industry has been enlarged with the recent revision in the definition of small, ancillary and export oriented small industries from December '97. Ceiling on investment in plant and machinery has gone up to Rs. 3.00 crore for these units from the earlier level of Rs. 60 lakh introduced in 1991, whereas for tiny sector and industry related service enterprises, investment level continues to be at Rs. 5 lakh. With these contours defined at the national level, many changes are taking place in the environment governing the SSI sector. The process is on for integrating the economy, particularly the industrial sector with developed and other developing countries through the process of globalisation. Competitive environment has resulted in severe competition within the small scale sector, between small and large scale sectors in the domestic market, and also in the international market. The entrepreneurs are aware of the new challenges, risks and opportunities. In the days to come, there will be considerable shift in the way entrepreneurs can perceive business opportunities.

While pursuing ED, it is not enough to think of promoting an enterprise. Growth and overcoming the problems faced from time to time are equally important. It is important to visualize the enterprise from a holistic viewpoint. Comprehensive theory of entrepreneurship encompassing all stages of growth needs to be kept in view for formulating strategies, conducting training programmes and devising monitoring, evaluation and escort services.

Specific pointers for action are listed here :

(i) Entrepreneurship development programmes of different duration should be more result oriented and keep in mind the challenges posed by the competitive environment.

(ii) ED should be an integral part of school education at plus-two level and in various professional, vocational and other courses at different levels. Relevant curriculum needs to be finalised. It is already being done in a number of institutions. This needs to be updated and extended to other institutions and states where it has not yet been adopted.

(iii) Distance learning and other forms of continuing education have significance in helping prospective and existing entrepreneurs acquire knowledge and skills on various aspects of their interest.

(iv) Emerging opportunities in various fields including computer applications and related aspects which offer scope for self-employment need to be given weightage in future ED activities.

(v) State level institutions have the advantage of reaching different districts and organizing programmes in remote areas as well. Through networking of apex national level institutions with the state and district level bodies, support is to be extended by the central institutions and all funding agencies to the state level institutes and implementing agencies.

(vi) EDPs can be organized for trade related programmes, product and process specialization, export orientation, rehabilitation of sick units, enterprise growth and diversification, etc. Growth-oriented programmes are essential for entrepreneurs who have undergone the preliminary programme for setting up an enterprise. The curriculum should include changes taking place in the economic scenario and the competitive environment in the dynamics of industrial development.

(vii) The present EDP model of six to eight weeks duration places great emphasis on getting an enterprise started. It does not pay attention for developing problem-solving skills needed to overcome as adverse situation, and evolve and implement turnaround strategies.

(viii) The revised EDP model should emphasise the need for training input that will equip prospective entrepreneurs with diagnostic as well as remedial skills to bring a floundering enterprise back to an even keel.

(ix) Future EDP Curriculum can include the following themes relevant in the current day context :

* Management Information Systems.
* Monitoring and evaluating the performance of an enterprise.
* Market research, with special reference to strengths and weaknesses of competing enterprises.

* Forecasting techniques to anticipate the future with reference to product changes, new technologies, quality improvement, training, etc.
* Emerging opportunities for self-employment.
* Diagnostic skills and turnaround strategies.
* Growth strategies.

7 Reviving Commerce Education — Need for a Radical Approach

—G. KOTRAPPA

We have had inherited commerce education from Britishers who invented the course mainly to produce graduates who would take up clerical positions in business enterprises. The commerce education has undoubtedly outlived its purpose. It is unfortunate that the basic structure of commerce education remained the same in spite of sweeping changes in the nature and conduct of business enterprises.

Reviving commerce education in tune with the ever-changing business and economic environment is the need of the hour. This is a dynamic world. Dynamism is a crucial component of any course structure if it is to be responsive to the present needs of our society. The very fact that commerce education being on top of the agenda of all commerce conferences and seminars is a pointer towards the seriousness of the problem. The major issues at stake are :

(1) **Obsolete :** The course is outdated and has lost relevance to the present circumstances.

(2) **Loss of Cream :** The cream of commerce education is being hijacked by professional courses, particularly by ICWA, ICA and ICS.

(3) **Traditional Outlook :** The course is bogged down by traditional outlook with little emphasis on specialization.

(4) **Emphasis on Teaching than Learning :** The course is over-burdened by theoretical orientation with little scope for imparting practical training.

(5) **End of the Road :** A commerce graduate faces 'end-of-the-road' situation with limited alternatives either to continue his/her studies or to seek employment. He/she is at a competitive disadvantage in the examinations conducted by UPSC and KPSC. Job opportunities for postgraduates are squeezed with the establishment of new colleges reaching a point of saturation and dwindling enrolment of students to B.Com. degree course.

(6) **Absence of a Body to promote Commerce Education :** In spite of a large number of commerce graduates and postgraduates, establishment of a strong body to promote and revive commerce education has never been thought of.

Accordingly, the revival of commerce education is to be based on the following criteria :

(1) **Nomenclature :** The very name of the course needs to be changed. Of all the alternative names discussed in the academic circles, 'Business Studies' (BS) is gaining more momentum. Existing B.Com. and M.Com. courses may be renamed as BBS and MBS courses.

(2) **Consolidation :** Different courses such as BHM (Bach. of Hotel Management), BCS (Bach. of Company Secretary) etc., being run parallel to B.Com. course to be consolidated and brought under one umbrella, *i.e.*, Business Studies.

(3) **Professional Status :** B.Com. degree should be elevated to the status of a professional course with the establishment of a separate body on the lines of All India Management Association (AIMA), may be named as All India Institute of Business Studies (AIBUS).

(4) **4-Year Course :** For strategic reason of gaining an edge over other degree courses like B.A., B.Sc. and particularly BBM the course duration of proposed BBS should be 4 years. This definitely helps rebuilding commerce education into a professional course complementary to Chartered Accountancy of ICA, Cost Accountancy of

ICWA, Chartered Secretary of ICS and Management of AIMA.

(5) **Specialization :** Specialization in areas such as hospitality mgt., bank mgt., quality mgt., business taxation, etc. is to be the hallmark of proposed BBS course. Specialization to start from II year BBS with 6 or 9 papers in each specialization evenly spread amongst three years.

(6) **Super-specialization :** A BBS graduate desirous of pursuing P.G., studies should be offered super-specialization in areas such as international trade and finance, corporate mergers and collaborations, etc.

Teacher training and development is at the heart of the plan to revive commerce education. Teacher knowledge and skills have to be expanded and improved, particularly in the specialised areas. This requires running a crash programme of training courses for our teachers. Besides, an additional investment for infrastructure development in the form of books and teaching aids is required. The funds thus needed may be mobilised by way of enhancing the fee to be collected from students.

By professionalising commerce education we have got nothing to lose, but the traditional outlook ! I feel it is an adventure worth experimenting and, perhaps, there may not be a better gift than this to our B.Com. graduates, sorry BBS graduates in the 21st century!!

8 Business Education for Rural/Semi-Urban Youth

—S. NARASING RAO

A French Statesman Mr. R.C. Fold has said that the thing that gives courage to men is idea. In other words, it can be said that knowledge is power. Out of 900 millions of country's population, 70% of the people live in Rural/Semi-urban centres; which also comprises of sizable number of youth. Many of the survey reports confirm that the urban people have got an edge over the rural mass — it is mainly because of higher infrastructure, advanced education, knowledge/exposure. The same rule holds good in respect of business education too. It is rightly stated that education is not something to induce into one's mind from outside, but to make a man realize what is already existing in him.

Here, my concern is not for those who are going to acquire professional/technical knowledge considerably for longer duration, involving higher expenses, to seek remunerative jobs/respectable placements in any established public sector undertaking. There are millions of youth despite having calibre/talent but for the compelling reasons, are denied of these opportunities and largely dependent on Private Enterprise for their livings. The important components of business education are : 1. Technical/Professional knowledge, 2. Financial and Managerial aspects, 3. Marketing knowledge, 4. Human Psychology. Unless a person acquires optimum knowledge under all these aspects, his business knowledge is incomplete; and this always comes in the way of his prosperity.

People who do not afford higher education consuming more time and money, largely depend on traditional system of education for their employment. To acquire this traditional business education, they put their children/dependents under the guidance of an experienced man in the field/master. This master craftsman not only renders business education, but also provides for day to day expenses. This mode of business education is found to be good, and cheaper one. Goldsmithy, Blacksmithy, Carpentry, Tailoring, Garland Making, in semi-urban centres T.V., Radio, Automobile Repairs etc., whole host of such activities can be listed under this category.

Intelligence is a capacity to learn the things, adoptibility to the changing environment, it is an ability to translate their job knowledge into a profitable proposition. Despite having rural background, lacking formal education, exposure to latest technology, many persons are found to be potential and talented. By their undaunted desires to become something in a society, they proved their existence and usefulness to the society. A few illustrious examples are given under :

1. Sri Yallappa Pujar of Hole Itagi (Tq. Shirahatti) prepares a very delicious Sohan Papadi for a competitive price and being sold through sweet marts at urban centres under their trade names. So also the Khava by our Ingali (Tq. Chikkodi) farmers. These rural people do not have any formal training on catering technology.

2. Sri Kammar of Hadli (Tq. Naragund) has hardly any formal education. He prepares thresher and other agriculture related farm equipments by using vernier calipers and other equipments.

3. Madabhavi (Tq. Athani) Chappals are internationally renowned as Kolhapuri Chappals.

4. Sri Goresab Jamader of Marihal (Tq. Belgaum) is expert at extraction of Rosa Oil by traditional method. The oil is being used by perfume industries at Pune.

5. Sri Mallikarjuna Chachadi of Ramadurg, a dynamic youth, was working as a pigmy collector in a Commercial Bank. Without any technical background/formal education, in a short span of 5 years proved himself a successful book manufacturer with an annual turnover of about 10 lakhs.

6. Sri Sunakappa Degalalli of Ramadurg is physically handicapped who doesn't know A B C of technology, has ventured into establishment of a plastic scrap Grating Project.

With the rapid advance of time and technology our globe keeps on shrinking and is no longer inaccessible to any part of the world. The process of liberalization in licensing, with the accent on Globalisation, has made the indigenous business face stiff competition from those who have access to the latest technology/ market knowledge. As a result it finds more and more bumps ahead and is often at sea. Any business concern not keeping abreast with the technical progress in its spheres of activity will soon become obsolete and lose out in the market over a period of time especially where exposed to competition.

Business is a game of risk, inherent as it is in any commercial activity, it is not possible to totally eliminate risk. At best one may have to work towards minimizing the impact of risk as much as possible. A pre-requisite to doing this effectively is to recognize the risks specific to that business activity.

In the present situation to run a business show effectively, a person should have an optimum knowledge relating to liquidity, funding, lending risk, maintaining the quality of assets etc. The entrepreneurs who wish to venture into a business, should develop the art of business growth, how to minimize general/administration expenses, to develop customer information system, etc. Of course a large number of colleges/Institutions are engaged in imparting formal technical education for a longer duration of time on almost all the activities. To name a few examples National Council of Educational Research and Training, NIRD, and NISIET Hyderabad, Indo-Danish Project on Technical Education on Tool and Die Making, Hotel Management and Catering Technology so on and so forth. Thanks to the Government that belatedly it has realized that major part of the people are not having money, time and eligibility to have education through such organizations.

With a view to mitigate economic and other hardships, to equip the youth with required technical know-how and other related aspects right from Government of India, State Government, Public Sector Undertakings, Private Philanthropic Organizations, have devised many schemes, and toiling hard to translate their dream into reality. A glimpse of such activities is listed as under :

Technical Institutions like ITI and other short duration job oriented courses are being started; but as compared to the facilities available to affluent class, taking into the magnitude of employment/ population of the country, the avenues made open for less privileged class is far from satisfactory.

NABARD has initiated many steps to develop relevant skills and managerial traits in the prospective entrepreneurs, so also in respect of escort services, linkage and market support to run a business on sound lines :

1. Establishment of Training-cum-production centres.
2. Rural Entrepreneurship Development Programme.
3. Market Oriented Training for Rural Artisans.
4. Training of/and by master craftsman.
5. Artisan-Guild.
6. Common Service Centres.

Training inputs will cover skills, learning, Elementary Book Keeping, Management of Production Finance, Labour, etc.

Entrepreneurship Development Programme (EDPS) are conducted by Technical Consultancy Organization.

CFTRI is providing valuable information/services on food processing technology.

SIDBI established "National Equity Fund" scheme in 1987. It provides equity support to entrepreneurs for setting up new projects in tiny/SSI. The Role of District Industries Centre is also significant in this regard. But, because of red tapism and other inherent weaknesses, the desired goals appear to have not been achieved.

Information-Technology Park, Bangalore is one such organization which disseminates variety of knowledge on International Standards to a large number of people on latest technology.

Small Industries Service Institute (SISI), a Government of India Undertaking, compiled scheme directory under Prime Minister's Rozgar Yojana which indicates 120 ways to become self-employed.

Council of Scientific and Industrial Research provides improvised project report on variety of subjects for the entrepreneurs.

Though food processing units have been mushrooming at a faster rate in the urban centres; these activities need to be given more fillip in rural and semi-urban centres. National Policy on Food Processing Industries aimed at augmenting employment opportunities. A head of the technical college opines that with a moderate amount of investment and little technical know-how a good number of activities can be taken up under this category.

Khadi and Village Industries Commission has identified 23 rural industrial activities. They are having their own system through which they provide business education, spread the knowledge of their activities and provide financial assistance for margin money.

KVIC established pottery training centre at Khanapur (Belgaum Distt.) in 1954 to give specialised training for pottery and ceramics. The services of Sri Krishnamurthy Mirmira, a good social worker of Bhadravati (Maharashtra) for the spread of pottery/ceramic education is really commendable.

His holiness Sri Veerendra Heggade of Dharmastala, with the joint sponsorship of Canara and Syndicate Banks, established RUDSET at six different places. Through this organization, Job Oriented Training Programmes on variety of activities are given to youth for period ranging from one week to one month. In addition they also take up post training follow-up measures, and initiate steps with Banks for financial support.

The BAIF of Urlikanchan (Pune) has been extending all types of support/extension services to the youth, who take Dairy Development activity for their economic improvement.

Lady entrepreneurs interested in tailoring no longer look up to the institutions like Royal School of Fashion, Bangalore, Fashion Designing and Management Courses. This task is taken up by a social worker Smt. Vasanti Pai of Manipal, through her Vikas Trust.

Self-Employment Women Association (SEWA) is a Voluntary Organization, in a modest scale committed to the welfare of women to alleviate their hardships by giving business knowledge.

Government Sponsored Poverty alleviation schemes like PMRY, TRYSEM, SUME, SEPUP are basically employment-oriented programmes. Provision for training to the beneficiaries is envisaged under these schemes; but they have not been able to generate fruitful results as a result of the following bottlenecks :

1. Disinclination of the beneficiaries.
2. Incompetency of the master craftsman.
3. Non co-operation by good private unit owners for the fear of facing competition by the same beneficiaries in the coming days.
4. Half-hearted attempts of the co-ordinators, etc.

Madhya Pradesh Government under Rajiv Gandhi Mission on Rural Industries, imparted employment-oriented training to over 4 lakhs of youth, and thousands of craftsmen.

The endeavour of small and big organization is one and the same to attract more number of customers. To boost up their sales promotion, they have permanent publicity arrangements. Through their house magazines, news latters they communicate the latest know-how and other relevant data. These magazines are helpful in enriching one's business knowledge.

Machinery Guide-Directory of manufacturers and suppliers of machine tools provides useful information on availability of machines.

Directories on Industries, market survey reports, Annual reports of the business concerns provide valuable business information.

Leading Dailies at regular intervals bring out their own special survey reports, publish special issues on business activities which give good insight into this vocation.

Ex. *The Hindu* — English leading daily — publishes variety of survey reports. Kannada Dailies are also bringing out special issues on business information.

Technical Officials at DIC, SISI, CEDOK, KSSIDC, KSSIMC, KSFIDC and other specialised branches, Commercial Bank Officials, are a very good source of business knowledge.

Government of Karnataka for the benefit of SC/ST youths, brought out a book in Kannada indicating facilities under various schemes.

Kannada magazines like Taranga, Diksuchi, Sudha, Karmaveera provide variety of business information to the aspirants through their regular features on job-oriented courses under various heads.

Research and Development Divisions, R.V. Engineering College, Bangalore, Manipal Press Corners play a supportive role on these counts.

Trade exhibitions, visit to Industrial Estates/Units give a fair account of business education.

Syndicate Bank, NABARD through their extension wings like Farm Clinic, Vikas Volunteer Vahini are disseminating business knowledge in their own style, to the rural people.

Renowned social workers like Sri Annahazare of Ralegansiddi, Sri Pandurang Altavale, and others have been channelising variety of information to the needy persons for their economic self-sufficiency.

Employment Information and Guidance Bureau, Karnataka University, Dharwad, is also said to be educating budding students to choose a right career path to shape their futures.

A person who is interested to have updated knowledge need not necessarily have classroom education. Institutions like Indira Gandhi Open University, Delhi, Annamalai Open University, Chennai, Institute of Management and Services, Delhi, Natraj Institute of Services and Technology, Chennai, Women Career Institute, New Delhi, facilitate distance education like home-study, hobby and career courses.

A learned person who has spent entire life in education field suggests that T.V. and Radio are like open universities. A person who has liking, certainly will get good amount of knowledge through these media.

While reviewing the performance under Government programmes, one of the learned person says that, the ultimate success of any programme would depend upon the human element implementing it. Even the best of the programmes would fail to deliver the goods if those entrusted with its implementation do not prove equal to the task. This rule equally holds good in respect of other fields also.

No amount of external infusion will make a man successful unless he has zeal to learn of his own initiation. Success always depends on ability. It must be sparked by ambition and sustained by integrity and determination. To top all these techniques, Sri Bhagavat Gita preaches that to get success in any venture, in addition to determination, art of doing the things, an element of luck is equally essential.

9 Business and Education : Interlinkage and Emerging Challenges

—M.R. PATIL AND T.M. POPKER

INTRODUCTION

The present economic reform measures generally described as liberalization, privatisation and globalisation (LPG) initiated since 1991, have resulted in a sea of changes in almost all the economic activities. As a result, all the segments of the Indian economy *viz.*, banking, investment, production, marketing, international trade, *et al* have been growing by leaps and bounds. However, it does not mean that prior to 1991 the Indian economy was stagnant. No doubt, even earlier to that there were changes and growth in the economy, but those changes and growth had not been felt as much as they are felt today. The continuing liberalized economic policies have not only brought in a rapid growth in economic activities, but more importantly, they have posed many 'challenges' before each economic activity. For instance, manufacturing units are considerably experiencing a challenge of producing the products of high quality at a competitive cost, marketing departments in the organizations are constantly struggling hard as far as marketing of their products is concerned and the financial institutions are finding more promising the task of disbursement of their mobilised financial resources for more profitable investments. Similarly, every economic activity is exposed to one or the other challenges.

One of the key factors associated with every economic activity *i.e.*, human capital (manpower) is happened to be the foremost to face those challenges. And many times the intellectual capabilities and innovative skills of managers and executives are being questioned as they are becoming deficient to meet the expectations of today's business. This kind of dissatisfaction with the performance of personnel has had a profound influence on the 'Business Education Institutions' as the personnel are the output of educational institutions. Thus, finally the educational institutions are happened to face those challenges.

Against this background, an attempt is made in this paper to focus light on the emerging challenges before business education and explore the possible measures to overcome those challenges. The paper is presented into four sections. The first section deals with 'Business : Its Evolution and Present Growth'. The second section speaks about the 'Education : Its Evolution and Present Scenario'. The third section establishes an interlinkage between business and education and emerging challenges before business education. The last section tries to explore the possible measures to overcome the challenges.

The term 'Business Education' in this paper broadly refers to all the institutions which are engaged in imparting business education. They include commerce colleges, postgraduate department of studies and research in commerce, business and management institutions and any other institutions engaged in imparting business education. Further, 'Business Education' term has been interchangeably referred to as 'Educational Institutions'.

BUSINESS : ITS EVOLUTION AND PRESENT GROWTH

The term 'business' has been considered as a super system with its two key sub-systems *viz.* 'Industry' and 'Commerce'. The term 'industry' refers to the aggregate of productive enterprises engaged in producing goods and services as desired or needed by the society at large. While the term 'Commerce' with its ancillaries *viz.*, banking, marketing, transportation, insurance, communication, packaging, advertising, etc. may be looked upon as an organized system engaged in supplying goods and services to the community. Thus an ultimate goal of both the key sub-systems is directed towards production and supply of goods and services to the community. The term 'industry' passed through different stages. Firstly, 'handicraft stage' where the manufacturing activities were based on manual labour. Secondly, 'domestic stage' where the craftsmen had to take up work on contract basis from the entrepreneurs and acted as intermediaries between the actual producers and the ultimate consumers. Finally, the new inventions in the textile industry and the development of steam engine, profit maximization motive of the entrepreneur, intense competition in the industry, etc. led to the new mode of production *i.e.* Factory System where mass production was carried on not only for local market but also for international market.

Similarly, the term 'commerce' also passed through different stages. Firstly, 'Self Sufficiency Stage' where man had to produce the things required for him and there was no exchange transactions. Secondly 'barter economy' where people began to produce more than required and the surplus was exchanged for other essential commodities. Thirdly, 'money economy' where money was introduced as a medium of exchange and finally, the scientific and technological improvement resulted in mass production which in turn led to the expansion of trade from town to nation and from nation to among nations.

Since independence, particularly after the introduction of economic reform measures like tax reforms, rupee convertibility, long-term liberalized import and export policy, new industrial policy (1991) characterised by removal of entry barriers, substantial reduction of areas reserved exclusively for public sector and abolition of industrial licensing, considerable inflow of foreign, capital, reforms in banking sector like reduction in Statutory Liquidity Ratio (SLR) and Cash Reserve Ratio (CRR) leading to release more and more lendable resources available to the banks, reduction in Prime Lending Rate (PLR), entry of private banks, etc. the growth and expansion of business is really remarkable. The economic indicators like 7 per cent average economic growth during the last three years placing India among the top ten performers in the world, as high as 12 per cent recorded industrial growth during 1995-96 which was the highest growth rate in the past 25 years, a historic peak record of $25.19 billion foreign exchange reserves during 1994-95 form the abnormally low level since mid-1970, etc. have further witnessed the present growth of Indian business.

EDUCATION : ITS EVOLUTION AND PRESENT SCENARIO

Initially, the education was aimed at just making the child to become a good member of his tribe or band. There was a marked emphasis upon training for citizenship as during those days people were highly concerned with the growth of individuals as tribe members and the thorough comprehension of their way of life. The curriculum during those days consisted of cultural values, tribal religion, etc. and the religious instructions took the most prominent place in the curriculum. During 1600, the Britishers established the East India Company with the main objective of trade, but the company did not recognize the promotion of education. Meanwhile, a new impetus was given by two important sources *viz*. 'Christian Missionaries' and the 'Semirationalist Movement'. In fact, the Christian missionaries had started their educational activities as early as 1542. It gave a new direction to elementary education with the introduction of instructions at regular and fixed hours, broad curriculum and clear cut class system. Similarly, in 1817, semirationalists led by Ram Mohan Roy started the Hindu College in Calcutta.

Indian education was further marked by the creation of a separate department for the administration of education in each province and establishing the Universities of Calcutta, Bombay (Mumbai) and Madras (Chennai) in 1857. At the same time institutions *viz*., the Anglo-Mohammedan Oriental College in Aligarh (1875), the DAV College in Lahore (1886) and the Central Hindu College in Benaras (1898), had come into existence.

During the 20th century events like international wars, rapidly spreading prosperity and affluence, immense increase in population, an explosion of knowledge, establishment of many professions, the growth of large scale science based industry, the enormous influence of mass media, etc. have had a sagacious influence on education.

Today, education has broadened its objective with a well-designed curriculum and imparts knowledge, develops skills, inculcates values and importantly promotes overall personality development of human beings whereby enables them to lead their lives independently and meaningfully. Over and above education has extensively expanded its scope to various specialised streams like engineering, medical, science, law, arts, commerce, management and so on. Furthermore, an enormous sub-specialisations like electronic engineering, surgery, taxation, economics, banking, sociology, marketing management, etc. are seen in each of the mainstream.

Higher education scenario including business education since independence has gone through a phenomenal expansion and growth. One can easily visualize the growth of education just going through the growth pattern of the number of universities, colleges, student enrolment and teachers during the last four decades. The number of universities have gone up from 21 in 1947 at the time of independence to 223 during 1996 recording 10.62 times rise, number of colleges including commerce and professional colleges have increased from 700 in 1947 to 8210 during 1996 registering 11.72 times rise, the student enrolment has been remarkably increased from 105,000 in 1947 to 6,100,000 during 1996 recording 58 times rise and number of teachers has been increased from 15000 in 1947 to 290,000 recording 19.33 times rise during the whole period. Further, on an average the number of students per teacher has gone up from 7 to 21 during the whole period.

INTERLINKAGE AND EMERGING CHALLENGES BEFORE BUSINESS EDUCATION

It is undeniable that business has got a close nexus with education. The efficient and competitive performance of business depends exclusively upon one of the important input factors *i.e.*, human factor since effective utilisation of other precious resources of business in accomplishing its varied socio-economic objectives depends in toto upon it. On the other hand, education institutions are the prime source of providing the personnel of skilled, capable, competent, innovative and trained for managing the business fruitfully. Thus, the degree of best performance of business relied upon the type of personnel, the educational institutions provide as an input for business.

In the changing economic scene in India in particular and all over the world in general, the Indian business is exposed to many challenges like global competition, technological upgradation, quality upgradation, cost consciousness, new combination of means of production, etc. As a consequence of those challenges, the owners and the proprietors of business enterprises started expressing their unhappiness with the 'products' of educational institutions as the graduates and postgraduates in business education may not be up to their expectations. On the other side, they expect the personnel possessing updated business skills and having an indepth technological knowledge besides their academic qualifications.

The business educational institutions have now felt seriously the growing disparity between what they impart to the students and what has been the demand from the employment market. This kind of gap between the supply and demand has turned into several challenges before the business education. Some of them are focussed here :

(1) Updating the Conventional Kind of Curriculum

An immediate emerging challenge before the business education is to update the existing traditional curriculum adhered to the prescribed syllabus, in line with the present needs and requirements of business. Imparting knowledge strictly as per the syllabus no longer continues to quench today's needs of employment market.

(2) Generating Willingness and Holding Interest in the Curriculum

Generating willingness and holding interest of younger generation (students) in the undertaken course has been really becoming the most promising task today. Many times, an uninterrupted flow of information in the lecture hall on to the students makes boredom which in turn keeps them out from the learning track. Hence it is too essential to ensure more and more opportunities to the pupils during lecturing for their self-initiative and self-development, instead of making one-way transmission without being established a proper feedback.

(3) Developing Technological Skills

An increasing development of technology in every field of economic activity has posed a pivotal challenge before business education. Business education, by and large, is imparting and training the students in selective functional areas like financial accounting, marketing, administration, personnel management, cost accounting, etc. but they impart a very little or no knowledge about technological concepts, issues and implications. A technology may be defined as a branch of knowledge that deals with methods and techniques of production, and industry highly expects from personnel to use newer and newer modern techniques of production. The main object of this is to make industry more efficient and thus to increase production and profitability.

(4) Developing Innovative and Creative Skills

In order to survive and compete efficiently in the present business environment, today's business requires managers with innovative and creative skills besides acquired knowledge from the stored package of information. But the present curriculum has hardly the place for such type of skills. Creativity may be viewed as the process of divergent thinking, the discovery and the identification of many alternatives. While innovation means introducing something new which has not existed, into the economy it may be either new method of production or new marketing technique or any other means of production.

(5) Elevating Moral, Ethical and Cultural Values

In today's changing scene, an acquired qualification of an individual would often be tested in the light of his personality and personal traits. Business also demands the personality possessing both an excellent qualification and strong personal traits. Thus, personal qualities like behaviour, character, good manners, politeness, gentleness, patience, peace, tolerance, etc. play a momentous role in establishing an excellent human personality which in turn ensures stability and credibility to business. But these values have virtually disappeared from the education text. It is, therefore, felt the need to restructure business education to evolve those values.

MEASURES TO OVERCOME CHALLENGES

The business education institutions in India have been imparting business education over the past several years with almost the same type of curriculum with some changes and modifications. Thus, the present challenges before business education cannot be overcome at once. It goes a long way to bring the changes in the curriculum as per the needs of business. There are certain key areas identified which may bring a meaningful change in the course of study. Those are as under :

(1) Restructuring the business education curriculum as per the needs and requirements of industry and commerce;

(2) Encouraging more and more research in the important problem areas of industry so that the research findings would be useful to tackle the problems. In order to achieve this, teachers may be extended with an opportunity to spend some time in industry to study the problems and actual needs of industry. This would be possible with the combined efforts of both industry and educational institutions;

(3) Syllabus-oriented teaching-learning needs to be broadened;

(4) Ensuring a common platform for industry and educational institutions to work out value-based curriculum taking into consideration the needs of industry.

No doubt, there are certainly some games to bring those measures into practice, but it would be possible with some concreted efforts of both business and business educational institutions.

REFERENCES

1. Aushuman Khare (1995), Rediscovering the Wheel, *The Times of India,* dated 14th Sept., 1995.
2. Arun, Nigvekar (1996), *Quality in Higher Education*, NAAC, Bangalore, pp. 9-10.
3. Economic Survey (1995-96), *Financial Express*, 28th Feb., 1996.
4. Economic Survey (1996-97), *The Economics Times*, 26th Feb., 1997.
5. *Encyclopaedia Britannica,* Vol. 6. William Benton & Helen Hemingway Benton (1943-73 and 1973-74), London, pp. 316, 17, 68, 69, 71, 72.
6. M.R. Shollapur (1997), University-Industry Interface in Business Education, *University News*, Vol. 35, No. 43, 27th October, 1997, pp. 1-4.
7. N. Vinayakam, M. Radhaswamy and S.V. Vasudevan (1982), *A Text Book of Business Organization*, S. Chand & Company, New Delhi, pp. 28-34.
8. P.N. Rastogi (1996), Cultivating a Change, *The Times of India Newspaper*, dated 26th Sept., 1996.

10 Management Education — Strategic Issues

—M.C. POORNIMA

INTRODUCTION

Management Education is one of the more significant components of Human Resources Development spectrum with great potential for adding value to products and services and for contributing to the national economy and improving quality of life of the people.

Management Education has acquired a vital prominence in economic activity towards the last quarter of the 20th century. Though Europe gifted the world with modern management tools and techniques in the 19th century, the US developed the science of management and handed over to the rest of the world what is known as Business Management.

Management Education in India has grown phenomenally during the last two decades and now it has become an important feature in our socio-economic and cultural life. Most of the industries employ professional managers. The number of academic institutions imparting Management Education and their intake are progressively increasing.

It would be interesting to note that after the United States, India has the largest number of management schools. We have made quantum jump in producing the number of management graduates. This quantitative expansion, without adequate preparation, had adversely affected the quality of Management Education.

With the liberalisation of economy, the gradual integration of local market into global environment the business is becoming more complex. For success in management, one can no longer look for individual brilliance or inherited skills. It is realised that managers are not born but are made. Systematic attempts are needed to identify, select, train and develop tomorrow's managers with requisite skills and abilities through systems approach in order to improve the quality of Management Education in India.

WHAT IS MANAGEMENT EDUCATION?

Various definitions of Management Education are given below :

Management Education can be defined as "Courses for practicing or intending managers, the purpose of which is to help the student to carry out management activities".

Management Education can be defined as "That area of the educational process which concerns itself with vocational preparation for a business career or *vocational* and professional preparation for a career in teaching business, and also with business information important for every citizen and consumer in order that he may better understand and use his business and economic surroundings".[1]

An education in business management can mean a number of quite divergent things depending on the context in which it is discussed. Political, geographical, social and temporal factors all have the potential to significantly influence what is meant by a higher education in business.[2]

"The task of developing ability to cope with more unstructured problems".

"Education for the whole process of Management".[3]

Management Education may be called for the specific preparation of an individual for a position of responsibility for the work of others in an organisation. It must also undertake the task of equipping the manager to carry out continuing and changing responsibility for the use of manpower and other resources.[4]

Management Education is the study of individual and group behaviour within the organisation and application of such knowledge. It is a way of thinking, a way of concerning problems and articulating research action solution. It is characterised by search for cause and effect orientation towards change, humanistic tone and scientific method. The field is becoming increasingly performance oriented. Management Education is not an old wine of industrial psychology put into a new bottle as some people have imagined. It has emerged as a field of study, research and application.[5]

Throughout this study "Management Education", is referred to preparing young people for future jobs in management, through university or management school degree programmes.

PAST AND PRESENT SCENARIO OF MANAGEMENT EDUCATION IN INDIA

Formal education in management is of recent origin in India. In early sixties, it was realised that investment in technology and training of engineers was not sufficient for implementing the plans for rapid economic development; managerial input was an important ingredient which was missing.[6]

Keeping in view the growing need for more competent personnel for managerial responsibilities the growth of management Institutes has taken place in India as below :

LANDMARK EVENTS IN THE DEVELOPMENT OF MANAGEMENT EDUCATION IN INDIA

1955	Setting up of Board of Management Studies.
1955	Part-time courses in four leading universities of India *viz.*, Madras, Delhi, Bombay & Calcutta.
1956-58	Management Courses in IISc. Bangalore, IIT Kharagpur, Victoria Jubilee Technical Institute Bombay.
1958-60	AIMA, NPC, Administrative Staff College of India.
1960-63	IIM Ahmedabad.
	IIM Calcutta.
1963-68	National Institute of Training in Industrial Engg. (NITIE) and MBA courses in university of Delhi.
1972	IIM Bangalore.
1984	IIM Lucknow.
1987	AICTE Act.
1988	All India Management Schools.

TABLE 1

Growth of Management Schools in India

Year	Number of Management Schools Established During the year	Total Number of Management Schools During the year
1	2	3
1954	01	01
1957	01	02
1961	02	04
1963	01	05
1964	04	09
1965	03	12
1967	02	14
1968	04	18
1969	03	21
1970	01	22
1971	06	28
1972	02	30
1973	02	32
1974	07	39
1976	06	45
1977	02	47
1978	08	55
1979	01	56
1980	04	60
1981	12	72
1982	08	80
1983	05	85
1984	12	97
1985	06	103
1986	05	108
1987	04	112
1988	05	117
1989	01	118

From Table 1 we can easily visualize the increase in the number of management schools in India. Today, there are over 450 management institutions in the country of the following categories :

- Central Government Established & Funded.
- State Governments Established & Funded.
- University Departments.
- University Affiliated Colleges.
- University Recognised Institutions.
- Private/Independent & Recognised by AICTE.

These institutes produce nearly one hundred thousand graduates and under-graduates every year of which nearly 9000 are post-graduates. The IBM's alone turn out more than 1000 MBA's every year.

This "Mushroom Growth" has, however, created severe concern about the goal or tasks in the direction of Management Education in India. It is felt that the Management Education is undergoing a period of "Soul troubles" *i.e.*, in search of an identity.[7]

CHALLENGES FACING MANAGEMENT EDUCATION IN INDIA

Management Education system should be designed to meet the current and expected demands of trained manpower for solving social problems. Societal systems are informant in all parts of the globe, and economic liberalisation is affecting the market size and complexity as well as the norms of international Business standards. The instances of mobility of professionals across the national borders have widened both the supply and demand perspective and problem solving horizon making it imperative for education planners to take a global view on both these counts and not to be restricted to national considerations alone. If management institutions remain static in this turbulent environment, they may be driven out of the market. If the customers' needs are not reviewed constantly they may refuse to do business with the institution which cannot produce quality graduates.

The following are the major challenges and hardships which need identification and steps to be taken for their alleviation :

- large scale expansion
- obsolescence of faculty
- curriculum design
- resource crisis
- library and infrastructure upgradation
- industry-institute interaction
- management transformation

The above challenges result in the deficiencies in the preparation of management graduates which may be in the following areas :

- problem formulating and solving skills
- decision-making skills
- communication skills
- motivation for lifelong learning
- professionalism and ethics
- inter-personal interaction
- computer usage
- maintenance philosophy and attitude
- entrepreneurial ability

STRATEGIES FOR FUTURE MANAGEMENT EDUCATION

Institute-Industry Interaction

The need for close collaboration between the Institutes of management and industry is unquestionable. The product user is the business and industry. Therefore, the customer's requirement is of great relevance in preparing the students who will ultimately provide the satisfaction. The course curriculum has to be updated continuously. For that linkages can be established through direct involvement of the practising executive in drafting and updating the relevant subjects. The views and options of the captains of industry and business magnates should be obtained and programmes should by shaped accordingly.

The academics should go over to business and industry and work on consultancy assignments or on specific projects. They should also have hands on experience. Sabbatical arrangements should be encouraged. Similarly, the practising managers with passion for teaching should go over to management schools and take up teaching and research assignments. The flow diagram to develop Industry-Institute Interaction is shown in Fig. 1.

For the benefit of practising managers at different levels specific seminars and workshops should be conducted from time to time.

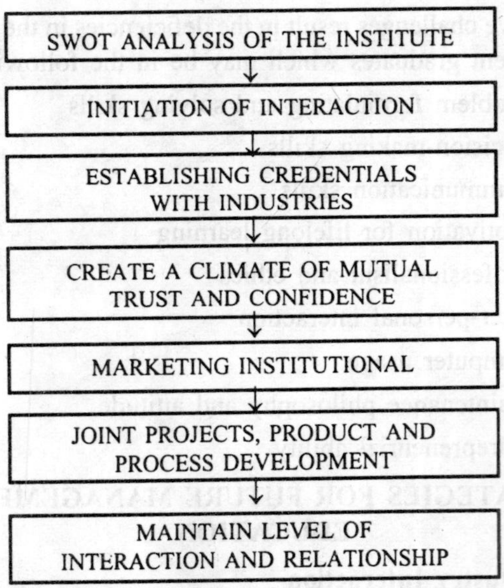

Fig. 1: Flow Diagram of process of Interaction.

This will provide an opportunity to learn, update and exchange ideas and benchmark the best practices. Students have to be exposed to such simulated situations.

Faculty Development

A faculty without a continuous professional enrichment programme will be a "fossilised practitioner". Providing attractive pay scales and ensuring strict entry behaviour qualifications without compromises of any sort, will attract people with efficiency to the profession of teaching. Merit pay scales such as bonus based on assessments, increments, incentives to teachers with proven efficiency in teaching, research, extension and publication activities may be provided.

Providing favourable environment for working will enthuse committed faculty members for better performance. Decreasing bureaucracy will strengthen intellectual adventurism and innovativeness among faculty members. Academic autonomy is a prerequisite for professional accountability. Exchange of faculty members among the institutes will help in exchange of information and ideas. Further promotion and incentives should be based on the following criteria. Set criteria may include :

* Professional accountability
* Management skills
* Commitment
* Consultancy assignments
* Research and development
* Attending seminars, workshops and conferences (national level)

Upgrading infrastructure facilities

Exchange of Library Collections/Research Findings/cases, etc. among different management schools. Inter-Library cooperation, Internet/Inlibnet, E-mail will boost development.

Control and Checks on Entry Points

In the present context in India the aspirants in Management Education centres are mostly fresh graduates unlike in advanced countries where candidates with a minimum of three to five years hands on experience are only admitted in business schools. It is an admitted fact that experienced candidates will be in a better position to understand and appreciate business education. They will be able to relate theory to practice. It is necessary to have checks and controls on entry points. For this purpose it is necessary to have National Admission Test like the one being conducted in America which is called "G-MAT".

Total Quality Business Schools

Total Quality Management has been tried out in Anna University, Chennai. It has signed a memorandum of understanding with the Lucas TVS group of industries which is an excellent idea for ensuring quality.

The application of the systems approach seems to be appropriate to bring quality requirement in Management Education based on customer expectations. Quality concepts have been recognised as the core of *Total Quality Management* (*TQM*). Quality systems try to standardise generic practices of quality management. The following proposal for building quality in a step-by-step fashion may be tried out :

- Self-appraisal of the individual
- Appraisal of the individual for improvement.
- Self-appraisal of the department to be done annually, both retrospectively and prospectively.
- Appraisal of department for improvement which may be regularly given in the annual report.
- Institutional appraisal of the department for judgment.
- Departmental appraisal of the individual for judgment.
- Institutional appraisal of the individual for judgment.[8]

Thus Total Quality Business Schools can be developed using Total Quality Management principles.

The ISO-9000 series of quality systems has been accepted worldwide to enhance the relative quality levels. Management Education cannot afford to ignore it. Its application may lead to a better utilization of all available resources in Management Education.

A General TQBS Model for Management Education is illustrated in Fig. 2.

CONCLUSION

Management Education processes and operations are undergoing several changes and many more changes are expected in the near future. There is, however, a general maxim which rules under this situation "Old Institutions either change or new ones emerge to take their place to meet Society's needs".

Management Education, requires a strong commitment by the University administration, close cooperation from business

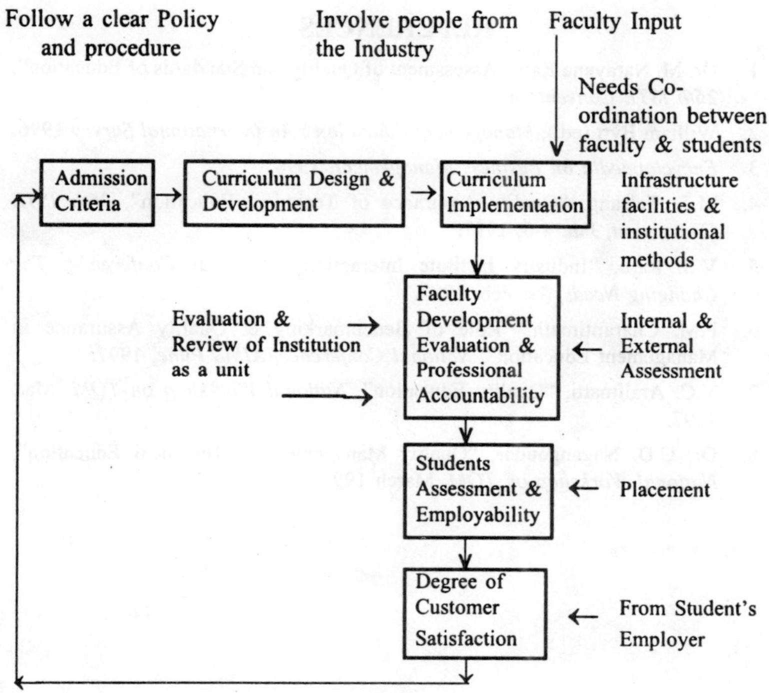

Fig. 2

organisations, sincere dedication by teachers and adequate resources allocation by the government.

Modern management plays a vital role in the rapid transformation of the society. But if we are to succeed in this area Management Education will itself have to be "managed" and made relevant and responsive to the environment which it seeks to serve. Achieving quality in Management Education cannot be an accident. It is possible through continuous and purposeful efforts. Systems approach will help in continuous improvement of the processes thus resulting in customer satisfaction. This will help in building "Total Quality Business Schools" in order to meet the challenges of the 21st century.

REFERENCES

1. Dr. M. Narayana Rao, "Assessment of Quality and Standards of Education", *26th ISTE Convention.*
2. William Byrt (ed.), *Management Education : An International Survey* 1996.
3. *Encyclopaedia on Business Management*, 1996.
4. M.T. Telsang, "Quality Assurance of Technical Education", *26th ISTE Convention*, Jan. 4-6, 1997.
5. V.S. Raju, "Industry Institute Interaction", *National Conference*; *The Changing Needs,* 1st Feb. 1997.
6. P.M. Charantimath, "Role of Benchmarking & Quality Assurance in Management Education", *National Conference, AIMS Pune*, 1997.
7. V.C. Aralimatti, "Quality Education", *National Workshop on TQM*, Mar. 1997.
8. Dr. C.D. Nagangoudar, "Quality Management in Technical Education", *National Workshop on TQM*, March 1997.

11 Business Education Through Information Technology : Virtual-Classroom and Resource Sharing

—H.K. SHUBHANGI

INTRODUCTION

Information is the crux of modern education. Business Education extensively uses various sources of information to enhance and impart knowledge. The conventional sources have been well documented books and other hardcopy records of information carefully preserved in libraries and archives. In conventional education system, this is effected by creation and maintenance of libraries. Further, the existence of the collection in the libraries is publicized through Information Search facilities provided by various Documentation Agencies. The conventional libraries have such disadvantages as massive infrastructure requirements, huge budgets for acquisition and maintenance of the hardcopy documents such as Books, Journals and other Periodicals, etc. In professional education, specially, this is a huge task as the useful life of knowledge has greatly reduced.

The development in Computers and Information Technologies have helped alleviate some of the problems in knowledge dissemination. In early days of the Electronic Revolution, such facilities as the microfilming and magnetic recording of the 'papyrus' documents, to some extent, solved the problems associated with the maintenance of the documents. The real gains of the electronic revolution have been seen only after the data communication technologies developed into cost-effective networks of small computers. The Internet and its associated technologies have further made 'global schools' possible.

The networking and data communication technology used in the libraries assisted in making this library information electronically catalogued. This electronic catalogue accessible to users spread over a large geographical extent. However, the knowledge itself was not accessible over the network as it still existed in hardcopy form.

The developments in high speed mass storage technologies and media conversion technologies assisted in converting and arranging the documents in libraries in electronic form. The mass storage devices like Fixed Disks, CDROMs, Magneto-Optical disks, Laser disks, DVDs, etc. made possible the transformation of hardcopy documents into electronic books. Conversion of documents into electronic form was largely expedited by media conversion technologies like scanners, CCD cameras and video recorders. The books in electronic form were, however, still accessible to a limited group of users due to networking restrictions.

The inter-networking of computer networks extended the accessibility of the electronic library to a larger group of users. It further made possible collaborative and co-operative libraries possible. Libraries could now procure and maintain documents without duplication and in a more orderly manner.

The deployment of Internet worldwide in the 1990's gave the real impetus to teleteaching and global classroom. Such Internet technologies as e-mail, ftp, telnet, Gopher, ARCHIE, VERONICA, World Wide Web (WWW) opened to the modern teacher and the student a new horizon of knowledge acquisition. The ever-evolving Internet is providing newer technologies to explore and adopt for teleteaching. Web sites with HTML, CGI, Java, etc. have made admissions, teaching, evaluation and appraisal possible on the Internet without manual intervention. INTRANET has further provided the necessary Internet tools to Educational Institutes for effective implementation of teleteaching.

There has been advancement in other electronic technologies such as Satellite Communication, Very Small Aperture Terminals (VSAT), Television Engineering, Radio Engineering, etc. An amalgamation of all these has led to such teaching aids as Radio

Courses and Teleconferencing. However, this paper limits itself to use of Computer Network Technologies as a tool for Teleteaching as it is believed that this provides a more effective multimedia teaching environment.

THE MODEL OF A VIRTUAL-CLASSROOM

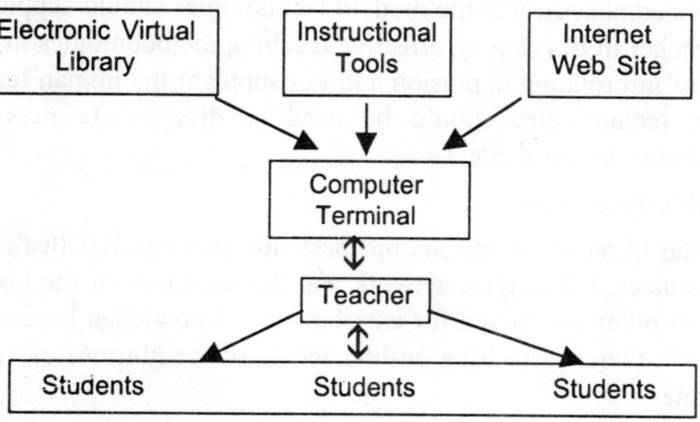

In this case the Instructor is facilitated by the Information Technology by virtually aiding him in his teaching work. Any textual matter from any book in the library to be used as a reference for instructions can be directly accessed through attaching to the Library Terminal in the classroom itself. Further the modern teaching tools like a overhead projector, or a LCD projector, or the computer-Projector Interface facilitate viewing of the information by the entire class as it projects and magnifies the computer console. The Reference text could be directly projected on the Interface.

Further, at any given point of time any clarification or doubt or any new addition to the knowledge base could be accessed through the Internet connectivity in the Classroom itself. It is possible even to communicate instantaneously to the faculty from other Institutes and even from the foreign Institutes while taking a lecture or imparting knowledge to the students. We also can access to the expert comments from the various faculty from different Institutes.

Telecommunication is a reality and the faculty from various institutes on the same subject can virtually share their knowledge on line and get clarified their doubts and enrich themselves through sound knowledge base.

This paper explores the possibility of resource sharing by various Institutes and build up a Virtual Educational Institute. However, the importance of a teacher-student interaction at human level cannot be ignored in this man-machine environment. The authors emphasize that the modern technologies should supplement the teacher in developing effective teaching methodologies in these days of information explosion and not supplant the human teacher. These technologies should be used to disseminate maximum knowledge to the student.

Library Resources

The libraries of various business and professional Institutions are connected through a network and the resources of the libraries of each other are shared for enrichment of knowledge base of one Institute, thereby ensuring on-line access of the libraries of various Institutes.

Technology Resources

The Technology can also be shared by various Institutes among themselves. In case of a technical Institute like Engineering College, where the Laboratories are already well set up with latest equipment. The Management or Business Schools can virtually share and access these resources specially the computer facilities. The Engineering Colleges normally are well set up with different types of operating systems and Network with different variety software and modern peripherals. The same could be accessed through the local telephone line through model by the Business Schools. Similarly, the huge library of the Management Schools could be accessed by the students of Technical Institutes.

Virtual Model

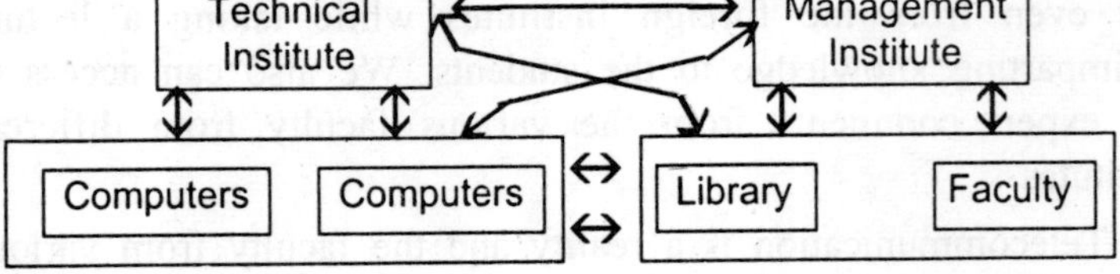

A VIRTUAL-CLASSROOM AND RESOURCE SHARING

A Virtual-Classroom could be visualized as a set of electronic tools provided to the teacher for developing a course, registration of students, delivery of the instructions, periodic and end-of-course evaluation of the student, teacher appraisal, research, etc.

General infrastructure for a Virtual-Classroom : A Virtual-classroom consists of a Web Site which can be accessed from a network running TCP/IP protocol suite. A number of HTML pages with Java and scripting tools support student registration, course material as animated multimedia documents, tutorials and tests. Evaluation and reporting is implemented as dynamic HTML documents with CGI.

AN ELECTRONIC CLASSROOM

Classroom teaching could be enhanced in terms of quantity and quality by use of modern electronic teaching aids such as Hypertext documents, LCD Projection systems and Video conferencing. Typically a teacher would connect to the appropriate Web site from a computer in the classroom and project the Hypertext documents, presentation slides, Video conferencing images to the students using a LCD Projection system. The students could interact with the teleteachers through a bidirectional communication channel in the form of tele-interviews, HTML form submission, etc.

IMPLEMENTATION

An *Intranet* is being set up at the authors' Institute with Network Operating Systems, TCP/IP protocol suite, Web Servers, HTML documents and CGI for implementing electronic teaching. The two Institutes are linked over PSTN to share the Engineering and Management resources. Faculty at the two Institutes share the available resources for a mutual exchange of information in classroom teaching and in research.

CONCLUSION

It may be summarized that use of modern computer, data communication and networking technologies, the Internet, Satellite and Television Engineering and their combinations has opened up new vistas for teaching in Professional Education where effective quality education can be imparted to students with the help of experts and libraries all over the world making Global Classroom a reality.

REFERENCES

1. Parag Diwan, Technological Blueprint for Distant Education, *Indian Management*, February 1997.
2. Pravin Prashant, Better Delivery, *Indian Management*, October 1997.
3. Fred T. Hofstetter, *Multimedia Literacy*.
4. S. Bhatnagar, Satyapal Anand, *Education and Technology*.
5. Robert A. Reiser, Robert M. Gagne, *Selecting Media by Instruction*.
6. S. Parmaji, *Distance Education*.

12 Case Study Approach as an Effective Tool for Teaching Business Studies : A Model Building

—M.R. SHOLLAPUR

INTRODUCTION

The main objective of this paper is to evolve and introduce the case study approach as a tool for effective teaching that is academically desirable and practically feasible at the +2 course in Commerce which is also called as Business Studies under the new curriculum which has come into force from the academic year 1995-96.

The paper is divided into four sections. The first section spells out the thrust issues of commerce education at +2 stage. The second section presents the highlights of the new curriculum in Commerce. The third section deals with the model building of 'case study approach' as a tool for teaching Commerce. The fourth section lists out certain pre-requisites for the meaningful adoption of case study approach for teaching Commerce.

As a part of model-building exercise, a sample questionnaire designed to study the structural and functional aspect of a business organization is given. The *modus operandi* of its use in teaching is referred to in the third section.

I. The Thrust Issues of Commerce Education at +2 Stage

Education is undoubtedly acknowledged as an input of development. Through imparting knowledge and infusing the sense of values with an attitude of reason, education produces the manpower that is more skilled and more adoptable to the needs of the nation. Commerce education is one such a branch of education which aims at injecting the business skills and talents and thereby prepares its learners to enter into the business field in different capacities, who in turn contribute to the overall well-being of the society. Over these years, Commerce education in India has grown in leaps and bounds especially due to growth of trade and industry, increasing emphasis on organizational problems, growing scientific attitude towards the problems of management, realization on the part of the business of the urgency of modernising the business organization, etc.

The objective of Commerce education is to prepare the students for personally fruitful and socially useful careers in related activity.[1] The primary objectives of Commerce education may be spelt out as below[2] :

1. To educate the future practitioners in trade and industry.
2. To train teachers and research workers.
3. To engage in research activities.
4. To perform a variety of service activities such as educational programmes for teachers and for persons in business and consulting service for business firms and government agencies.

These objectives encase in them a vision of Commerce education as a whole, reflecting the broader aspirations to be fulfilled. Since the Commerce education is imparted in three different strata *viz.*, +2 or pre-university, undergraduate and postgraduate stages; the broader vision of Commerce education should be ideally spread over to each strata so that effective and workable operational objectives at each strata can be set.

Since the +2 stage is an entry-point to the stream of Commerce education, the following primary objectives can be attached to the Commerce course of this stage :

1. To introduce the course in terms of what it is all about.
2. To present an outline of the course highlighting its significance, *i.e.*, the role of business and its contribution to society.

3. To specify the job areas associated with the course.
4. To equip the students with elementary skills relating to various business activities.

In addition to these primary objectives, the following subsidiary objectives can also be enlisted :

1. To provide a thorough conceptual foundation relating to the subjects taught under the course.
2. To provide exposure to the students as much as possible, relating to the real life situations in business.
3. To make the students competent enough to undergo successfully the foundation courses leading to professional degrees in view of the present facility of pursuing the professional courses like CA, ICWA, ACS, etc. soon after the +2 stage.
4. To make the students 'the exact fit' to the undergraduate course in Commerce.
5. To motivate the students to stay on in the stream of Commerce education without taking any switch-over to other courses.

These objectives in the ultimate analysis aim at the noble task of the requisite skill-building through which the realization of vision of Commerce education is ensured. The skill in this context is nothing but an ability to use one's own knowledge effectively and readily in the satisfactory performance of a task assigned. It is a power of doing any particular thing competently. The +2 stage being the foundation stage, the skill building exercises should begin from here onwards on gradual and phased manner. Hence, the content of the Commerce course and its orientation at +2 stage go a long way in building skills in the students.

II. Highlights of the Restructured Curriculum in Commerce

Karnataka is one of the first states in the country to introduce the two-year pre-university course as a separate department in the year 1971-72. In April, 1971, the first of the syllabi, the course of the study and the scheme of examination were framed. The syllabi have undergone subsequent revisions in 1981 and 1986. The latest restructuring of the course which has come into force from the academic year 1995-96 has taken a major departure from the previous attempts of revisions both in terms of content and orientation. The Board of Pre-University Education has conducted orientation trainings to the teachers in Commerce all over the state for a period of almost two years before it was brought into force so that the teachers could know and equip themselves with the novel teaching skills which the new curriculum necessitates.

The Underlying Spirit of the New Curriculum. The highlights of the new curriculum in Commerce are :

1. Changing the nomenclature from 'Commerce' to 'Business Studies'.
2. Evolving a participatory curriculum : group discussions, interactions with business professionals and practitioners, etc. are made mandatory.
3. Setting a business laboratory where business practicals are carried out.
4. Stressing on exposure through business visits, interactions, etc.
5. Emphasizing skill building through innovative and effective teaching techniques like case-studies.
6. Making the course-contents more balanced *i.e.*, 40% of the contents relate to basics in Commerce, 30% relate to undergraduate course in Commerce and the balance 30% relate to professional courses like CA, ICWA, etc.
7. Incorporating well-defined instructional objectives[3] wherein 30% is knowledge-oriented, 40% is understanding-oriented, 20% is application-oriented, and 10% is skill development-oriented.

It is evident from the aforesaid highlights of the new curriculum that the prime focus of the new curriculum is to make the course in business studies application-oriented by providing practical involvement to the students in different avenues of business. It is suitably designed with a view to equip the students with the skills needed in setting up of own enterprise, planning, organizing and executing any business activity, raising needed funds, promoting and selling products successfully. Accordingly, the teaching techniques need to be streamlined. Of the various teaching tools and techniques like discussions, arranging guest lectures of business professionals and practitioners, conducting practicals at business laboratory, business visits and case studies as spelled out in the curriculum; the case study approach is more novel and unique at +2 stage as an effective tool of teaching.

III. Case Study Approach : Conceptual Foundation and Practical Application

A case study is an indepth, comprehensive study of a person, a social group, an episode, a process, a situation, a programme, a community, an institution or any other social unit.[4] The case study in its broader perspective is designed to gather descriptive information of the respective unit of the study aimed at identifying the various characteristics/essentials, understanding its life-cycle, explaining the interaction between the factors that explain the present status or the development over a period of time. It gives a total view or an overall generic picture of the unit or process or programme selected for the study. It studies everything about something rather than something about everything. Intensive analysis of specific details provides answers to questions like what, where, when, how and why. Discovery of facts through these questions and their interaction contributes to our understanding of realities. The information needed for such an intensive investigation is collected through different techniques *viz.*, observation, personal interview, etc.

The broad objectives of teaching-oriented case studies are :

1. To provide conceptual clarity,
2. To improve understanding and grasping faculty,
3. To develop analytical skills, and
4. To foster those qualities that can improve the decision making skills.

In a bid to bring home the fundamental concepts to the students, a teacher is found in quoting the live instances of presenting hypothetical situations or making use of pictorial/graphical tools which broadly come under the ambit of case studies. Since they are being quoted within the four walls of the classroom, drawn from the imaginative faculty of the teacher, such instances may fail to import the intended message effectively. Hence, a need is felt to involve the students in the process of learning.

Modus Operandi of Case Study

For the purpose of teaching, case study can be undertaken in respect of any unit.[5] The objective of the study in each case should be spelt out clearly. The different activities/steps that are involved

TABLE 1

Mechanism of Case Study and its Significance

Sl. No.	Steps involved	Time frame (Approximate weeks)	Resultant learning output obtained in execution of each stage of the case study
1.	Introduce the concept of proprietary concern in the classroom	1	An idea of proprietary concern.
2.	Ask the students to select a concern	2	Observation and comparison of the units locally found.
3.	Prepare a simple questionnaire involving the student in this process	1	Reasoning and testifying.
4.	Students asked to collect the information according to the questionnaire	2	Observation, collection, comprehension, interpersonal skills.
5.	Monitor and process	In Routine course	Alertness, honesty, doubt-clarifications.
6.	Writing down the observations by the students	1	Reasoning and understanding skills, analytical and interpreting skills, communication skills, decision-making skills.

in the process of case study and the significance of each of the activities/steps in the overall process of learning is given in Table 1. (The unit selected is a sole proprietary concern and the object of the study is to know its structural and functional apsects.)

Thus, it is quite obvious that, the case study approach provides a platform of learning through experiencing. The students are made to undertake a scientific inquiry through observation, collection, analysis, interpretation, and decision-making. It enhances the analytical ability, broadens the breadth and flexibility of mind, fosters imagination, develops interpersonal contacts, improves communication skills and in its ultimate analysis imbibes decision-making skills, which is badly lacking at present, with the students of business-studies.

IV. Pre-requisites for Meaningful Adoption

Despite the significance of case study approach, its introduction at Pre-University stage raises certain doubts and fears too. The important among them are as follows :

1. Suitability of the topics for understanding through case study.
2. Willingness of Pre-University students to undertake each study.
3. Time factor involved in successful completion of the study.
4. Practicability of the teacher to supervise each case study.
5. Cost factor involved in the studies.
6. Response from the local units selected.
7. Authenticity of the data furnished.
8. Fear of data duplication and manipulation by the students.
9. Provision of academic infrastructure.
10. Motivational aspect of such studies.

There are, however, certain pre-requisites which go a long way in making the case study approach the most successful and meaningful exercise. It is the readiness of the teachers to equip themselves with the new skills of teaching that the new curriculum warrants, the readiness of the business community in particular to extend their helping hands in furnishing the information about their business, the whole-heartedness of the authorities in motivating the teachers, the initiation of the concerned authorities in filling the gaps of the academic infrastructure, etc. have a salutary effect on making the case study approach a success.

Annexure

Questionnaire for Studying the Structural and Functional Aspects of a Proprietary Concern*

I. Identification

1. Proprietor's name :
2. Age :
3. Name of the concern :
4. Date of commencement :
5. Place of business :
6. Nature of business (mark the appropriate one) :
   (a) Próduction :
   (b) Buying and selling :
   (c) Service seller :
   (d) Others :
7. Goods dealt in :
8. Size of business : Small/medium/large
9. Is it ancestral business? : Yes/No

II. Organisation and Management

A. *Organisation*

1. How was the idea to commence business conceived?
2. Time gap between the conception of the idea and its execution.
3. Whose help was sought in executing the idea and how?
4. Permission from local authority taken : Yes/No

---

*This questionnaire can be made use of in studying a proprietary concern which is engaged in trading.

B. *Management*

1. Qualification of the proprietor :
2. Different types of activities involved in the business :
   (a)
   (b)
   (c)
   (d)
3. Who assists in managing the business : Family member/Paid Manager/Others
4. In what way the family members assist in the business? :
5. How are business decisions taken :
   (a) Independently :
   (b) On consultation with : Family members/ manager/fellow businessmen
6. Is it possible to supervise the business personally? : Yes/No

III. Raising of Capital

1. Total capital invested :
2. Source :
   (a) Owned funds :
   (b) Borrowed funds :
3. How owned funds were pooled? :
4. Particulars of debt :

Sl. No.	Sources	Amount (Rs.)	Rate of interest
1.	Relatives		
2.	Friends		
3.	Bank		
4.	Others		

5. Do you feel the capital adequate? State reasons :
6. What plans are made to tap up the additional capital? :

IV. Purchasing Function

1. Source of purchase : Local/outside
2. Total annual purchase (Rs.) :
3. Purchase expenses, if any, and the amount thereof : (a)
   (b)
   (c)
   (d)
4. Is credit facility available? : Yes/No
   (a) Amount of credit purchase (Rs.) :
   (b) Repayment of credit : Instalment/Lumpsum
5. Problems involved in purchasing function : (a)
   (b)
   (c)

V. Selling Function

1. Place of sales :
2. Coverage of market :
3. Total annual sales (Productwise) : (a)
   (b)
   (c)
   (d)
4. Expenses to effect sales and the amount thereof : (a)
   (b)
   (c)
   (d)

5. Are goods sold on credit? : Yes/No
6. Problems of credit collection : (a)
(b)
(c)
7. Problems faced in selling function : (a)
(b)
(c)

VI. Accounting Information

A. *Relating to purchase and sale of goods* :

1. Total annual purchases (Rs.) :
2. Total purchase expenses (Rs.) :
3. Total annual sales (Rs.) :
4. Total selling expenses (Rs.) :
5. Stock (Rs.) :
   (a) Opening :
   (b) Closing :

B. *Relating to general incomes and expenses of business* :

Expenses	Rs.	Income	Rs.
Salary/wages		Interest	
Rent		Commission	
Repairs		Bad-debts recovered	
Commission		Others	
Bad debts			
Interest on loan			
Others	______		______
	______		______

C. *Assets held by the business concern* :
(a)
(b)
(c)
(d)

D. *Outside Liabilities payable by the concern* :

(a)

(b)

(c)

(d)

REFERENCES

1. Pierson *et al.*, : "The Education of American Business", *Carniege Series*, McGraw-Hill Publications, (1959), p. 27.
2. Ghosh, A.B., *Commerce Education*, S. Chand & Sons (1969), pp. 23-34.
3. This weightage is the outcome of the five days' workshop conducted by the Board of Pre-University Education in Bangalore from 5th to 9th Dec., 1994, for evolving the concepts and criteria for setting the model question papers in Business Studies.
4. Krishnaswamy, O.R., *Methodology of Research in Social Sciences*, Himalaya Publishing House (1993), p. 64.
5. For the sake of simplicity, the word, 'unit' is referred to. It may cover any organisation or any unit of study as specified in the course-content.

13 Innovations in Management Education — Some Structural Issues

—A.H. CHACHADI

Management education essentially aims at developing managers who can face the challenges posed by the external environment. Management is universally relevant to the extent that all organizations, profit-making or non profit-making, need management to survive, grow and expand. Ever since the concept management education was evolved, there have been sincere attempt to develop need based methods which can prepare managers to face tomorrow's challenges. When compared to management of non-profit organizations, management of profit-making organizations has received wider attention and effort. In this paper essential focus is on innovation in management education.

There are four participants in the process of management education. They are :

1. Students or participants
2. Trainers
3. User organizations (represented by executives)
4. Training organizations.

Innovations are response to the stimuli received from the environment. Field of management has been subjected to many changes on account of changes in the relevant environments such as economic, political, social, cultural and technological. It is these environments which bring about changes in management practices. Since management education is essentially user-based, the changes in the environment have to be noted and suitable changes made in the methods of management development. The relevance of management education depends on how well the training institution, trainers and participants interact with user organization which itself is influenced by the external environment apart from its own. Fig. 1 illustrates these linkages. M.B.A. by far is the most popular programme in management education and naturally most talked about. In a recent issue of Fortune[1], Alan Dentsman says "Business schools are not giving them skills that employers need — leading, creating, communicating — so companies are doing it themselves or looking elsewhere". Peters and Waterman writing on the rationality which led the American industry astray, talks of 'Paralysis through analysis' a phenomenon for which rational thinking is held responsible. They say that professionalism has hindered risk-taking and thereby resulted in more of procastination. A recent article in Business India[2] talks of a project envisaged by Indo-German Chamber of Commerce which proposes to recruit fresh graduates and subject them to rigorous on-the-job management training in tune with the German traditions as they feel that prevalent practices in training managers do not have the needed touch with practice.

Discussed above are the warning signals which make us think again on issues involved in management education. As warned by Herbert Simon[3] Management Education and Practice are like water and oil unless mixed continuously they will separate out. It is in this context that existing mode of interaction between user business

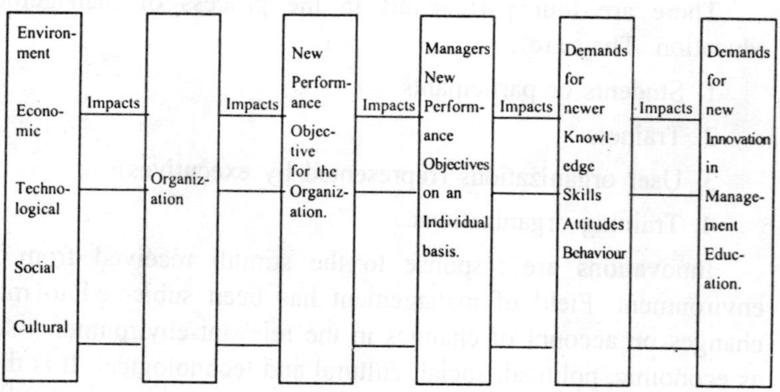

Fig. 1

organizations on the one hand and training institutions, trainers, participants involved in management education on the other hand has to be re-examined to evolve more effective rapport so that the gap can be reduced. See Fig. 2.

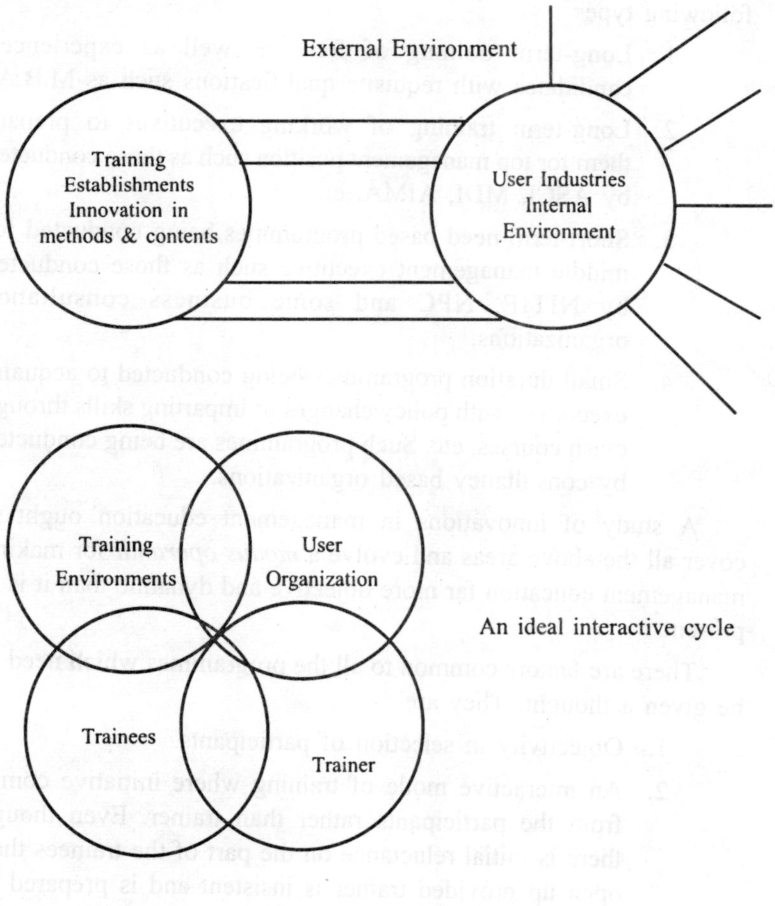

Fig. 2

Following areas need to be studied in greater details :

1. User organization and management development institution linkages.

2. Trainers and user organization linkages.

3. Students and management development institution linkages after training.
4. Student and user organization linkages during training.

General management development effort can be classified into following types :

1. Long-term training of fresh as well as experienced candidates with requisite qualifications such as M.B.A.
2. Long-term training of working executives to prepare them for top management position such as those conducted by ASCI, MDI, AIMA, etc.
3. Short-term need based programmes being conducted for middle management executive such as those conducted by NITIE, NPC and some business consultancy organizations.
4. Small duration programmes being conducted to acquaint executives with policy changes or imparting skills through crash courses, etc. Such programmes are being conducted by consultancy based organizations.

A study of innovations in management education ought to cover all the above areas and evolve a *modus operandi* for making management education far more objective and dynamic than it is at present.

There are factors common to all the programmes which need to be given a thought. They are :

1. Objectivity in selection of participants.
2. An interactive mode of training where initiative comes from the participants rather than trainer. Even though there is initial reluctance on the part of the trainees they open up provided trainer is insistent and is prepared to tolerate the initial 'dullness' in the classroom.
3. Any lasting impact on people being trained for managerial positions can be made only when the knowledge base on which they are operating is examined and corrections are begun from that end rather than the skills, attitude and behaviour which are more of an outcome than basis.

4. In essence, it can be said that while developing people for management, the focus need be on the 'personality factors' rather than techniques and processes as those are outcomes of deeply embedded personality traits.

Based on this hypothesis a survey was conducted.

1. METHODOLOGY

In order to assess the impact of changing environment, a survey including sixty students, ten teachers of management, ten executives and five training organizations was conducted. A questionnaire followed by personal discussions, wherever possible, was used.

2. SURVEY DETAILS

Students : All the students except 2 persons *i.e.*, 96 per cent of them felt that business environment was changing and needed corresponding changes in the training system. More than half of the students at 60 per cent opined that M.B.A. curriculum should be standardized through a professional monitoring organization like Institute of Chartered Accountants or Institute of Cost and Works Accountants. Advantages cited include :

1. There will be some degree of responsibility attached to the award of M.B.A.
2. Through a national level body of experts syllabi can be changed often to reflect the latest thinking in business area.
3. There can be a common entrance test of all the students which will bring down the large variety in approaches.
4. There will be a code of ethics for M.B.A. which is highly essential, failing which he or she can be disqualified from practising as a manager.

With regard to the existing structure of M.B.A. courses following changes were suggested by the remaining 40 per cent of respondents. Some of the improvements cited were as follows :

1. Government should decide and allocate specific areas for developing managers. It was felt that existing courses were too generalized and more specific attempt could be made to train manager for different areas of industry.

Citing the example of textile industry whose problems differed considerably from other industries, a case was made out for a separate management institute which will prepare managers with focus on textile industry and problems.

2. On the lines of Institute of Rural Development Management, it was felt that Institutes should have relevant themes and should be in the area where such efforts are concentrated.
3. It was suggested that every institute should have advisory committee consisting of eminent industrialists from the area around and they in consultation with academicians advise on what changes should be made in the methods and contents of the training based on the current trends and experience. Such an ongoing effort on a continuous basis was felt a must for improving the quality of trained managers.
4. As each institute can gain considerably from the experience of the other institution it was recommended that there should be closer co-operation and collaboration on a systematic lines leading to exchange of views by the teachers and students. This will instill more confidence while bringing in new ideas.
5. In order to ensure balanced development of the region in which the institute is situated, it was recommended that a quota of seats should be allocated on industry basis for the sponsored candidates.
6. Regarding admission procedures it was felt that focus should be more on conducting unstructured stress interviews as it was felt that ability to manage stress was an important prerequisite for good performance of managers.
7. Dearth of good Indian cases was felt as an impediment in management education. In this regard setting up of National Care Development Fund was recommended to ensure development of sufficient number of cases as dearth of time and dearth of funds were cited as major

impediments in case development particularly for management institution coming under University administration.

8. It was suggested that a more balanced approach is necessary in funding management institutes since there is a lot of imbalance between funding of National Institutes of Management and the schools coming under the University setup.
9. Long standing interaction with industries around on a continuous basis was felt essential to ensure testing of concepts and ideas.
10. It was also suggested that there must be encouragement given to experts both in industry and academicia to write books on management through a special fund or a book trust and the existing over-reliance on foreign books is proving too irrational.

Following are some of the views expressed by the teachers of management :

1. Business management institutions should be delinked from University setups. This was the view of 70 per cent of respondents. The reasons cited in favour of this observation were :

1. Business management education is a multidisciplinary effort which requires pooling up of efforts more particularly from outside the university.
2. The hours of work, style of work and methods of training differ substantially from other departments in the university.
3. In the administration of a business school, there has to be continuous interaction with the outside world, this requires that quick decisions have to be made. The existing setup of university has an elaborate decision-making system thereby rendering divisions obsolete.
4. Business school has to compete for funds with other departments as an equal while its needs and programmes are entirely different.

2. Institutions should be autonomous with liberal funding by industry. Such institutions should receive grants directly from University Grants Commission or from Ministry of Education.

3. Existing system of examination should be abandoned. Focus should be on joint assessment by teachers on the lines of group interview. Weightage of final examination should be gradually brought to nil while increasing the focus on performance in field work, case studies, etc.

4. Eighty per cent of respondents felt that there be less focus on use of lectures and more on role play, discussions, seminars, etc.

Following were the observations made by the executives. Out of the ten executives interviewed four were professional managers with prior training in management and six were technical men who had come through ranks. Eighty per cent of the executives were of the opinion that present methods of training and selection, M.B.As. are inadequate. They had the following observations to make :

1. M.B.As. lack human skills particularly skills of interaction and team building.
2. There is poor understanding of ground realities leading to non-performance and a good lot of troubles to start with.
3. Specializations offered are leading to compartmentalization thereby producing serious imbalance in understanding the total problem.
4. Experience prior to management education is not being given enough importance whereas such candidates are likely to respond much better to the management education programmes.

Following suggestions were given to overcome the existing limitations :

1. There should be more vigorous interface with industry. Students should work in close liaison with industry on live management problems.
2. Regular exposure to the changing environment through interaction with executives on the job. For this it was suggested that the students must visit the industry

concerned rather than expecting executives to visit Institutes as it is very difficult for them to get time off for such jobs.

3. Rigid specialization should give way to sandwich type of courses where a student has exposure to all the areas of managements while he may have special knowledge in one area.
4. There should be a fixed quota for sponsored candidates in the regular M.B.A. courses so that industries can improve their manpower through regular deputations.

Of the five training institutions chosen for interaction two belonged to banks, one belonged to educational foundations, two belonged to industry as training departments of which one was in private sector and the other in public sector.

Three of the five institutions expressed dissatisfaction with what was happening *i.e.*, the quality of training. The reasons cited were :

1. Not enough funds and time are devoted to training functions. Much is sought to be achieved in a short time thereby limiting the quality of effort.
2. Very often faculty drawn from within and outside, lack training skills thereby resulting in obvious lack of interest by the trainees.
3. Trainees are often not physically or mentally prepared to undergo a rigorous exercise thereby limiting the response and in turn reduce the levels of motivation reached by trainers.
4. Line managers lack adequate interest in training function and do not involve themselves in the formulation of training, thereby isolating training from realities.

Following were some of the recommendations to improve the training function :

1. The existing awareness of the importance of training and development is too inadequate to ensure due importance to the function. There should be a national level effort to bring about such an awareness, through a systematic campaign through media and otherwise.

2. There is a dearth of organizations to train the trainers particularly in the field of management education. There should be more such institutions at regional and national levels so that professionals can sharpen their training skills to increase their effectiveness.
3. Right from recruitment focus should be laid on active interest to be shown by the participants in improving their career profile by active participation in training and development efforts. Response to training and development should be given due weightage in performance evaluation.
4. Active involvement of line managers in developing training programmes should become a criterion in their performance evaluation.

Limitations of the Study

The size of the respondents in each case was limited keeping in view their proximity and willingness to interact personally with a researcher. This was based on the personal experience of the researcher that total dependence on questionnaire response can sometimes be misleading. Here the survey has been used to test the ideas and generate ideas wherever possible. The responses of the student community was most satisfactory as many creative ideas were put forward on the subject.

3. ANALYSIS

Analyzing the total function of management education it can be said that 'today management education is in a state of flux'. Past assumptions and presumptions are being put to serious test and the whole field is looking for a serious overhaul to make management education more responsive to ground realities. When glanced through, the responses give a feeling that something must be done to redefine the role of trainer, trainee, training establishments and the user organizations. To illustrate, N.R. Seth in a recent contribution on the subject says "Management education needs to be organized and promoted in relation to the national priorities".[4] This substantiates some of the views expressed by students. In another context N.R. Seth[5] lauds the performance of institute of Rural Management and National Institute of Bank Management as they are able to develop indigenous teaching material considered highly essential in teaching of management. While accepting the dearth of adequate teaching material he laments non-establishment of National case clearing house. V.A. Panadikar[6] writing on the same theme advocates a more pragmatic approach to manage the information revolution leading to a knowledge based society, rather than one involved in just producing and selling goods. In this regard he deplores the rigid classroom approach and lack of an open-ended approach to teaching of management. K.C. Sahu[7] writing on the theme Reorienting Management Education says, concurrently, the education system must be based on full faith in teachers, like those prevailing in IISCs, IITs, IIMs and other such autonomous institutions to plan, execute and control the total process including evaluation of students by the concerned teachers. This goes well and substantiates the view of teachers that existing system of examination in management education must be slowly abandoned to pave way for more objective methods of evaluation.

4. RECOMMENDATIONS

A. Trainee

1. The methods of selecting candidates for undergoing training in management particularly the M.B.A. courses must change giving more scope for candidates' ability to read surrounding environment on one hand and managing stress on other.

2. Preference needs to be given to prior work experience of candidates as it helps the learning process by providing a good 'learning model' otherwise management education could become vague and uninteresting. Similarly effort needs to be made in selecting candidates for ongoing management training programmes from within the industry. An effort to understand and match the background of the candidate with the programme is a must. Candidate's or Participant's response to and performance in training programmes must become a criteria for his performance evaluation otherwise learning processes will slowly become extinct.

B. Trainer

3. More freedom must be given to teacher in the training process and there should be less reliance on examination as a

system. Management education must be made more dynamic by keeping it open-ended and giving scope for use of new methods already known and development of innovative methods, not known presently with the sole aim of improving the quality of management education and achieving the objective of developing a prudent, warm and responsive manager in this fast changing world.

C. Training Establishments

4. Training establishments particularly the business schools must be liberated from the clutches of monitoring organizations such as the universities and functional and to some extent administrative autonomy needs to be given to enable them to function effectively.

5. Creation of a national level institution of professional managers and giving it the required status to devise the syllabi from time to time and conduct examination will greatly reduce the existing anomalies in management education and increase the status and prestige of the course.

6. A code of ethics must be developed for professional manager and a failure to live upto it results in his being discredited from membership of the proposed national level professional body. This is essential to curb fraudulent practices in the name of 'professionalism' wherever they exist.

7. A fund should be established by the Ministry of Education to promote development of indigenous cases as well as teaching material in the form of books, audio tapes and video-cassettes as well.

8. A national level case clearing house is long over due and must be established to pool the existing scattered effort and direct the future effort.

9. A national level organization in the form of Indian society for training and development is already existing. Its efforts must be supported through policy as well as funds to create awareness about training and development as a function on one hand and creating facilities for training the trainers in management education thereby improving the quality of training process.

10. Tax incentives may be given to organization, for assigning funds for training and development thereby augmenting the national effort of human asset creation.

11. Existing setups of business school under the University system can be augmented through a management education advisory board consisting of entrepreneurs, Chief executives, Functional Managers apart from institutes' own faculty. This board will guage the changing performance expectations of the functioning manager and bring about appropriate changes in the content and methodology of training. These are some of the innovations which can be given a thought in restructuring of management education.

REFERENCES

1. *Fortune*, July 29, 1991, p. 122.
2. *Business India*, Aug. 5-18, p. 30.
3. Herbert Simon, *Administrative Behaviour*, Harper and Row.
4. *Economic and Political Weekly*, Nov. 30, 1991, p. m126.
5. *Ibid.*
6. *Ibid.* p. m132.
7. *Ibid.,* p. m136.

14 Progress and Problems of Business Education in India Since Independence

—Z.U. KAHRIOOWALA,
RAIS AHMAD KHAN AND
M.S.M. AL-SHAIKH

Commerce education in India has passed through several vicissitudes in the past one century. Commerce education has more relevance with changing business environment and has become a part of it which means the knowledge about various business activities like industry, trade, transport, banking, insurance, etc. It mainly relates with educating and training the operations of all these business activities.

COMMERCE EDUCATION IN INDIA BEFORE INDEPENDENCE

Commerce education began in India as early as 1886 when the first commercial school was set up in Madras by the Trustees of Pachiapp's charities. The Madras Government instituted examinations in commerce at about the same time. The Government of India started a school of commerce in Calicut (Kerala) in 1895. In 1903, commerce classes were started in the Presidency College, Calcutta. Between 1903 and 1912, Commercial institutions were also started in Bombay and Delhi with facilities for training in Type-writing, shorthand, correspondence and Business Methods, Commerce education at the university level began with the establishment of the Sydenham College of Commerce and Economics in Bombay in 1913.

GROWTH OF COMMERCE EDUCATION IN INDIA AFTER INDEPENDENCE

After Independence in 1960 there were 35 universities offering commerce as a special subject and at the school level there were 15 Secondary Education Boards in India dealing with commerce education. With an increase in trade and commerce in the country, the commerce education has also spread rapidly. In India there were about 17900 students in B.Com. courses in 1950. This number increased to about 10 lakhs in 1992.

ENROLMENT OF STUDENTS IN COMMERCE

The following table shows the details of enrolment of students in commerce from 1950-51 to 1991-92.

TABLE 1

Enrolment of Students in Commerce

Year	Enrolment in Commerce	Total Enrolment
1950-51	17,915	165,359
1966-67	1,23,119	11,55,548
1972-73	3,18,888	21,68,107
1976-77	4,25,459	23,59,670
1977-78	4,63,957	25,64,972
1980-81	5,54,253	27,52,437
1981-82	6,28,031	29,52,066
1982-83	6,69,813	31,33,093
1987-88	8,57,971	39,10,828
1991-92	10,09,832	46,11,107

Source : Annual Reports of University Grants Commission.

The above noted table reveals that in 1950-51 there were only 17,900 commerce students, which rose to 10,09,832 in 1991-92 showing an overall rise of 5542 per cent. While the total enrolment of students in all the subjects in 1950-51 were 1,65,359 which has gone up to 46,11,107 in 1991-92 showing an overall increase of

2688 per cent. This leads to a conclusion that the overall growth of enrolment of students in commerce has been about thirty-five times over 1950-51.

MALADIES

The commerce education in India has been facing numerous problems which are as follows :

Present system and courses of commerce education do not have any occupational source; it lacks practical orientation while determining curriculum hence unable to solve industrial problems; apathy of Government and U.G.C., towards commerce education; the present system of commerce education not suited for the growing complex of the organization and social needs of the growing economy; university education is supposed to impart conceptual knowledge, not professional knowledge; lack of uniformity in curriculum; indiscrimination in admission; non-availability of suitable text books; lack of interaction with industry; no job opportunities are available to commerce graduates in rural areas and management education is considered as professional education though it is an extension of commerce education.

REMEDIES

To improve the commerce education and making it suitable to the changing business environment, the government should take the following measures :

1. Government should provide financial support for practical commerce education;
2. to redesign the commerce courses by introducing practical areas, vocational or career-oriented in commerce education;
3. present syllabus must be parallel to professional courses like CA, ICWA, etc.;
4. to redesign the commerce courses at par with the requirements of modern industries and other organizations;
5. to reduce the classroom strength;
6. to provide regular training to commerce teachers to update their knowledge;

7. selection of the commerce teachers should be on the basis of their performance;
8. low standard of higher secondary education;
9. to provide training to commerce students to have a practical knowledge; and
10. financial and infrastructural support to business education should be provided by business houses; Teacher's orientation programme may be undertaken in co-operation with business houses; commerce teaching should be practice-oriented and accordingly system of practicals should be introduced.

Further, a number of measures can be undertaken by the universities to improve the scope of business education, which are as under :

1. The commerce education in universities should seek cooperation from the professional bodies, *e.g.*, ICWA, ICA, ICS, and also interact with Industrial houses;
2. to revise the syllabus of commerce courses from time and time and make it up to date with changing business environment, by involving the representatives of industries, Governments and professionals like Chartered Accountants, Cost Accountants, Company Secretaries and Managers, etc.;
3. the student should be given opportunity of role play live cases;
4. enforce the inspection of commerce colleges by the team of experts in commerce;
5. professional and noted industrialists should be invited to discuss practical situation;
6. university should conduct all examinations in time and declare results in time;
7. universities should organise seminars and workshops for commerce teachers to update their knowledge;
8. to promote vocational courses for providing practical guidance to the students;

9. emphasis must be given to practical training in the area of specialization both at graduate level and postgraduate level.

To improve the scope of commerce education in changing business environment some more suggestions are as under :

1. enforce strict discipline among the commerce teachers;
2. enforce knowledge oriented teaching rather examination oriented coaching;
3. enforce enrichment of commerce teachers by reading books and magazines;
4. develop libraries with rich collection of books and periodicals;
5. conduct examinations under strict supervision and control;
6. organise industrial visits to commerce students;
7. introduce job placement cells for commerce graduates;
8. provide audio-visual aids to the teachers;
9. enforce internal examinations for commerce students;
10. organise seminars and workshops for teachers and students;
11. enforce compulsory computer education to commerce students;
12. enforce compulsory 75 per cent attendance of students;
13. introduce teacher evaluation schemes for every year;
14. commerce and management being the two branches of business education should maintain a close contact and act in a cohesive manner rather than conflict and rivalry amongst themselves; and
15. commerce departments should diversify its functioning and should provide extension services like providing training to manpower for industrial and Government departments, consultancy services, etc.

CONCLUSION

Due to fast changing business education, *i.e.*, privatisation, liberalization and globalisation of Indian economy, it has become imperative on the part of business educationists to cater to the need of the market by imparting business education in a realistic manner with practical touch. This can be achieved by developing better linkage between Universities and Industries. The measures are required to be taken at different levels and develop commerce education as it is desired by business and industry.

REFERENCES

1. Prof. Jena, R.K., *The Indian Journal of Commerce*, A Quarterly of the Indian Commerce Association, Golden Jubilee Conference Issue (1996).
2. B. Narayan, *Commerce Education in India*, Devdas Bhorali (Ed.), Deep and Deep Publications, New Delhi (1987).
3. Mathur, M.V., *Report of the Special Committee on Commerce Education*, New Delhi (1981).

15 Computer Based Business Simulation Games — A Method of Teaching

—M. MANICKAM

INTRODUCTION

A review of the existing teaching methods reveals that most of them invariably keep the students to be patient listeners than active participants as regards the subjects dealt in a classroom situation are concerned. While such methods assume the credibility of leading the students towards their course completion, when it comes to a situation of relating the theoretical knowledge accumulated to the practical requirements the methods turn to be helpless. Under this condition it is imperative that there must be proper linkage between theoretical knowledge and the practical situation, in order to make the subjects more purposeful and meaningful. Business simulation games emerge as a new instructional method to fulfil the said need.

BUSINESS GAMES — A BRIEF DESCRIPTION

The job of business executives is closely associated with four important aspects : (i) Decision, (ii) Application, (iii) Revision and (iv) Reaction. The focus of the business game is mainly to provide the students a planned learning experience on the said four aspects. The participants in the game are expected to undergo the process of dynamic sequential decision-making, implementing, revising and reacting.

A business simulation is dynamic sequential decision-making problem structured around a model of business operations in which students make a number of inter-related decisions in managing the operations. The model describes the mechanism whereby the decisions of the players are translated into results. A game is intended to reproduce certain aspects of real life and through the operation of the decision-result cycle, the creator of the game establishes the fact that the result obtained in the game is expected to occur in real life situation also. The mechanism is built on the pattern existing in the creator's mind about how the real world behaves.

THE MEANING OF BUSINESS SIMULATION GAMES

A simulation game is designed to provide the players with an overall feel for the flows of costs, cash, profit, etc. through a business. The actual management of these flows in competition with other players gives the player a chance to learn through making a variety of decisions in simulated environments. A player learns through making mistakes but without the concomitant loss in time and risk of money. The advantages of making decisions in simulated environments are now becoming practical for classroom utilization due to widespread use of computers in teaching.

As an individual or a member of team, a player/student of management game is confronted by a situation that requires him to decide and act. The resultant consequences may either be good or bad; but then he faces a new situation which is at least, in part, of his own making. From this decision-result cycle he has the opportunity to learn. All games have some form of decision-result consequence and all are designed to create the learning opportunity; but the nature of the learning made possible can vary. This is influenced both by the actual design of the game and also by the manner in which it is used on each occasion. The players attempt to learn how the variables in the environment behave by a thorough analysis of the data provided in the simulation itself and thereby master the concepts and techniques which the simulation is designed to teach.

Winning and losing is a sensitive subject. But one aspect commonly observed is that those who lose in the games are to gain more from experience than those who win. The competitive instinct is so powerful that a player wants to identify himself as the winner and others as losers do. By repeating the play several periods games help the students find that the benefits of sound long run decisions offset those results of superficial short run decisions.

OBJECTIVES OF SIMULATION GAMES

Business games are designed to fill the gap between the theoretical ability to solve specific problems and the inability to implement this knowledge to real world problems. Business games are designed so that the degree of complexity-simplicity is determined and limited by the knowledge of the players. As a consequence of an intentionally designed environment containing certain characteristics, games provide many areas where highly technical and sophisticated concepts may be applied in order to select the optimum course of action. Irregularities are introduced into the statistical behaviour of several important areas of activity so that the student cannot deduce the absolute optimum course of action.

Hence the primary purpose of a business game is to place the students of managerial decision-making in a simulated real world environment so that the learning experience of students can be enriched. Through this environmental conditioning the element of realism — a real situation, a real benefit, and a real detriment — is drawn up on :

1. To capture the imagination and interest of the students,
2. To implement theory into practice, and
3. To allow the students to live with the consequences of their decisions.

In general business simulation games are used to :

1. Cause enjoyment.
2. Release knowledge already possessed.
3. Present new knowledge.
4. Encourage the practice of skills.
5. Provoke behaviour.
6. Stimulate thought.
7. Communicate a vision.
8. Practise teamwork and
9. Assess performance

BENEFITS OF BUSINESS SIMULATION GAMES

1. The student learns through mistakes without the concomitant loss of time and money.
2. Business games provide the student with a vehicle upon which to practise his Analytical tools.
3. The student is immediately provided with an integrated view of the firm's total operations. This integrated picture is a welcome contrast to the piecemeal approach used in teaching.
4. The importance of the functional areas and the necessity for maximizing the objectives of the total firm can be presented through management system approaches to decision-making within the firm.
5. The classroom competition stimulates interest in business courses.

CHARACTERISTICS OF MANAGEMENT GAMES

1. Good games create greater involvement from students bringing higher motivation to study and learn.
2. Competitive spirit existing in the majority of human beings gets people interested in games.
3. People are also interested in them because of the dynamic nature, always creating new problems to solve and new opportunities for success.
4. As the game develops by the strategies of the players and by the authority of the instructor, it gets rid of the classroom atmosphere and the students 'own' the training situation.
5. Management games allow physical movement and they tend to be less formal than other methods. Players rather than sitting in a particular place get up and move about, form committees, prepare graphs, conduct research, argue and relax in a way that is similar to their on-the-job behaviour.
6. Motivation is usually high and without the slightest encouragement from the instructor management games are played for long hours.

7. As management games are played by a number of teams, different problems crop up and they undergo changes several times according to the reasons at the moment of decision-making which makes the policies genuine. Thus there are more situations available for study than one in a case study.
8. Students have an opportunity to examine and reflect on their own behaviour — and to do it within a short time span when it has greater reality and has not had time to be rationalised away.
9. Prediction of human behaviour can be made easily through the use of management games.
10. The more the players become involved in the game the more the thoughts are devoted to the immediate object of winning and the less they reflect up on possible applications of their learning to the outside world.

ADMINISTRATION OF MANAGEMENT GAMES

The students of the simulation firm face the challenge of running the entire operations of the firm. Individually or as a member of the management team, he is charged with the responsibility of optimally managing the activities of the firm. The management simulation requires both current and long-run decisions on the part of the participants. Only through forcing an integration of the necessary period-to-period decision-making with long-run profit planning can a proper managerial frame of reference be obtained. In order to make good short-run decisions; management is required to forecast into the future. Thus, in each period the participant is required to make both long-run and short-run decisions. Any decision not compatible or consistent with the master plan must be modified. The decision for the current period must be further revised to assure that they attempt to maximize the long-run objectives of the firm.

A primary task in managing the firm will be the acquisition of relevant decision-making information. There are three sources of information. The first source of data is provided in the form of History Data. This Data will provide background information on the firm's operations from which one can discern how the different phases function and observe the influence of the decisions on the business. To start with, this data, provided to the teams, is uniform and depending upon the decision-making ability of the managers they change for the next period.

The second source of Information is contained in the instructions which explain the general range of the behaviour of the variables like Price, Production, and marketing expenditure.

The third and most important source of information will be the reports that will be received after each period of decision-making. These reports will be in the same form as the initial history and will give full and precise information on the firm. At the beginning of the simulation relatively little information is available about the market and competition. Although the simulation's design incorporates many general characteristics of actual industry, it is not a reproduction of that specific industry. Each team will be supplied with a statement showing comparative performance of all the teams.

CONCLUSION

In the context of the needs of the present day business education a method of teaching-learning will be considered as suitable only when it encourages self-learning, motivating for further learning and the outcome of the teaching-learning is more relevant to practical situations. Also the learning process is expected to be flexible and enjoyable. Business games place the students in a simulated environment wherein the students encounter the problems representing reality. Thus business games emerge as a new teaching-learning technique which suits to the needs of the present-day business education.

Keeping in line with the various aspects discussed above a simple, yet a comprehensive game is presented below. Students, teachers and business executives used the game on several occasions. Students and faculty can easily computerise the game operations.

GAME — PRICE, PRODUCTION AND MARKETING STRATEGY

Fire Works Limited is one of several companies selling crackers during Deepavali season. The crackers are manufactured once in a year well in advance so that retailers get the crackers before Deepavali week. Hence sales are made only from supplies on hand and Fire Works Limited normally ends up with some closing inventory. Fire Works Limited keeps these packs for use in the next year but incurs an inventory carrying cost of Rs. 5 per pack.

Fire Works Limited has been charging Rs. 40 per pack and has been selling 3000 packs each year. Analysis of production costs shows that Fire Works Limited has Rs. 30,000 in fixed costs each year and a variable cost of Rs. 16 per pack.

Fire Works Limited has recently conducted a market research study to determine the effect of price on the sales of crackers. This has revealed that sales are affected both by the price charged and the sales the team had in the previous year. As long as the price is not increased by more than 50% of the previous year's price then one-third of the previous year's sales would be maintained. Additional sales for each team are determined by the equation :

(20,000 × Average price of the teams)/(Team's Price^2)

Thus the potential sales of each team in a year are :

(Team's sales in the previous year/3)+[(20,000 × Average price of the teams)/(Team's Price^2)]

Due to the increased demand for crackers, Fire Works Limited has recently decided that they could greatly increase their sales by a vigorous sales promotion programme. The programme is aimed at supermarkets, industrial co-operative societies, retail grocery stores and temporary sales agents. A combination of direct mail solicitation with newspaper, magazine, radio, and TV advertisements programme is to be launched. Analysis of expenditures for marketing indicated that sales as previously determined could be increased by a multiplying factor of : (30,000+Marketing expenditure)/30,000. Thus total potential sales (no. of packs) for a team in a year are :

(Team's sales in the pre/3) + [(20,000 × Average price of all teams)/(Team's Price^2) × (30,000 + Markeing expenditure)/ 30,000]

Actual sales are determined by either potential sales or available supply whichever is lesser. The game may be played by 4-6 teams competing with each other and the results of each team will be influenced by the prices set by the other teams. The game will last for 6 to 8 periods with the winning team being the team with highest cumulative profit at the end of the game.

For the first year each team will be assumed to have had a price of Rs. 40, sales of 3000 packages, no inventory carried forward and no marketing expenditures in the previous year. Each team will decide price per packet, production quantity and marketing expenditure. Price increase of more than 50% of the previous year's price will not be permitted in any one year. Marketing expenditure cannot be increased or decreased by more than Rs. 5,000 in any one year. After each session each team will be informed of the price, marketing expenditure, inventory, sales and profit of all the teams.

16 Computer Application in Business Education — A Forward Linkage

—C.S. RAYUDU AND
S.B. NAGESWARA RAO

DO NOT TEACH WHAT CANNOT BE PRACTISED

Teaching of some spiritual and religious doctrines like teachings of Lord Krishna in *Bhagavat Geeta*, of Jesus Christ in the *Bible* or of Budha might have had global influence. But an organized attempt to take them to classrooms, in recent years are resented by career-oriented professional students. This is not to demean the Great teachers or their philosophy but its appropriateness of *place, time and age* are being looked into.

FLAWS EXISTING

The problems faced by the business graduates in recent years have been a great concern for the parents, students, Government, employers, etc. The reasons are :

1. Exposed and oriented towards classroom theoretical teaching.
2. Not practical, work-related and action-oriented.
3. Lack of interpersonal and communication skills.
4. Parochial and not global in values and thinking
5. Lack of greater education base of information and communication technologies, office automation and electronification of other operations.
6. They lack broader range of practical work-related abilities required for effective work.

CHANGES NEEDED

Higher education in business studies has to undergo a significant and traumatic change. This process of transformation is likely to take up a new area of academic world untouched. The stress on the need to develop guiding innovation with a vision of learning-cum-teaching should be the basis of curricula.

Considering the complex socio-economic milieu of business education, it is time now to think on driving forces and impediments. If we continue the way we are going, we should expect it to be obsolete after sometime. Unless we drastically change our business education priorities we are likely to end up with business education without utility and social purpose. Business education should revolve and reorient on and around.

ELECTRONIC EDUCATION

Value-added education is also moving towards paperless education or electronic education and certificateless degrees. Employers today are not interested in paper degrees anymore, but are very certainly interested in the skills of information technology widely applied. Gone are the days when traditional business education degrees were considered of immense use. But today society attaches less importance. The point is business education should help the individuals to transform their innate and infinite potentials into a demonstrable application skills in automated office.

Computers are deployed by many organizations. It would be very hard to find a large company, governmental agency, or educational institution that is not using computers. People working at different levels require skills of management information systems using office automation, decision support systems. Computer application to business is widespread and all organizations today are totally dependent on computers for numerous administrative functions, as diverse as business is complex.

Computer literacy is a must now-a-days for every business discipline and it is indispensable particularly for corporate jobs. The need for computer fluency and literacy has been growing among the executives after getting a job. It is found that computer knowledge is important among all levels of professionals, middle and senior management employees. Unless they acquire such literacy in education career only, it is very difficult for them to cope with the organizational requirements and to be successful executives.

In these days just a business education gives nothing and cannot make competent and not fit to the requirements of the employers.

IN-HOUSE AND OUT SOURCE

Organizations, institutions and educational institutions today do their word processing, electronic spreadsheets, dBASE, desk top publishing, graphics, animations, audio and video works and other applications in-house. The course content should be designed in such a way to impart computer awareness. There is a wide job potential for out source also. Unless business graduates are well-versed in these fields they are unwanted in the employment market. In these fields there are wide possibilities for self-employment. Home office and small offices generate wide employment opportunities. The self-employed run at out source have much avenues for their computing such as departmental stores, wholesalers, retailers, small traders, etc. The technical knowledge acquiring along with regular curricula can sell their services better.

BUSINESS APPLICATIONS OF COMPUTING EDUCATION

In these days of complexity of functional areas, operations have been mechanized through computer and computer related systems. For instance : Information Technology (IT) is increasingly applied in accounting and finance. For instance : vouchers preparations, automatic numbering of vouchers, billwise tracking of trading, non-trading accounts, track party accounts, loan accounts, new bills raised, payments, receipts, adjustments, etc., analysis of bills, multi-currency accounts, multi-company accounts, electronic debt servicing, cashless trading, cashless credit collections, electronic fund transfer, electronification of accounts presentation by using multi-media elements like audio, video, graphics, animations and other features. In elementary accounts computers are applied as well as in multi-godowns inventory, multi unit inventory, multi valuation inventory, batches and lots, etc.

To meet the requirements of the employers, and suitable to the available job opportunities the business education system must adjust itself with the changing trends to work with innovative applications of IT to impart such skills.

STRATEGIC EDUCATION IN STRATEGIC APPLICATIONS

A number of electronic points of sales (pos) machines are in operation for strategic application which are widely used in departmental stores, supermarkets, retail stores, hospitals, distribution transportation, etc. They are used for register control, inventory, incoming and outgoing order control, delivery control, sales support etc. Syllabi on these aspects are necessary.

Computer awareness is indispensable because this is used in issuing receipts, sales slips, journals, debits, credits, cheques, invoices, daily reports, periodicals, inventory reports, etc.

There are two aspects of information technology. They are computer education and computer use to practical situations which is also gaining momentum. A transformation is taking place from blissful manual to total electronification. Value addition has generated lots of interest in all, value is being talked about and business education is no exception. Public awareness on computer education in business application has been growing.

IN DIVERSE AREAS

Without computer appreciation a business graduate is not competent in an environment where functional operations are electronified, such as cost and budgeting control, stock control and sales distribution, payrolls and personal records, project management, finance, and accounts, materials management, inventory management, product planning and control, purchase, manufacturing and marketing. Sound decisions cannot be made without decision support systems and our education is not teaching.

In Infocity Hyderabad alone 50,000 jobs of computer professionals of various categories are available as estimated. It is also estimated that 4,00,000 jobs are available abroad for Indian computer professionals, 2,00,000 jobs in the United States alone and the computers would show the path to progress to the business education professionals.

ACTION PLAN

The present system of business education needs relook, rearrange, redefine to the changing needs to meet the needs and aspirations but not our own.

The economic reconstruction has added a global dimension to the Indian industry. At the backdrop of such changes the heritage of business education has remained constant and could not respond to the advancement of Information Technology in business application such as virtual reality, internet, networking, worldwide web, electronic commerce, electronic data interchanges, e-mail, cellular phone, paging, mobile communications and other media.

For proper development and growth of business education quality institutions should go for experimenting which are needed to reform and restructure the course with the consultation of industry and other professional institutions.

Development of new curricula consistent with the social needs evolving new methods in education and training would set into motion new frame. Top priority needs to be given to reestablish the social credibility of business meant for the public.

17 Current Issues in Commerce Education

—S.S. HUGAR AND S.G. HUNDEKAR

INTRODUCTION

Quality-oriented need-based commerce education is a vital input factor for all-round economic progress of developing countries like ours. Basically, whether it is commerce or science, it aims at sharpening thinking power and increasing productive capabilities of the people in the country. The level of economic prosperity of any country is predominantly influenced by the level of human resource development, because human being is a resource which gives life to lifeless resources to bear fruits towards the economic development of the country. This is more so in case of commerce education. Commerce education aims at brightening human power in the direction to increase in the wealth of a nation. Viewing from this angle only, the planners have framed new education policy with main focus on human resource development through the instrument of education thinking that there would be happy linkage between the theory and practice of commerce education in India. But, it is shameful to remark that much remains to be done by the planners at the implementation level and the so-called educational institutions in the country in designing course curriculum to suit the requirements of practical business world. No doubt, our country is spending in terms of crores for providing existing bookish information rather than application-oriented and solution-oriented education. It is the perfect matching between the man-traits and job-traits which goes a long way in increasing the productivity of any activity. Unfortunately in our country neither there is matching nor mechanism of imparting application-oriented education. This fact is supported by several facts, one or two for example may be a graduate with B.A. degree is appointed as commercial tax officer. Similarly a graduate who does not know anything about ledger or entry is appointed as Accounts Manager in Banks or Insurance Companies.

Against this background, the present paper encompasses three parts :

Part-A highlights the present scenario of commerce education in the country. Part-B provides the structural changes to be effected and Part-C throws some light on implementation modalities of the re-structured course.

PART-A

At present the commerce education in our country is plagued with innumerous problems. Some of them are highlighted here :

(1) Multiplicity of Courses and Institutions : In our country multiple courses like BBS, BBA, BBM, B.Com., DBM, etc., at graduation level and M.Com., MBA, MBM, MMS, etc., at post-graduation level with more or less same focus on the same curriculum, thereby creating confusion in the minds of employers about the selection of right candidate with the right degree for the right job. Similarly at the institutional level there has been mushroom growth of multiple institutions like IIM, Universities, Institutes of Management, Institute of Chartered Financial Analysts of India, Institute of Chartered Secretaries of India, Institute of Chartered Accountants of India, etc., which impart same curriculum with slight change in their focus. Such a state of affairs creates a confusion in the minds of learners as to which course is to be studied in which institution for what type of job. Therefore, it may be said that there has been overlapping and duplication in the efforts of imparting commerce education in our country.

(2) No Co-ordination between Theory and Practice : Our present commerce education is imparted just to provide the information about theoretical aspects of the course ignoring their practical utility. This is the main reason as to why the products of commerce education are not sold out in the employment market.

(3) Absence of Specification of Job Areas : The type of the job which can be efficiently and effectively done by the commerce graduates is specified neither by the planners of the country nor by the practical businessmen. Freedom is given to the graduates of other disciplines like Science, Arts to make an encroachment in the job market.

(4) Irregular Updating and Revision : The present system of commerce education, in the wake of rules and regulations either from the Government or from higher educational bodies, does not permit to effect essential changes in the curriculum at regular but frequent intervals.

(5) Encroachment of Academicians of other Disciplines : Under the umbrella of inter-disciplinary approach, there has been an encroachment into the commerce discipline by the academicians of other disciplines like Arts, Science, etc. These people with the absence of the fundamental knowledge about commerce and business would be ineffective to adopt their teaching styles to the requirements of the commerce students.

(6) Lethargic Attitude of Course Teachers : Again, it is shameful to remark that there has been lack of activism on the part of the course teachers in making a change in curriculum and also in the subjects to be taught at regular intervals. Lack of integrative attitude on the part of the teachers *i.e.*, teaching the same subject by the same teacher until his retirement or keeping the same subject for the sake of a single teacher until his retirement, makes teaching ineffective and course becomes obsolete. Teaching as a learning process is said good-bye by the teachers.

(7) Undue Influence of Non-commerce Academicians in Policy Decisions : In the present system, most of the academic matters and issues are discussed and decided by the academic bodies like Academic Council and Syndicate at University where the proportion of commerce teachers would be poor or sometimes nil. Naturally this results in approval of unwanted decisions for implementation or rejection of useful decisions.

(8) Poor Communication Skills : In the guise of teaching a particular course in the regional language, there has been deterioration in the communication skills. The learners are becoming neither perfect in the regional language nor perfect in common language. Sometimes, instead of teaching a particular language as a medium of expression, it is being taught as literary subject. Such a practice does not strengthen the commerce graduates to improve their communication skills.

PART-B

The present commerce education needs thorough re-structuring of the curriculum. Relevant, need-based courses in the light of national survey of employers' requirements are to be introduced. A proper sequence of the subjects to be taught should be specified without giving any scope for overlapping and duplication. Similarly, the essential and desirable traits of teachers for teaching different courses must be clearly defined. An admission for undergraduate course may be sought only by those who have studied atleast four basic subjects of commerce at their plus two (PUC) level of education.

There is an acute need for judicious combination between theory and practice. There must be provision for practical work, case studies, etc., so that decision-making skills would be developed among the students. Practical training for two or three months may be made compulsory at part III level before awarding the degree.

Financial Accounting, Computer Application, Business Mathematics, Business Statistics, Business Research, Management Information, etc., should be part and parcel of curriculum for commerce education. At part I and part II (*i.e.*, I year, II year) of undergraduate levels of commerce education, these core papers may be made compulsory. At part III level (*i.e.*, III year), there may be a provision for specialization in the main functional areas like Accounting and Financial Management, Marketing Management, Production Management, Human Resource Management, Banking, Insurance, Taxation, International Trade, etc.

A serious thought may be given for the replacement of nomenclature of the stream of commerce education as Bachelor of Business Science (B.B.Sc.) at undergraduate level and Master of Business Science (M.B.Sc.) at postgraduate level to make the courses more attractive and competitive in the job market.

PART-C

For making the implementation of the restructured curriculum more effective and useful, the following measures may be undertaken.

(1) Full freedom is to be given to the Dean of the Faculty for updating the curriculum in the Board of studies meeting without waiting for approval by bodies consisting of non-commerce academicians.

(2) For the purpose of injecting recent changes relating to the discipline into the regular coaching, there must be a provision for regular faculty development programmes without seeking either approval or financial assistance from any other higher educational institution like UGC as is being done at present.

(3) There must be periodic change in the subjects to be taught by the course teachers in such a way that the subject once taught is not taught again by virtue of either replacement or updating.

(4) For updating the knowledge of course teacher and also of the students, there must be a provision for yearly addition of new books, journals, etc.

(5) The contents of the languages to be studied by commerce graduates be designed by the Board of Studies in Commerce rather than Board of Studies in the particular language.

(6) There must by change in the teaching methodology *i.e.*, from lecturing method to either discussion method or lecturing-cum-visual-audio method. Such a practice enables to make use of several software packages developed in the field of industry and business.

(7) Besides regular teaching classes, there must be some minimum practical periods every week. For this purpose a Business Science Laboratory may be maintained in each study centre so that the students would be in a position to develop the skills for preparing the accounts, analysing the statements and drafting the reports, etc.

(8) There must be liaison between business units and the educational institutions so that there is perfect linkage between what is taught by the institutions and what is needed by the practical businessmen.

18 Training the Trainers in Business Education — Impact of Refresher Courses in Commerce and Economics

—M.R. CHANDAWARKAR

Business Education has been emerging as the most crucial field of contemporary knowledge and practice, since the past four decades. India's total student enrolment[1], for the academic year 1995-96, was 64,25,624 out of which, enrolment in commerce was 14,10,119 *i.e.*, 21.9% of the total. Out of the total 3 lakh college and University teachers, more than 40,000 are Commerce and Management teachers.

Liberalization of the economy in our country, rapid strides in the field of information technology, gradual integration of local markets into a global environment, have paved way for revolutionary changes in Business Education and research in terms of both — methodologies and concepts. There has been a growing appreciation of the importance of quality and its assurance in every sphere, be it industrial or educational. The ability to produce goods and services and register development, sustainable over long periods of time, in the global market, necessitates a regular supply of trained, committed and motivated manpower, equipped with working and managerial skills. Are we, as teachers in Business Education, empowered with requisite professional skills, to mould the lives of our future corporate citizens and prepare them to meet the emerging challenges? The Education Commission (1964-66) stressed on the qualitative improvement in teacher education. Strengthening teacher education was considered a prerequisite, not only for qualitative improvement of education but also for the blossoming of human excellence. The National Education Policy 1986, envisaged a systematic and comprehensive attempt at staff development, Academic Staff Colleges (ASCs) were set up and subject-oriented refresher courses (RCs) for senior lecturers, were started in 1988. The Prof. Mehrotra pay revision report (1986) envisaged participation of teachers in Refresher Courses as prerequisite for career advancement.

At present, 45 Academic Staff Colleges are actively involved in conducting Refresher Courses for college teachers. A survey was conducted, to evaluate the impact of Refresher Courses in Commerce and Economics, conducted by the Academic Staff Colleges of University of Hyderabad, Goa and Karnataka Universities. Though Business Education occupies a core position today, there is increasing awareness and concern for the need and importance of improving the quality of Business Education. This study aims at evaluating the impact of these RCs and suggesting measures, with the sole aim of bettering the system, to effectively train the trainers in Business Education, to meet the problem and prospects of the 21st Century.

RCs CONDUCTED BY THE ASCs UNDER STUDY

These ASCs have been conducting RCs for various subjects. But this survey covers participants of Commerce and Economics RCs only. While RCs in these subjects, are conducted by ASCs Goa and Karnataka Universities, the ASC of University of Hyderabad conducts RCs in Economics only, alongwith other subjects not covered in this study.

Refresher Courses are normally of 3-week duration and mainly aim at upgrading the knowledge of the content of the subject, improving personal and scholastic competence of the teachers and their pedagogic skills. Another crucial objective of RCs is to awaken their dormant probing attitude and motivate them to be research-oriented.

On an average, the ASCs covered in this survey have conducted one RC per year in each subject, involving around 35-40 participants in each course. The per participant cost incurred during the VIII Plan by the ASCs of Goa, Karnataka and Hyderabad Universities on RCs was Rs. 2960, Rs. 3144 and Rs. 4140 respectively.[2]

RCs consist of lectures, demonstrations, lecture-cum-discussions, participants' seminars and field work. While Lecture-cum-Discussions have received priority in the Academic Staff Colleges of Goa and Karnataka Universities, the University of Hyderabad lays more stress on lectures. Some field work activity and participants' Seminar is also undertaken by the two former Universities.[3]

The following Table gives the subjectwise distribution of teachers trained in different ASCs in RCs, during the VIII Plan, in Economics, Commerce and Management.[4]

TABLE 1

Subjectwise Distribution of Teachers trained by all ASCs

Subject	:	No. of Teachers Trained in RCs.
Commerce	:	5517
Business Administration	:	87
Accountancy	:	90
Management	:	146
Investment Management	:	47
Business Management	:	58
Economics	:	4028
Total		9973

The committed efforts of all the ASCs have resulted in 9973 teachers in Commerce, Economics and Management being trained during the VIII five year plan. The UGC proposes to conduct 60, 50 and 8 RCs respectively, through Goa, Karnataka and Hyderabad Universities, covering 1800, 2250 and 1600 participants respectively during the IX five year plan.[5]

Thus, the UGC has been formulating ambitious plans for staff development. But unless the impact of its programmes is evaluated, they cannot be efficiently managed. Hence, this survey was conducted to study the impact of RCs in Commerce and Economics conducted by the ASCs of Goa and Karnataka Universities and University of Hyderabad.

Objectives of the Study

This study has been conducted with the following objectives :

(1) To evaluate the effectiveness of Refresher Courses in Commerce and Economics conducted by the ASCs of Goa, Karnataka and Hyderabad Universities.

(2) To suggest measures to make these programmes more useful and effective.

Methodology

The study sample consisted of about 300 teachers, who attended Refresher courses on these subjects, conducted by the Academic Staff Colleges of Goa, Karnataka Universities and the University of Hyderabad.

300 questionnaires were despatched by post, out of which responses were received from 226 teachers. Out of these, 187 were male and 39 were female. Among the respondents were 45 lecturers, 133 Senior Scale lecturers and the remaining 48 were Selection Grade lecturers, 43 teachers came from rural place of work, 115 belonged to colleges located in semi-urban areas and 68 belonged to urban colleges. Further, 93 teachers had less than 10 years teaching experience and 133 teachers had above 10 years teaching experience.

Personal discussions and interviews, with about 20% of the 226 teachers, were also held and have been greatly relied upon, to reach conclusions.

Questionnaire/Interview Schedule

The questionnaire was divided in 3 components, representing the main benefits of RCs. Each component was measured by 4-6 items. The components were :

(1) Professional skill (measured by 4 questions).

(2) Personal Development (measured by 6 questions).

(3) Interpersonal skills (measured by 4 questions).

The respondents were asked to rate the items on a 6-point scale from 0 to 5, representing Dissatisfaction to 'High Satisfaction'.

Besides these, some general questions reflecting expectations of participants from the RCs, were asked.

Statistical Tools

Standard statistical tools like the mean, 't' test, ANOVA and Chi-Square, have been used to interpret data collected. The 't' test has been used to test the significance between 2 groups and Analysis of Variance (ANOVA) has been used for testing the significance between 3 groups.

Chi-Square values have been computed to study the association between the recommendations suggested by respondents against sex, status, place of work and experience.

Findings

This study has been conducted to analyse the impact of RCs in Commerce and Economics. Accordingly, the questionnaire highlighted the 3 main benefits of RCs *i.e.*, improvement in Professional skills, Personal development and Interpersonal skills.

The respondents were classified on the basis of sex, status (lectures/senior scale/selection grade) place of work (rural, semi-urban and urban) and experience (less than 10 years/more than 10 years).

TABLE 2

Table showing the MEAN OPINION 'PROFESSIONAL SKILL'

Increase in	:	Mean Opinion
1. Subject information/knowledge	:	3.64
2. Expressional/communicative skills	:	3.51
3. Motivational levels	:	3.05
4. Problem solving abilities	:	2.93
		13.13

The above table throws light on the mean opinion of the respondents regarding the increase in their professional skills, as a result of participation in RCs. The maximum satisfaction is regarding increase in subject information/knowledge where the mean opinion level is 3.65, closely followed by increase in communicative skills (3.51). Least satisfaction is observed in case of problem-solving abilities as denoted by a low mean of 2.93.

TABLE 3

Table showing the 'Mean Opinion' — 'Personal Development'

Improvement in	Mean Opinion
1. Time Planning Abilities	1.96
2. Creative Potential	2.54
3. Career Development	2.36
4. Attitude towards the job	3.25
5. Computer knowledge	2.53
6. Ability to involve in research, through project work	2.69
	15.33

Table 3 makes is clear that the teachers are highly satisfied regarding their improvement in attitude towards their job, denoted by high mean level of 3.25, followed by an improvement in their ability to involve in research through project work (2.69). This is one of the crucial objectives of a RC and is achieved here. However, a low mean opinion of 1.96 is observed regarding improvement in Time Planning Abilities.

TABLE 4

Table showing the Mean Opinion — Interpersonal Skills

Improvement in	Mean Opinion
1. Managerial skills	3.06
2. Leadership Ability	3.11
3. Relation with colleagues and superiors	3.37
4. Ability to guide students through innovative research	3.20
	12.73

Awakening the dormant research potential of the teachers and encouraging them to motivate students, too, in that direction, is an important objective of RCs and this has proved true in this study, which evidences a high mean opinion level of 3.20 regarding this aspect. But maximum satisfaction is observed regarding improvement in relations with colleagues and superiors. It is worth noting here that the best part of our life and the best part of the day, are spent in the work place. Hence, it is of utmost significance to ensure that the work atmosphere is congenial and conducive to growth. The high opinion on this score highlights the benefits of RCs and the sincere efforts of the UGC aimed at staff development.

A comparison between the mean opinion levels regarding the above mentioned 3 benefits of RCs reveals that maximum improvement is in personal development of participants (Mean = 15.33), followed by improvement in professional skills (Mean = 13.13) and then in interpersonal skills (Mean = 12.73).

A status-wise comparison between the three benefits of these RCs has thrown light on the fact that lecturers have benefited the most from RCs followed by Senior Scale lecturers and then by Selection Grade lecturers.

Similarly, place of work-wise comparison between the three benefits of these RCs has evidenced that mean opinion level of satisfaction of teachers coming from rural colleges, is highest followed by opinion of those coming form semi-rural colleges and then by urban colleges. Facilities such as access to varied books/journals and exposure to latest developments in the subject, are restricted in rural areas. This explains high level of satisfaction.

TABLE 5

't' test — Sex and Increase in Satisfaction Levels

Variable	Number of cases	Mean	S.D.
Male	197	41.3636	10.217
Female	39	40.3846	10.156

Mean Difference = 0.9790
t = 0.54, d.f. = 224, p = 0.586 Not significant.

The 't' test was applied to study if gender of the teachers had any association with their satisfaction levels.

The above table clearly depicts that there is no significant difference between the opinion levels of male teachers and female teachers regarding increase in satisfaction pertaining to the 3 benefits.

TABLE 6

Analysis of Variance — Status and Increase in Satisfaction Levels

Source	D.F.	Sum of Squares	Mean Squares	F Ratio	F Prob.
Between groups	2	2697.6642	1348.8321	14.5521	.0000
Within groups	223	20669.7694	92.6895		
Total	225	23367.4336			

Multiple Range Tests : Duncan test with significance level .05. The difference between two means significant if Mean (j) = Mean (I) > = 6.8077 *Range *Sqrt [1/N(I)+1/N(J)]

with the following value (s) for Range.

Step 2 3

Range 2.79 2.94

All three groups differ significantly.

The ANOVA test was used to study if there was a significant difference between the status of the teachers and increase in their satisfaction levels and this has been confirmed, as shown in the above table.

TABLE 7

ANOVA — Place of Work and Increase in Satisfaction Levels

Source	D.F.	Sum of Squares	Mean Squares	F Ratio	F Prob.
Between groups	2	4097.3502	2048.6751	23.7080	.0000
Within groups	223	19270.0834	86.4129		
Total	225	23367.4336			

Multiple Range Tests : Duncan Test with Significance level .05. The difference between two means is significant if Mean (J) – Mean (I) > = 6.5732 * Range * SQRT [1/N(I) + 1/N(J)] with the following values for Range

Step 2 3

Range 2.79 2.94

All the three groups differ significantly.

Table 7 gives the results of the ANOVA test which was done to study the possibilities of a significant difference between the place of work of teachers and the enhancement in their satisfaction levels. It is concluded that all the three groups differ significantly.

The following Table 8 gives the values of the 't' test which was applied to analyse if experience of the teacher had any relation to the increase in his satisfaction levels. The mean level of satisfaction of teachers with less than 10 years experience was found to be higher at 48.3333 than those with more than 10 years experience at 36.2030. Thus, it is concluded that less experienced teachers have benefited more from the RCs.

TABLE 8

't' test - Experience and Increase in Satisfaction Levels

Variable	Number of cases	Mean	S.D.
Experience less than 10 years	93	48.3333	7.565
More than 10 years	133	36.2030	8.725

Mean Difference = 12.1303

t = 10.85, df = 224, p = 0.000 Differ significantly.

TABLE 9

General Opinion of Participants

		YES		NO	
		No. of Participants	% Total	No. of Participants	% of Total
1.	RCs must be repeatedly conducted	209	92.5	17	7.5
2.	Project work must be assigned to each participant	140	61.9	86	38.1
3.	More exposure to computer literacy programmes	121	53.5	105	46.5
4.	Discussions about changes in Syllabus to be an integral part of the RC	111	49.1	115	50.9

The general opinion of the participants regarding RCs, is summarised in Table 9. A striking majority of the teachers *i.e.*, 209, representing 92.5% of the sample, are of the unanimous opinion that RCs are beneficial and must be repeatedly conducted. This is thus in unity with the UGC's goal to provide opportunities for serving teachers to exchange experience with other teachers, benefit and learn from each other, and develop better ways of disseminating existing and new knowledge.

This opinion is closely followed again by a majority of 140 teachers (61.9%) out of total of 226, unitedly agreeing that project work should be compulsorily assigned to each participant of the RC, and the relevant project reports should be collected from them, before its completion. One of the crucial objectives of RCs is to stimulate the probing attitude among teachers and make them research oriented. Such project work will contribute positively to meet this end and has been agreed to by a majority of the teachers covered in this study.

The quantum jump in science and technology, particularly in information and communication technology, has made it necessary to train our students in a manner that would enable them to keep pace with modern global requirements. In this direction, computer awareness and knowledge has become the need of the hour and is confirmed by 53.5% of the teachers who feel that this knowledge should be imparted in RCs. However, the majority is not as significant as in the case of the previous two cases. About 46.5% of the teachers have expressed that specialised and practical aspects of computer literacy, cannot be satisfactorily imparted during the short duration of RCs. Hence, more exposure to computer programmes, in RCs, is not desirable nor feasible.

One of the measures of improving the quality of Business Education, is periodical revision of the syllabus, to bring it in conformity with the needs of the present-day complexities. Regarding this aspect, 49% of the teachers have expressed that discussions about the syllabus need not form an integral part of the RC programme. The syllabus for various courses differs with universities. Besides, changes in the syllabus are normally discussed and effected by bodies like the Board of Studies, Academic Councils of the

Universities and other Bodies. Very few college teachers get an opportunity to have a say in such academic discussions. Perhaps this is reflected in their opinion.

TABLE 10

Chi-square Table

Responses	Se	Status	Place of Work	Experience
1.	0.00196	2.899	1.3135	6.555*
2.	0.6129	5.3932	1.1810	4.2323*
3.	2.9674	9.6298**	2.9851	1.6868
4.	0.4221	6.3803*	9.36829**	0.0335

*Denotes Association. **Denotes Strong Association.

The above table gives the chi-square values, which were calculated to study if there was any association between the variables — sex, status, place of work and experience of the teachers and their responses to the four general questions. It is clear from the table that there is no association between sex and any of the responses. However, a strong association exists between status of the teachers and their opinion about computer literacy in RCs (Response 3). Similar is the case between the place of work of the teachers and their opinion about including discussions on the syllabus in the RCs. It has also been established that there is a close association between experience of participants and their opinion about conducting regular RCs and assigning project work to participants.

Major Findings

The Major findings of this survey are :

(1) RCs are an essential pre-requisite for effective staff development.

(2) Sex of the teachers does not influence their satisfaction levels, in any manner.

(3) Lecturers with lesser years of experience, have benefited from the RCs, to a much greater extent than their more experienced counterparts.

(4) Enhanced levels of satisfaction, to a greater extent, are observed among teachers coming from rural place of work.

(5) Maximum benefit from RCs is the increase in subject information/knowledge, followed by increase in expressional/communicative skills and an improvement in relations with colleagues and superiors.

(6) Least benefit from RCs is observed in case of improvement in Time Planning abilities and in problem solving abilities of participants.

(7) Majority of the participants are of the firm opinion that:

(a) Project work should be assigned to each participant of the RC and reports should be submitted by them. This will motivate research orientation.

(b) Imparting basic computer knowledge should form an integral part of every RC.

(c) Discussions about changes in the syllabus, need not be included in the RC curriculum.

Suggestions

The findings of this study and interaction with some respondents, have encouraged the researcher to make the following suggestions, to improve the effectiveness of RCs in Commerce and Economics:

(1) College teachers should repeatedly participate in RCs, once in 3 years, upto a maximum age of 55.

(2) The linkage of RCs to career advancement has created circumstances where teachers attend the RCs for the sole purpose of getting a certificate rather than benefiting from participation. This situation is aggravated by the fact that aspirants for attending RCs far outnumber the vacancies available in the ASCs. Hence, more opportunities to attend RCs in ASCs must be created.

(3) To achieve this end partially, Universities, Institutes and colleges should be permitted to conduct need-based RCs on a self-financing basis and thus provide more opportunities for participation. This will also help to ease the financial crunch faced by the U.G.C.

(4) It would be desirable if each ASC conducts RCs in most of the common subjects, more frequently. Attending a RC in a place nearer to the place of work will increase participant's convenience and reduce expenditure on their Travelling Allowances paid by the U.G.C.

(5) Once the backlog created on account of excess demand for RCs and less opportunities, is cleared, there will be more involvement and a sense of purpose, on the part of teachers. The essence of RCs is to effect staff development and this will be possible due to their wholehearted participation.

(6) Out of the 3-week duration of RCs, two weeks may be devoted for the thrust area and one week for non-specific but crucial areas like Human and Intellectual Property Rights, computer awareness, Human Resource Development, quality in education through accreditation, environmental studies and population control. This will contribute to qualitative improvement of RCs.

(7) Post RC evaluation of the programmes and also of participants, must be periodically undertaken to improve their effectiveness. That which is unmeasurable is certainly unmanageable. Hence, professional development among the participants could by analysed through suitable entry and exit evaluation.

(8) RC participants should not be silent observers but take active part in the discussions and proceedings. Lack of communicative skills caused by language problems, pose a serious threat to their active participation. Hence, improvement in communicative skills must from an integral part of the RC curriculum, to ensure reciprocal interaction.

(9) It is a common observation that some resource persons at RCs are from local colleges/university departments with less experience and mastery in their subject. The financial restraints placed on the ASCs, result in such arrangements. The resource persons should be persons of authority and should be invited from outside, if necessary.

For RCs in Commerce and Economics, professional managers, bankers, consultants and industrialists must necessarily be invited as resource persons, to enhance the equality content of the programmes.

Industrial visits and visits to stock exchanges where possible, seminars with Chambers of Commerce and Productivity councils, will help in lending a practical touch to the academic programmes. It is also desirable to provide the participants, international perspective of globalisation *vis-a-vis* liberalisation.

Focus should also be on training the teachers to develop entrepreneurship skills among their students so that they may be self-employed, particularly in the growing sector of the economy.

(10) The time schedule of RCs is fixed in such a manner that participants are left with no time to visit the library to read and think over the topics discussed during the day. Hence to facilitate these activities, the timings may be so fixed as to finish the academic sessions by about 2 p.m. This will enable participants to interact with others.

CONCLUSION

We, as teachers of Economics, Commerce and Management have to inform, instruct and inspire our students and equip them with requisite skills, not only to work efficiently or manage their business professionally, but also provide service to society. As we approach the 21st century, we have to be sufficiently equipped to train future corporate citizens to meet the emerging challenges. RCs are a means made available to us by the UGC, to sharpen our abilities, widen our capacities and update our subject knowledge. Crores of rupees are being spent by it, to conduct such programmes. It is up to us to attend the RCs with wholehearted involvement, proper perspective and receptive frame of mind and ensure that the U.G.C.'s efforts towards staff development, are not reduced to a futile exercise.

REFERENCES

1. U.G.C. *Annual Report* 1995-96.
2. Academic Staff Development — Facts and Figures. *Report of the Review Meeting of ASCs*, Jan. 28-30th, 1997, National Institution of Educational Planning and Administration, New Delhi, p. 30.

3. Chalam, K.S., *Performance of Academic Staff Colleges in India*, Rawat Publications, Jaipur, 1995, p. 36.
4. *Report of the Review Meeting of ASCs*, Jan. 28th-30th, 1997, NIEPA, New Delhi, p. 26.
5. *Ibid.*
6. Gujrathi, R.J., 'Role of Commerce and Management Teachers in Changing Times', *The Indian Journal of Commerce*, Vol. No. 190, Part I, March 1997, Bhubaneshwar, p. 14.
7. Sisodia, M.L., *Educating the Educators — Vitalizing from Experience*, Devika Publications, New Delhi, 1998.
8. Hariharn Meena and I. Ramabrahman, 'Professionalising the Orientation, Courses', *University News*, New Delhi, Aug. 15, 1994.

19 Progress and Problems of Business Education During 50 Years of Post-Independence Period

—K.K. KURIAKOSE

CONTEXT

Business Education in India is now at a turning point. After years of stagnation it is beginning to take a new turn. The pressures on Business Education are high on account of the liberalisation, globalisation and privatisation all over the world, especially in India since 1991. The new economic and financial reforms are aimed at achieving rapid economic growth through liberalised economic environment in the country. To facilitate process of economic development in the country, institutions imparting Business Education are supposed to effect structural changes in their educational polices so as to suit the structural adjustments made in our country. In this context, it is quite apt to trace the progress and problems of Business Education in India during the 50 years of post-independence period.

Business Education before Indian Independence

The Business Education system of our country has its roots in the colonial past. The Universities of Presidencies of India were established on the model of London University. The University of London was not like the Oxford and the Cambridge. Those were conservative Universities run by the Church to impart knowledge to the Aristocrats who did not need to care about money or job. By and large London University was different, satisfying the thirst of the middle class who were responsible for the Industrial revolution.

The Industrial revolution in England really paved the way for imparting Business Education for improving the human resources, which is highly essential for boosting the industrial growth of England.

In India British system of education commenced in 1835 on the basis of Macaulay's minute. According to Macaulay "English education was to make Indians British in every respect except the colour of the skin". The establishment of the Universities of Calcutta, Bombay and Madras as affiliating Universities in 1857 was the outcome of this need. The general purpose of education was to create a cadre of Indians who would be educated enough to be useful in helping the British to rule India more effectively. By the time of the First World War we had four Universities — Bombay, Madras, Calcutta and Delhi.

Post-Independence Perspective

One year after Independence when Radhakrishnan Commission gave an Indian touch to our higher education, we had 20 Universities. During this period we began looking around the world for models to adopt. A nationalistic perspective for Business Education emerged during this time. Inspired by the views of Mahatma Gandhi and Jawahar Lal Nehru, efforts were made to bring changes in education, primarily to suit the Indian situation. When Kothari Commission was set up in 1964, there were around 50 Universities. Kothari wanted to do away with the pre-1947 model. The main attempt was to diversify the system with the introduction of technological education. National Policy of Education 1968, 1986 and 1992 emphasised the need for social liberation and economic development. A majority of the higher education institutions like the IITs, IIMs, ICAR, etc., were established based on this principle. The main features of business education during post-independence period are :

1. Unplanned, unhealthy and unprecedented quantitative expansion of Universities and Colleges.
2. Deterioration in quality of Business Education.
3. Ivory tower mentality of those in Business Educational Institutions.

4. No link with the developmental needs of the society.
5. Imbalance between skilled requirements of business and the curriculum followed.

The Liberal Syndrome

The horrified emphasis on liberalization and globalisation put our education system also under threat. The advocates of this policy say that we must make profit out of structural changes in education. The logic is quite simple : It is that the business education should also be made a real business. Our central funding agencies seem to echo this when they say that we must welcome self-financing institutions. There is a mushrooming growth of BBA, MBA, BCA and MCA courses thinking on these lines. They run these institutions by 'extracting' money from the students. Profit-oriented programmes will take the education system away from the desired goal of preparing youth to participate in nation building process. Business education system should be streamlined in such a way that the fruit of the education should be shared by all.

Need of the Hour

In order to wipe off the maladies in business education there should be revitalisation in business education system. The steps necessary are :

1. Those who man the educational institutions have to campaign against the 'mass culture'.
2. They should create an awakening among the youngsters to use their vitality not in the "creation of their own kind", but in the making of things that are useful to them and the community.
3. The business education should promote not only pure learning but also professional training to suit the needs of the 21st century.
4. Changes have to be made in the curriculum to meet the needs and expectations of the people.
5. Institutions imparting business education must have departments which train young persons in sophisticated business related areas like computer, management, marketing, finance etc.

6. Should consider the all-round development of the young students' personality in order to challenge the international competition.

CONCLUSION

The centres of business learning should do their lot in making these students, 'skilled persons with a human heart'. Knowledge can be transmitted through various means, but love of knowledge can be imparted only by personal contact. So a better slogan for business education is to "sharpen the knowledge and widen the vision through interactive methodology, research and human resource development programmes".

20 Business Education : A Manifesto for Rethinking

—SHREEDHAR SHETTY AND
MANJUNATH KOTIAN

Business education, or management education is a delicate balance between theory and practice. In a dynamic and complex environment, this balance becomes particularly important. If theory and practice are constantly changing, the curriculum needs to be very flexible. More importantly, one has to make a distinction between education and training. Business education is not merely training to induct the graduates into the practice of management. It should lay stress not only on the practice but also on the theory and principles based upon rigorous foundation and empirical evidence. Liberalisation, privatisation and globalisation, more popularly known as LPG, of the Indian economy had made it imperative that business or management education also has an 'international perspective.' Various premier business schools of our country are making special efforts to "internationalise" their programmes. In this context, this paper attempts to present a manifesto for a rethinking in business education in India.

In the 1990s, there have been dramatic changes in the competitive environment within which businesses take place. Two of the major drivers of these changes have been the intensification of global competition and the rapid changes occurring in the technology. Increased global competition can be traced to the opening of previously closed markets, primarily in Eastern Europe and Asia, and the maturation of the existing industrial markets throughout the world. In addition, technological changes have brought about new business processes and paradigms as well as given birth to a range of new industries. Fields as diverse as communications and entertainment in addition to computing related areas have witnessed a transformation in the form and content of competition in the respective industries. Against this evolving backdrop, institutions of higher education must prepare future business leaders. Over the years, there has been a gradual movement towards increased internationalisation of business programmes as well as the use and integration of technology into business programmes. However, in most instances, the steps taken have been more a matter of show than of substance. At this juncture, we call for a rethinking of the process of educating business leaders and a revision in the content and delivery of business education using the **"7-S framework"** of McKinsey consulting firm.

Management education has a key role to play in changing business scenario. As education is a means of change to be effective, it must change 'mindset' and inculcate new ideas of independence and entrepreneurship, and ability to cope with the change and meet the global challenge.

The new frontiers of science and technology all over the world, more specially in India, have opened up a great challenge to Indian management education. Hence, there is a need to understand higher education in traditional universities and industry-linked management institutions. The private sector management institutions are supported by industrial groups like, Usha group, Modi group, Kirloskar group, Amity group, Pai Industries group, Nirma group, etc. The actors in the management of these institutions are students, faculty and employees. Everybody seems to use 'placement' as a best way of judging the quality of an institution. Main interaction among themselves and with the society has got a greater impact. Therefore, they are all interdependent and have got greater role to play in building management institutions.

We should draw your attention to various mundane questions. How these institutions have been created? What are the infrastructural facilities created? How do they draw the faculty? What courses and contents they have? What is the placement myth? What management problems they have? What are their future plans? Suggestions will have to be made to improve their performance, quality, placement, interface with industry, etc. to compete with the international business schools and impart Indian management education in the 21st century.

The McKinsey Consulting Firm offers a **"7-S framework"** for business success.[1] The first three elements – strategy, structure and systems – are considered the "hardware" of success. The next four – style, staff, skills and shared values – are the "software". Institutions imparting management education today will have to 'do right things' (effectiveness) rightly (efficiency) first time and all times. The 'process' and 'results' of imparting worldclass business education are briefly analysed below.

1. Shared Values

The core values of imparting management education should emanate from a sound mission and vision statement of the institution. Business school should provide students with forward-looking, dynamic business education that is equipping them to meet the challenges of the next century. It should prepare them to make a contribution to the business world and to their communities. Fostering excellence in business education should be the primary goal. These business schools should nurture the mission of providing accessible high-quality programmes to students that are relevant to the world in which they live, work and contribute. It should acknowledge the central role teaching and research play in educating and graduating "employable" students. It should commit the institution to a path that strives for excellence, innovation and leadership.

Of all the kinds of programmes and initiatives undertaken by a college or university or business school, curriculum development is perhaps the most important. Curriculum development requires faculty who have specialised knowledge of course content and methods of instruction. It is also important to appoint a programme advisory committee, consisting of future employers of graduates, which understands the terminal competencies needed by graduates of the programme.

With increasing number of institutes and programmes of business in India, it is worth-while to examine a need for 'professional accreditation' of business programmes. The evolving accreditation paradigms in the United States are worth exploring for continuous quality improvement in our institutions. Accreditation proclaims the quality of our institutions to external stakeholders such as students, their parents, and the businesses that hire our graduates. Comparison with international accreditation standards can affirm the value of education in India and the value of Indian educational institutions in the world. In a global market place, world class education can be a strong competitive advantage for an individual, for a company and for a country. This long-term map of our intentions must be made very clear through the mission and vision statement, and this 'identity of interest of imparting relevant world class management education' must be shared by all people in the institution.

2. Strategy

A business school is evaluated on four important criteria : the reputation of the school, the relevance of the curriculum to today's business world, the academic and professional credentials of the faculty, and on-the-job performance of the graduates. Hence, the strategies of achieving the mission, goals and objectives of imparting worldclass management education should be measured and managed in the light of these criteria.

A judicious blend of concepts, theory and practice offered through lectures, case studies, group presentations, business games, role plays and industry-related research projects provide an insight into the issues of implementation, administration, and other practical concerns that surround managerial action.

Similarly, understanding students' career ambitions, helping them redefine their professional needs, and bringing the corporate clients and the student community together to evolve a mutually meaningful, win-win, trusting career progression is the core objective and strategy of campus recruitment programme of business schools.

3. Structure

Business schools need a flexible, user-friendly organisational set-up instead of rule-minded, rigid, bureaucratic hierarchies. Otherwise, instead of facilitating the process of imparting worldclass management education, the structure may hinder the intended performance of these business schools. Hence, colleges and universities offering management education should think in terms of altering and modifying the administrative arrangements.

4. Staff

Management education calls for an interactive and innovative educational processes. Educational institutions should strive hard to create and sustain an intellectually stimulating environment that attracts and retains the finest faculty and support-service staff.

5. Skills

Business schools should prepare students to read and gather information critically, a skill that industry has deemed essential in the 'information age'. They have a responsibility to graduate students with the right mix of business, technical, and analytical skills, ready to assume their role as 'critical and informed' corporate citizens. Employers (both in India and abroad) expect four essential skill-sets to be possessed by a performer :

1. the ability to work in teams;
2. the ability to communicate;
3. the ability to become leaders; and
4. the ability to continually update business skills by gathering and assimilating information.

Many industrial and academic experts point out that universities teaching these skill-sets will be preparing their students well for the next millennium.

6. Style

Business schools need progressive, result-oriented leadership styles on the part of the administrators. Autocratic, power-centred, reactive approaches will do more damage than any good to the process of imparting high-quality management education. All supervisors must constantly undergo leadership and management development. This is extremely important for the department chairperson; the hub of the academic family. Most department chairs are promoted from the ranks of department faculty. Therefore, a department chairperson should receive special training at the time of initial appointment and should continue to receive additional training periodically to make him ready for 'proactive thinking, feeling and actions'. Innovative processes in management education are fundamental to progress. Leaders should use every opportunity to encourage and reward innovation at every level of the institution. They must learn that innovation means failures must be accepted, and even welcomed, to achieve successes. They should possess a mindset of "hating to lose" rather than just "loving to win". They must realise that most innovations in public-service institutions are imposed on them either by outsiders or by catastrophe.

7. System

Since education, research and service are the university's most important products, each system must consider its own impact on the student and faculty first. This does not mean that the system must neglect other considerations, but it does mean the system must produce a "quality result" in its central mission. If the system produces a responsibly educated graduate, delivers quality service, and produces quality research, then funding, increased student applications and an enhanced reputation will result.

Once a system is in place, it should be allowed to work. No single person should attempt to control the system. The system produces results — unsatisfactory results should dictate changes. System defects should be constantly sought out and eliminated. A bad system should be replaced by a good system. The enemy of a good system is a very good system. There should be no scope for system complacency or arrogance.

To conclude, the primary function of any educational institution is to prepare students to meet the challenges that lie ahead. Competing in a global market place, staying ahead of change, becoming a knowledge-based economy are challenges that have to be addressed by the institutions that are educating tomorrow's business leaders. Finding people who have the tools necessary to meet the demands of an ever-changing market is the Number 1 challenge business faces. Business today is looking for the best and the brightest young talent. Your institution is more than just a place to look for talented young people. It is a partner — working with the business community to constantly adapt and keep pace with their changing needs. Make sure the business education you provide is "relevant" to the "real world". If we wish to be worldclass, we cannot but have deep and strong links with the rest of the world, in research, practice, and teaching. We should earn a unique place in the community of leading business educators.

REFERENCE

1. McKinsey, 7-S Framework from "*In Search fo Excellence : Lessons from America's Best Run Companies*" by Thomas J. Peters and Robert H. Waterman, Jr. 1982.

21 Challenges Before Business Education in India in Open Regime

—C. KISHAN RAO

I. BUSINESS EDUCATION IN INDIA

Present Scenario

In this era of liberalization, industrial and economic policies are undergoing lot of changes in several countries in the world. The financial markets in the industrially advanced countries have undergone far-reaching changes in 1980s. De-regulation and liberalization have facilitated innovations. The Indian economy too is passing through a period of transition and undergoing rapid transformation. Financial Sector in our country has become highly competitive and market driven. Commercial banks are diversifying their business into several activities, *viz.*, merchant banking, portfolio management services, leasing, hire-purchase, factoring, forfeiting and custodial services. Computers and communication technology are being made use of on a large scale with the ultimate objective of improving productivity and customer service. Financial liberalization, competition and diversification have exposed banks to new risks and opportunities. Offices of 'OMBUDSMEN' have been set up to provide satisfactory redressal of customer grievances relating to banking services.

Technological changes in the field of electronics, telecommunication, computers have had a profound impact on the emerging society. Change in business environment has forced business units to reconsider traditional strategies, policies and routine method of conducting/managing business. The forces of growth, diversification, globalization and technological developments have made decision-making process in business management more and more complex. These relate to bringing down costs, increasing productivity, improving customer service, keeping quality high and designing/launching of new products. On account of globalization, Indian manufacturing units have been forced to compete in international markets both in terms of price and quality. These developments which are taking place in trade, commerce and industry, banking and technology have direct impact/bearing on business education that is imparted to students in the universities/ B-schools. It is, therefore, necessary for us to look into the present pattern of business education and also in the process make an attempt to redefine the role of business education and its relevance to the current developments taking place in the country.

Today business education degrees seem to be the most sought after degrees which have become popular than medicine and engineering. It may not be out of place to mention here that recently British Council had organised 'Education Fairs' in 5 Indian cities. Representatives from 40 British universities and colleges spent a fortnight shopping for student in New Delhi, Calcutta, Chandigarh, Ahmedabad and Pune. Despite an entry fee of Rs. 50 nearly 3000 students made enquiries and the quality of candidates was reported to be extremely good. Roughly 50% of the enquiries were for management/commerce courses, 20% science and technology, 12% medicine and the rest were distributed against humanities, fashion design, hotel tourism management and law. This only shows the importance that is being accorded to management/commerce education in the country and the emerging trends in the future.

Business education in India started when the Britishers came to India and wanted to recruit clerical and accounting personnel from local sources. Business education got prominence soon after the establishment of universities in several states in the country. Though universities started teaching business education, the real impetus for it came only during 1960s and 1970s, when IIMs came to be established. The contribution made by the universities and IIMs in the cause of spreading business education has been really impressive and notable. Probably recognising the importance of business education, Government of India has taken initiative to start 2 more IIMs, *viz.*, one at Indore and another one at Calicut. It is stated that more than 600 institutions including universities and IIMs are offering business management education in India. In the wake of growing industrialization in the country, there is going to be heavy demand for managerial personnel/expertise at all levels. With the kind of highly educated and professional manpower we have, we should be able to move into international markets with greater confidence and acceptability. In view of the massive dose of investment in industry and infrastructure, there would be good demand for Indian talents for managing multi-national/big corporate houses in India and outside. Therefore in this context, business education has to play a key role in proper and efficient management of industrial units.

II. OBJECTIVES OF BUSINESS EDUCATION

The objective of business education is to develop the following skills which in the long run would benefit the country, corporate world and the individual :

* To gain self knowledge and confidence;
* To broaden one's viewpoint of work and the world;
* To understand, manage complex business propositions;
* To accelerate managerial and leadership development by providing potential business leaders with skills, knowledge and expertise;
* To develop/evolve proper behavioural pattern and value systems;
* To develop profound understanding and cultivating intellectual integrity in dealing with complex business situations;
* To highlight the qualities of adaptability, innovation and dynamism.

III. EXPECTATIONS OF THE CORPORATE WORLD FROM BUSINESS EDUCATION

A first ever survey of campus recruiters conducted by the Xavier Labour Relations Institute (XLRI) at Jamshedpur revealed that unconventional skills are most in demand. Some of the extracts of the survey published in 'Business To-day' (December 7 – 21, 1997) reveals a whole lot about the expectations of the corporate world from students who successfully complete their education in B-schools. Responses for this survey were collected from 61 managers working for 58 companies that regularly shop for talent on campus. This survey attempted to discover the competences, functional specialization and knowledge base that companies want their MBAs to come equipped.

(A) *MBA Skill sets for tomorrow :*

1.	Human Resources Development Skills	83.6%+
2.	Infotech & Systems Skills	82%
3.	Financial Management Skills	62.3%
4.	Marketing Management Skills	62.3%
5.	Sales Management Skills	27.9%
6.	Production Management Skills	26.2%
7.	Materials Management Skills	19.7%
8.	Maintenance Management Skills	4.9%
9.	Industrial Relations Skills	3.3%
10.	Accounting Skills	1.64%

-+ % of respondents rating the specialization important

- Figures exceed 100% because of multiple responses.

(B) *Management Techniques in which CEOs are most interested* : (MBA concept maps for tomorrow)

1.	Customer Orientation	65.6%+
2.	Learning Organization	65.6%
3.	Networking and Systems Management	52.5%
4.	Total Quality Management	47.5%
5.	Business Process Re-engineering	41%
6.	Globalization	26.2%
7.	Activity Based Costing	18%
8.	Managing Supplier Relations	3.3%

9. Change Management 1.64%
10. Product Management 1.64%

+ % respondents rating the concept important.

- Figures exceed 100% because of multiple responses.

(C) *What the MBA must learn :*

1. Human Resource Development 83.6%
2. Infotech & Systems 82%
3 Financial Management 62.3%

(D) *What the MBA must know :*

1. Customer Orientation 65.6%
2. Learning Organization 65.6%
3. Networking & Systems Management 52.5%

(E) *What the MBA must display :*

1. Ability to work in a team 62.3%
2. On the job performance 55.7%
3. Leadership Skills 32.8%

To conclude, the survey revealed that the corporate world wants the students to get fully equipped in the various functional areas as also in leadership styles, problem solving abilities and human resource development skills. The package of expectations contains three important components, *viz.*, what MBAs should learn, know and display.

IV. CHALLENGES BEFORE BUSINESS EDUCATION

1. Attainment of international standards in business education in terms of contents, teaching methodology is considered a top priority in the present competitive and complex scenario in the country.

2. Continuous process of evaluation of curriculum to find out its relevance to the ground realities and evolve appropriate packages for development of business education. Business management education should strive towards reaching still higher levels of excellence/performance.

3. The programmes/contents in business education should meet the criteria of innovation, novelty, relevance in the context of present-day happenings inside the country as also outside world. The programme evaluation must undergo modifications periodically. Business education programme should have more practical orientation. It should facilitate development of open minded and intellectually independent business professionals. Pragmatic steps are needed in this direction.

4. Industry and academic interaction has not been fully explored. Efforts are required to be made to transfer research findings from business schools to industry and bring business education closer to the ground realities.

5. The electronic media has made a powerful impact on the society. Its relevance for further advancement of business education needs to be studied in depth.

6. There appears to be some gap in the quality pattern of business education offered by the universities and IIMs. The business education offered by IIMs seems to have an edge over what is offered by the universities. This needs to be looked into.

7. The education that is imparted to the students at present is oriented towards administration/management of industry, *viz.*, manufacturing sector. But today service sector has also come to play a very important role in the economy of the country. Today banking, insurance, capital market, airlines, transport, health, tourism, etc., are some of the service industries which are gaining popularity and are in need of management personnel to look after these services. The type of business education they need, orientation they require are entirely different from what is imparted to management personnel in manufacturing sector. Therefore, there is need for all the universities as also B-schools to think in terms of finalising a distinct and unique curriculum for these service sectors.

8. Today 'Consultancy' is another field which is gaining importance. The services of consultancy firms from abroad are in heavy demand. Their services are being utilised by the corporate houses, banks, financial institutions, public sector undertakings, etc. to name a few. This only indicates that not much efforts have been made to develop consultancy sector in India. This is another area

where universities and business schools have to do some serious thinking in giving it a much needed boost to develop the field.

V. HOW TO MEET CHALLENGES IN BUSINESS EDUCATION (AGENDA FOR THE FUTURE)

1. There is need to promote and develop research activities in the context of changing domestic and global economic environment. Business education cannot afford to remain purely academic. Efforts should be made in the right direction to give it more practical slant. In industrialised countries university/Business school and industry linkages are strong. Management events/exhibitions should be organised periodically on a regular basis to provide an interface between the corporate world and business schools. The business schools should develop a network of practising management personnel, retired senior officials to provide inputs to improve the practical relevance of business education curriculum.

2. Business schools should encourage admission of students from other countries as this will provide much needed flavour in the classrooms. There should be regular interaction between the faculty working in foreign business schools and students here, so as to facilitate the students in India to hear and learn about other countries culture and business financial systems. Students and faculty exchange programmes with some of the advanced countries should be encouraged.

3. Major portion of teaching materials should emanate from our work situations. A portion of the material could also be from other countries. Teaching methodology should be oriented towards real life situations. This would facilitate the students to get a better understanding of what is going on in the real world and enhance the ability of the students to grasp problems and suggest solutions.

4. Technology is bound to move to all the countries in the near future and technological advancement is bound to have its impact on the prosperity and well-being of the society. Hence technology selection, technology management and innovation should become a key element in the curriculum of business schools.

5. Attempts should be made to develop proper ethical values in the curriculum. A strong ethical foundation is necessary in every sphere of activity. The course contents should emphasise on the

development of right attitudes in managing day-to-day problems and situations. The curriculum in respect of HRD & communication should *inter alia* stress the following aspects :

- how to initiate a change;
- how to motivate and guide people to work in a team;
- how to handle critical situations that confront the management and workers;
- How to develop objectivity;
- how to respond to proposals and suggestions for change and innovation; and
- how to be good at communication.

6. The students from business schools should be able to operate in this vast changing competitive environment comfortably. This calls for a drastic shift in the structure and thrust of the curriculum. The curriculum should give more emphasis to HRD, leadership skills, ability to work in a team, infotech and system skills, financial and marketing management, customer orientation, total quality management, business process re-engineering, etc.

7. Recently, some of the public sector banks have been given freedom regarding recruitment of supervisory staff. As a result of this liberalization and autonomy, banks may go in for campus recruitment. In the light of this development, there is need to include some inputs relating to the following areas in MBA/ Business Management programmes to be in tune with the changes taking place in the financial sector :

1. Customer Service/Bank Marketing.
2. Management of risk products.
3. Capital adequacy and income recognition norms.
4. Financing exports in the liberalised environment.
5. NRI funds/NRI investments.
6. Factoring, forfeiting and custodial services; portfolio management, merchant banking, leasing, hire-purchase and debt securitization.
7. Nayak committee recommendations and financing mechanism for small-scale units.

8. Assessment of working capital requirements in the context of freedom given to the banks in this regard.

9. 'Ombudsman' scheme for resolving customer grievances.

8. The gap that exists between Universities and B-schools in the curriculum of business education should be bridged by having dialogue and discussions. This sort of interaction between the universities and B-schools would facilitate maintenance of uniform standards in business education. It is also necessary that universities and business schools meet periodically to take stock of developments taking place in India and abroad in economics, business and social fields. The idea is that these institutions should keep themselves abreast of the developments taking place in this competitive world.

9. Recently Government of India has announced the enhancement in the ceiling limit of investment in plant and machinery for small scale industries (upto Rs. 3 crores). The practical implication of this step is that a unit would be called a small-scale unit even when the investment in plant and machinery is of the order of Rs. 3 crores. So far these SSIs were mostly in the form of sole proprietary, partnership, etc. Now they may modernize their organizational structure and become private and public limited companies. Immediately their financial position may not permit induction of professionally qualified personnel but they may require the services of these experts in the form of consultants/advisors, etc. Consequently B-school students may have to think in terms of serving not only big corporate houses but also mid-cap companies and fairly large-sized small-scale units. In this context the universities and B-schools may have to take cognizance of this development and make necessary changes in the programme contents/curriculum so as to be in tune with the latest trends.

10. Since the 'Consultancy field' has bright prospects in India, efforts should be made to include this area in the programme contents. In future, most of the mid-cap companies and small-scale units may require the services of consultants to advise/help them on a regular basis. In the light of this steps may be taken to treat this subject as a separate discipline and offer degrees/diplomas.

22 Towards Restructuring Business Education

—P.S. YADAPADITHAYA AND
M.P. HRISHIKESH

In the Indian way of thinking, a human being is a positive asset and a precious national resource which needs to be cherished, nurtured and developed with tenderness and care, coupled with dynamism. The Catalytic action of Business Education in this complex, competitive, and dynamic growth process needs to be planned meticulously and executed with great sensitivity.

Formal management education which started in India in 1950 with the opening of Master of Business Administration (M.B.A.) curriculum in the Deptt. of Commerce of Andhra University, has come a long way since then.[1] The current decade has been marked by tremendous growth in the number of Management Educational Institutions, most of which have come up in the private sector. At present there are more than 520 such institutes offering business education in India.

NEED FOR RESTRUCTURING

It is disheartening to note that there is a general decline in the academic standards and the quality of management education in India. No doubt, there are several excellent centres of business education and research like the IIMs, ITIs, some universities and departments of universities, deemed universities and some colleges. They make a very valuable contribution, but standards are not uniform in our vast management education system.

The quality of management education depends on several interlinked variables such as quality of the content and technique of imparting business education; the quality of teachers, the quality of infrastructures and the quality of students seeking business education.

The success of management institutes and thereby management education, would largely depend on how quickly and effectively they are able to adapt and address themselves to the needs of the society and the changing business environment.

PRINCIPLES OF RESTRUCTURING

The restructuring of business education in India should be based on the following principles :

1. The course should be up-to-date and in tune with the latest developments in the field.
2. The course should be relevant to the real business world with a global outlook and appropriate in the context of liberalisation, privatisation and globalisation (LPG) of the Indian economy.
3. It should incorporate modern techniques of imparting management education such as computer simulation, audio-visual labs, case studies, role plays, group discussion and presentation, and management games. These techniques will assure '*hands-on-experience*' to the management students.
4. The course should attract, develop and retain professionally qualified and committed faculty members who have got a flair for management teaching.
5. The course curriculum must be continuously reviewed and updated incorporating interdisciplinary and international perspectives.
6. The programme must have state-of-the-art computer laboratory, high-quality library, need-based career-management centre, and a very active industry-institution interaction centre.
7. Classroom business teaching should be reinforced by practicals, summer training, internship, extension education (socially useful and desirable activity) and a project report.

8. There should be a close, purposeful, trusting, win-win mutually beneficial industry-institution partnership which would enhance the quality and credibility of management education in India.
9. Towards internationalising the course, management institute should strive hard for international accreditation and strategic alliances with the world class business educational institutions.
10. The course evaluation has to be made on a continuous basis so that there is no cramming at the last moment leading evaluation only of the skill in memorizing.

MISSING LINK BETWEEN BUSINESS RESEARCH AND PRACTICE

Again it is quite disheartening to note that the results of management and business research conducted by various institutions are not well communicated, understood, nor effectively utilized in the working world of business management. It is needless to say that business management teachers and researchers need to understand and involve themselves in the activities of real organisations, and practising managers need to understand and appreciate the nature and outcomes of such research studies through a genuine, meaningful, and rewarding industry-institution partnerships.

It should be clearly noted that the science and practice of management can be brought closer together, in an effort to effectively integrate business theory, research, and practice. Several approaches have been proposed to bring science and practice of management closer together by doing research that is useful.[2]

It is also suggested that progress in the organisational sciences has been limited by many management scholars' strict adherence to the "*scientific method*" in the design and conduct of research, which often does not fit the realities of "real world" sittings.[3] It is recommended that academics should not insist on choosing settings that fit their methods, but instead should consider altering their research design to fit the setting or environment being investigated.[4] Doing this could have interesting and important implications for both management research and practice. Research on organisations can contribute to our scientific knowledge base as well as to practitioners who are interested in the effectiveness of organisations, according to Lawler and his collegues.[5] Indeed, Lawler has established two fundamental criteria that all management research projects must meet : the project must help practitioners understand organisations in a way that will improve practice, and it must contribute to a theoretically and scientifically useful body of knowledge about organisations.

Industry-Institution Research Partnerships

Even though, formation of a number of partnerships has occurred in U.K. and USA, there is an insignificant growth of cooperative efforts between management education and industry in India. Such cooperation should be viewed as an important means for increasing India's competitive position in the global market place. During the 1980s, in the developed countries, the value of linking university and corporate research and development to increase competitiveness became widely recognised by many government, business and educational leaders.[6] This recognition resulted in the emergence of many cooperative R & D Programmes between American businesses and educational institutions.[7] Typically the business-university partnerships are called 'centres', are organisational units of business educational institutions, and have a number of corporate sponsors who provide funding for research and other activities. The predominant purpose of these partnerships is to generate applied research. Other activities include joint meetings of management researchers and practitioners, training and development programmes and conferences, and recruiting of management students by the sponsors. These 'centres' provide an unparalleled opportunity to bring management researchers and practitioners together to address problems facing the management field. The 'centres' provide faculty members with an increased awareness of real world problems and opportunities to conduct research that will contribute to both the science and practice of management. In turn, this value-added knowledge can be better fed to the management students. For management practitioners, these 'centres' provide access to faculty expertise, and opportunities to be involved in, and directly benefit from, innovative research. This appears to be the "*Weakest link*" in our business education system.

We feel that a natural product of the growing relationships between management academics and practitioners will be an increase in joint management research and publication. One can witness a growing ability and desire of professors and managers to jointly conduct management related research projects. We agree that an essential requirement for greater integration between science and practice of business education is increased interactions between researchers and practitioners, and exposing the students to the practical ground realities of managing organisational processes and results.

REFERENCES

1. Althaf Khan and Kamal Yadav, "Management Education in India : Emerging Issues", *University News*, Vol. 35, No. 15, April 14, 1997, p. 13.
2. Lawler, E.E. III, Morhrman, A.M., Jr., Mohrman, S.A., Ledford, G.E., Jr., and Cummings, T.G. (eds.) (1985), *Doing Research that is useful for Theory and Practice*, San Francisco : Jossey-Buss;

   Hekel, M.D., Sorcher, M., Ber, M., and Moses, J.L. (1982), *Making it Happen : Designing research with implementation in mind*, Beverly Hills, CA : Sage; and

   Bochm, V.R. (1980), Research in the "Real Work" — A Conceptual Model, *Personnel Psychology*, 33, 495-503.
3. Bochm, V.R. (1980), Research in the "Real Work" — A Conceptual Model, *Personnel Psychology*, 33, 495-503.
4. *Ibid.*
5. Lawler, E.E. III, *et al.* (eds.), op. cit.
6. Morrison, C., Mcguire, E.P., Clarke, M.A. (1988), *Keys to W.S. Competitiveness*, New York : The Conference Board Inc.
7. Fairweather, J.S. (1988), *Entrepreneurship and Higher Education : Lessons for Colleges, Universities, and Industry*. As HEERIC Higher Education Report No. 6, Washington, D.C. : Association for the Study of Higher Education.

23 Challenges Before Business Education in India

—A.B. KALKUNDRIKAR

1. Business education today is passing through a critical phase. With the advent of new economic policy in 1991, the demand for business education is increasing. It may continue to rise as we enter into the twenty-first century. The number of business schools has tremendously gone up and different dimensions are being added to their structure and curriculum design. These business schools are now confronted with new challenges.

2. In this paper, an attempt is made to assess the present position of business education, challenges before it and how to meet these challenges.

BACKDROP

3. Business education broadly aims at imparting knowledge, developing skills and qualities to make a person successful manager, businessman *or* an industrialist. In fact, managerial inputs have become essential in every walk of life.

4. Business education mainly comprises of commerce and Management education. In the early phase of 1980s, commerce education had become quite popular and this led to quantitative expansion of business education in terms of student enrolment, number of institutions and faculty status. Students joined the course thinking that it offers better job opportunities. Unfortunately this did not happen. Those of such students who decided to pursue professional courses such as Chartered Accountancy, Company Secretary, ICWA and allied disciplines found that the knowledge imparted was not adequate enough to support various careers and vocations available. The students from other streams also started

joining these professions and the demand for commerce started declining.

5. In the initial stages, the destiny of commerce faculty was guided by economics teachers who felt that commerce should not be a fully professional course. As a result, it was treated as a part of economics discipline. People with economics background provided logical thinking to commerce faculty, but it did not provide practical solutions to business. With the growth of business and industry, the demand for business skills started growing. Mere knowledge base was not enough. Commerce education provided a very narrow perspective.

6. The decade of 1990s marked by liberalisation, globalisation and privatisation added a new dimension in the form of mushroom growth of Management Institutions offering MBA/PGDM/PGDBA programmes and also BBA programme. Diploma courses also made their appearance on the scene. Business education acquired more a formal character than what really business and industry need. The absence of need-based education, lack of industry-institution interface, inadequate efforts to vocationalise the system of business education and improper practical inputs have distorted the whole process of our business education.

PRESENT STATUS

7. Since Management education has become a major component of business education, it is worth-while assessing the present position of Management education. To exploit the opportunities created by new economic environment, the number of management education institutions has increased.

Type of Institution	Total Number
1. I.I.M.S.	06
2. Management Edn. Depts./National/ Sector specific Central Universities	43
3. Management Depts. of State University	84
4. Other Institutions	367
Total	500

8. The present structure of business education in India is as follows :

Top Level		I.I.M.S.
Middle Level	—	Sector specific Institution
	—	National Level Institutions
	—	Universities
	—	Central Universities
Bottom Level	—	Management Education Depts. of State Universities
	—	Autonomous Institutes
	—	Other Institutions

9. No doubt there has been quantitative expansion of business education facilities, but the quality has suffered/deteriorated. The number of business schools has increased from 32 to 500. These institutions are recognised by the All India Council for Technical Education, a statutory body under the Ministry of Human Resource Development, Govt. of India. In addition, there are many more institutions not recognised by AICTE but run as Autonomous Institutions, conducting their own programmes. The recognised Institutions, whether affiliated *or* unaffiliated to Universities, are under the control of State Governments, Department of Technical Education and other such bodies. In some states, there is co-ordination between these agencies and in some there is total absence of co-ordination.

MAJOR CHALLENGES

10. The Indian economy has witnessed remarkable changes in the post liberalization period posing new challenges to almost every sector. Educational sector is no exception to this. The major challenges before business education in the coming era of 21st century would be :

1. Competition
2. International Perspective
3. Information Technology

4. Placement
5. Quality and Academic Standards
6. Industry-Institution Interface
7. Image Building
8. Knowledge Management
9. Autonomy.

1. Competition

11. Competition is a buzzword of liberalization era. There is a sudden shift from. 'Protective Environment' to 'Competitive Environment'. The subsidized education in a protective environment has failed to keep pace with changing times. Business education pattern in India did not deliver the required results. Business education has to now adapt to changing condition. It should make the students more competitive by developing their overall personalities. The spirit of competition needs to be inculcated in the students community. This calls for participative mode of education entailing more involvement of students in the process of education.

12. Institutions imparting business education are already facing crisis of identity, character and quality. They will have to re-design their courses and adopt innovative methods for imparting education to suit the changing needs of the society. T.Q.M. principles need to be applied and value-based business education has to be imparted.

2. International Perspective

13. Globalisation has added a new dimension to business education. Internationalisation of business, changing profile of trade and commerce, knowledge explosion and demand for smart products require our business schools to redefine their goals and mission. There is a need to provide international perspective to the students by upgrading training methods to global standards.

3. Information Technology

14. Another greatest challenge before business education is Information Technology. The rapid strides in the growth of IT-industry has created deep impact on the working of almost every sector. Information technology has revolutionalised the entire

operational process in economy. Business education will be required to keep pace with this kind of a change. Sinet, Intranet, Internet and Cyberspace would call for modernisation of library facilities, teaching pedagogy and upgradation of infrastructure by the business schools. The networking within and outside the organization would become the need of the hour. Computer with L.C.D. overhead projector, cable T.V., local area network (LAN), worldwide web, WAN electronic media would change the face of business education. The nature of support services would also undergo a radical change.

4. Placement

15. Unlike other spheres of education, placement is at the heart of business education. The image of business schools depends largely on their placement activity. In a competitive situation, industry and business have shown preference for lean organization which calls for downsizing thereby helping the process of cost reduction. To this is added, Cyclical fluctuations. In the wake of recession and depression, employment gets adversely affected and placement becomes very difficult. The mushroom growth of business schools on the one hand resulting in increased supply of business graduates and compression of demand due to changing business environment on the other is going to pose a big challenge before business educationists. The existing jobs may become obsolete and new jobs may emerge. The job content and skill requirement may go on changing. Business education should focus on preparing students for these new jobs and keep pace with changing times by operating "an accordion factor". In a competitive market, placement is going to be really a big challenge.

5. Quality and Academic Standards

16. International perspective resulting from globalisation would demand high quality education in the 21st century. The quality of education and academic standards of business education will be of a very high order. Admission criteria, selection of students, training inputs, teaching pedagogy, industry interaction, industrial visits, faculty development through practical experience in industry, computerisation of library services and application of ISO-9000 standards will be a part of business education. Electronic Commerce

and Office Automation, paperless documentation will be the order of the day. Obviously the business education should focus on all these aspects to provide required inputs. Resources sharing avenues will have to be tapped. Library resources, books and journals, research papers, technical reports and case materials will have to be obtained through computer network. Faculty collaboration, conferencing, placement information and subscription to electronic journals will be common components of business education.

6. Industry-Institution Interface

17. Unfortunately business schools in India have weak linkage with industry due to conventional approach to business education. There is a need to build strong interface between industry and business schools. This linkage has to be on a continuous basis. It is not enough to sign only Mous between industry and institutions. Industry should sponsor research projects, send professionals for interaction with faculty and students, organise Seminars and Workshops in collaboration with each other, develop an environment of industry and academia exchanges, provide summer placement to students and train them in problem-solving techniques, provide industry exposure through placement of faculty for practical experience and provide information for developing live cases. Academic should focus on industry-oriented practical research, provide inputs for development of industry and undertake effective consultancy work. There is a need for involving people from industry in designing need-based curriculum and courses.

Industry should provide funds for building strong infrastructure to business schools. Total involvement of industry and business persons in business education will be required to meet the challenges of globalisation.

7. Image Building

18. In the wake of increasing competition and globalisation, each business school will be required to develop its own image. This would call for designing some uniqueness for the institution. Every institution should distinguish itself from other similar institutions imparting business education. A monopolistically competitive situation that would emerge from cut throat competition would require special efforts for image building.

8. Knowledge Management

19. The twenty-first century is going to witness knowledge based business. There is already knowledge explosion. Information technology has facilitated free and excellent dissemination of information. The volume of information available is likely to create confusion and chaos. A scientific and careful knowledge management will be a challenge that would emerge from this type of situation.

9. Autonomy

20. In a market-free liberalized economy, unwanted regulations by the Government, Universities and other bodies would make our business education irrelevant and keep business institutions out of place. Autonomy in respect of course designing and operational aspects would become essential without divorcing and diluting, of course, quality and academic standards.

CONCLUSION

Business education in the 21st century will be totally different than what it is today. The economic policy has opened up new vistas and added different dimensions to business education. There are many challenges as well as opportunities ahead. Business educationists will have to face these challenges and use opportunities to their own advantage. A new culture with ethical base will be required to be developed to survive in the twentyfirst century.

REFERENCES

1. Chaudhary, H.C., *Management Education in India Past, Present and Future.*
2. Harish Kumar, "Globalisation of Business Education," *University News*, Aug. 11, 1997.
3. Singh, Amrik, "Challenges of Higher Education," *University News*, Dec. 1, 1997.
4. Shejwalkar, P.C., "Commerce Education — A Shift in Paradigm," *University News*, Aug. 25, 1997.
5. Tripathy, Nalini and Mangaraj, Sujata, "Challenges of Management Education in India," *University News*, Nov. 3, 1997.

24 Skill-Building : A Key to Curriculum Development in Commerce Education

—S.G. HUNDEKAR AND M.R. SHOLLAPUR

Commerce education is a form of instruction which aims at injecting business skills, talents and knowledge into the minds of the students to inspire them to assume entrepreneural risks confidently and launch their own business successfully or prepare them to take a career as a business professional competitively with an emphasis on specialised knowledge.

The fruitfulness of a discipline like commerce can be ensured only when it succeeds in meeting the contemporary needs of the society. Any mismatch between the focus-contents of the curriculum and the societal needs interrogates the very existence of such discipline. The peripheral outlook reveals that commerce education has secured the balance between these two ends. This is evident from a sea-change in the focus areas of commerce from the erstwhile typing, shorthand, book-keeping, etc., aiming at producing the clerks to as many as 115 subjects like Management, Finance, HRD, Computers, etc., as spelled out in the Report of the UGC sponsored Curriculum Development Centre in Commerce, so as to meet the varied needs of the society in general and the business world in particular.

It is high time now to introspect ourselves regarding the competitiveness of commerce students and their ability in reaching the desired expectations. Despite a change in the composition and direction of commerce curriculum, how many of our students are capable of launching their own business independently? How many of them can fairly do well in non-business market areas like

Finance and Accounting, HRD, Computers, etc., when compared with their counterparts coming from the professional and management institutes? It is disheartening to note that the present day products of commerce education are hardly accepted by the industries in their different job areas. The University Education Commission in India has observed as early as 1949 that "the graduate education in Commerce was manufacturing graduates who could not properly be fitted into occupational structure which is rapidly changing towards technical and vocational pattern". It is unfortunate to note that the malady still persists today without being cured after having traced it out half a century back.

The crux of the problem is that the students are not well-equipped with those skills needed. The skill in this context means the ability to use one's own knowledge effectively and readily in execution or performance, technical expertness, a power or habit of doing any particular thing competently. The emphasis is that the skills are based on knowledge and the objective should be to bring that knowledge to the level of competency. As far as knowledge component is concerned, commerce education contains the varied aspects of business and its managerial practices exhaustively. There are, however, a host of factors which have come on the way to carry over the 'knowledge' into the layer of 'competence' culminating into 'skill building'.

Against this background, the present paper aims to explore the skill-building approach in the development of the commerce curriculum. The paper is divided into two parts, covering the measures for skill-building and the consequential tasks to be performed to realise the goal of skill-building.

I. Measures for Skill-building

Firstly, the time honoured method of imparting instructions within the four walls of the classroom where the students are the passive listeners need to be revamped. In a bid to get exposed, the students may be asked to write success stories of the businessmen to whom they are accessible. Besides, they may be asked to collect news items relating to their subject. The use of audio-visual aids can give a better standby to the students in getting themselves exposed to business-situations.

Secondly, group-discussion should be made mandatory (say one hour a week), where the students interact with their teachers as well as with their fellow-friends. Such interactions infuse not only the understanding of the subject but also develops communication skills which are badly lacking among commerce students.

Thirdly, there should be close interaction, between the students and the business professionals/practitioners at regular intervals. These professionals/practitioners from among the locality itself (let be a successful sole-proprietor) are to be invited to share their experiences in the field of business which enlightens upon the life experiences in business. The report of the Special Committee for Commerce Education also called as Rao Committee (1961) has revealed that the commerce education in educational institutions in U.S.A. is conducted with an active co-operation of business community. If it is attempted in our country too, it adds greater empiricism to the course.

Fourthly, the practical-assignments should be the regular feature of the curriculum. The students, for instance, may be asked to work upon the documentation aspect of a hypothetical firm/company or collect the copies of the shares and debentures from those who possess them or visit the banks to collect the brochures relating to different deposit/loan schemes, etc. Such assignments carried on either individually or in groups, help the students to forge linkage between the theory and practice.

Fifthly, compulsory visits to industries, financial institutions, etc., should form the core component of the curriculum. Through such visits, the students get an opportunity to observe and interact with the real life situations in business. This live experience provides a platform to compare between the theory taught within the four walls of the classroom and the real life flux in business.

Last but not the least is the case-study approach where a student should be asked to study a business unit or a situation or a programme. During the period (around a fortnight) of case-study, the student becomes one among the functionaries of the unit, observes it, collects the relevant information for his study, attempts to comprehend the same and in the ultimate analysis comes out with his own conclusions. Such an exposure broadens the knowledge base, fosters analytical and judgement ability, develops imagination, promotes interpersonal relations and improves communication skills. Above all, it gives personal motivation to accept the responsibilities in business whenever and wherever they arise. This approach goes a long way in imbibing the business-skills because the skills as we understand cannot be taught in the classroom but are to be learnt on a job.

II. Tasks Ahead

The skill-building in commerce education as examined above is not a single time job, but an ongoing process. Hence, certain preliminary tasks need to be performed and doubts ought to be clarified before the skill-building programme is launched. Following are a few important things to be looked into in this context.

Firstly, the teaching fraternity of commerce education itself primarily need to be equipped with the necessary skills to impart the skill-development-oriented curriculum. Hence, they need to be trained in methodology of teaching with an added focus on innovative methods.

Secondly, the teachers need to update their knowledge on continuing basis. Hence, the refresher courses are to be arranged on regular basis.

Thirdly, the *modus operandi* of funds needed for academic infrastructure *viz.*, audio-visual aids, business magazines and newspapers, etc., need to be spelled out in clear terms.

Fourthly, the periodicity of inviting business professionals/ practitioners should be determined, in the absence of which it may take away the effective teaching hours. Selecting the business professionals may pose a problem especially in rural areas. The urbanites may be too busy to attend such programmes.

Fifthly, unending and untiring rapport is to be established with the industry. The industries to be visited, the formalities to be completed with, etc., are to be completed before the commencement of the academic year.

Sixthly, regarding, case-study, the different avenues that can be covered, the methodology to be adopted, etc., are to be clearly elucidated. The local business community needs to be convinced regarding their role in accommodating the students in their business units during the case-studies. The time factor, marks allotment, mode of evaluation, funding, etc., are to be decided upon in clear terms.

CONCLUSION

If the aforesaid measures of skill-building are implemented in right earnest, the commerce education is sure to infuse the required amount of competitiveness in our students. The participatory methodology of teaching as reflected in group discussions, interaction with business professionals and practitioners not only clarifies the doubts of the students but also fosters to comprehend, act or react in right perspective thereby improving their communication skills too. The business visits provide platform of real life flux in business spectrum. The case-studies facilitate the application of theory and concepts, inspires scientific outlook and finally develops the decision-making skills. In order to materialise this noble goal of skill-building through these measures, the teaching fraternity has to bear an added burden and to discharge it sincerely. In conclusion, it is apt to quote here the saying of Dr. S. Radhakrishnan, the renowned Indian philosopher and educationist : "The true end of education is not the acquisition of information important though it may be, or acquisition of skills though they are very essential in modern society. One must have that superior outlook which goes beyond information and skill. It is the teacher who gives the spark which will enable one develop a new outlook on life and draw a new kind of a being."

25 Challenges Before Business Education

—M.R. HEGDE

The fundamental aim of Education is the all-round development of a human being. Education aims at providing the essential skills and qualities to enable us to live better. The aim of Business Education is to impart the essential knowledge of business and business skills to the students and to make them personally fit for business and socially fit for community life. Therefore, it is axiomatic that Business Education aims at promoting efficient teachers and dedicated researchers in the field of Business Education.

Business Education includes Commerce and Business Administration. It encompasses education in the areas of Trade, Service Sector (financial institutions, insurance, transport, etc.) and Industry. The various branches of Business Education are Marketing Management, Service Sector Management, Financial Management, Business Administration, Computer Application, etc. The different areas of education in the field of Commerce and Industry are thus brought under a single discipline, *viz.*, Business Education.

The New Economic Policy has brought about a sea change in the Indian Economy. The Globalisation, Liberalisation and Privatisation, have drastically changed the situation in the business world. Of course changes are very common in the business world as this field is highly sensitive to variations in economic, political, technological and other parameters. It is this ever-changing phenomenon of business that has posed varieties of challenges to Business Education. The main task of Business Education is, therefore, to make students fit to face the challenges of ever-changing business environment. This warrants a dynamic approach on the part of all concerned serving in different areas of Business Education.

Business Education should mainly be targeted towards building necessary work-skills among students opting different occupations and professions and of course, making them conscious of their social responsibilities. This indeed is the main aim of Business Education. Following are the six important thrust areas to be taken care of in order to realise the aims of Business Education :

(i) Framing a suitable course content.

(ii) Providing required Infrastructural Facilities.

(iii) Having necessary Faculty Improvement Programmes.

(iv) Obtaining healthy co-operation of Industries and Professional Institutions with Educational Institutions.

(v) Conducting 'On the spot Research' periodically for improvement of curriculum, and

(vi) Making timely changes in syllabi to suit the needs of dynamic business situations.

These six thrust areas also happen to be the main challenges before Business Education.

The specific suggestions under each of the six thrust areas cited above to meet effectively the challenges before Business Education may be enlisted as follows :

FRAMING A SUITABLE COURSE CONTENT

* conduct a thorough survey and find the needs of the course in different branches of Business Education before framing the course content.
* restructure the course content in such a way that students of Business Education going out of educational institutions are suitably accepted in the concerned employment market.
* impart specialised education and training to the students in different branches of Business Education after their completing an initial stage of common curriculum so that the students of Business Education are made fit exclusively for specific jobs and professions.

* avoid the entry of graduates from non-business faculties in the jobs intended for business graduates by making the business graduates armed better for such jobs.
* motivate graduates of Business Education for self-employment and also for setting up industries on their own.
* provide enough scope in curriculum for the students to know and understand the international business environment.
* include practical classes/project work wherever necessary for different papers of Business Education.
* set the curriculum and teaching of language papers in such a way that the students of Business Education acquire reasonable command over the language.
* include compulsory papers on Computer Applications to all the students of Business Education so as to season them in software skills.
* take proper care in framing the syllabi for inter-disciplinary papers and also in teaching them.
* build in the students proper awareness of social responsibility and moral values along with the Business Education.

PROVIDING REQUIRED INFRASTRUCTURAL FACILITIES

* get the contents of the infrastructural facilities determined by a panel of Business Education Experts.
* provide proper infrastructural facilities required for Business Education in all educational institutions.
* let the universities grant/extend the affiliation to such institutions only where the required educational infrastructure is provided.

HAVING NECESSARY FACULTY IMPROVEMENT PROGRAMMES

* find out proper instructional methods to different subject areas.

* equip the teachers with advanced knowledge of business and economic concepts and principles.
* make the teachers aware of latest business technology and workplace requirements of the job aspirants.
* encourage the teachers to have a feeling of commitment dedication involvement and a mindset non-resistant to learn and teach new things.
* arrange a thorough revision of books on various branches of Business Education from time to time in order to fit the changes taking place in the field.

OBTAINING HEALTHY CO-OPERATION OF INDUSTRIES AND PROFESSIONAL INSTITUTIONS WITH EDUCATIONAL INSTITUTIONS

* ensure continuous and regular interaction between the educational institutions on the one hand and industries and professional institutions situated close by, on the other so as to produce the business graduates in the most desired manner.
* make it obligatory, if need be by legislations, on the executives of industries and professional institutions to offer students the work skill exposure by providing training and guidance.
* arrange alliance with outside bodies for recruitment of business graduates through campus selection, etc.
* have a proper and realistic evaluation of business graduates based on the all-round assessment of their academic excellence as well as practical work skill.

CONDUCTING 'ON THE SPOT RESEARCH' PERIODICALLY FOR IMPROVEMENT OF CURRICULUM

* conduct thorough research on issues directly connected with business practice in general and Business Education in particular.
* carry out a prospective field survey periodically with regard to the type of personnel required by the different

areas of business world for a stipulated span of time (say 10 years).

* apply the findings of periodical investigations for updating the course content.

MAKING TIMELY CHANGES IN SYLLABI TO SUIT THE NEEDS OF DYNAMIC BUSINESS SITUATIONS

* get regular feedback at definite intervals to keep track of changing business situations.
* restructure the syllabi to suit the needs of the time.
* include in the syllabi the necessary contents to enlighten the students about the real life problems in business and also about the latest technological and institutional changes in business environment.

Business Education is essentially a discipline with everlasting challenges mainly due to everchanging business environment. It is this element of dynamism that requires Business Educationists to have a dynamic approach on all matters related to business. In addition, the changes to be incorporated in Business Education are perennial features as the course contents are required to be overhauled time and again with changes in business environment. Unless we understand and appreciate the challenges before Business Education and make a sincere attempt to face such challenges in pragmatic and systematic way it will not be possible for us to combat the confusing and outmoded situation presently prevailing in the field of Commerce Education.

In a word, the need of the hour now is to act swiftly and decisively to effect drastic and innovative changes in the contents of our Commerce Education to bring it in tune with the modern developments in the world of Commerce and Industry. Earlier we realise this and respond appropriately to the challenges confronting us, better it would be for all.

26 Business Education in India — Forward and Backward Linkages

—A.C. BHAWSAR AND M.K. RAKIBE

The Oxford dictionary defines the word 'COMMERCE' as the exchange of merchandise. Thus the Commerce Education can mean education in the areas of trade like exchange of merchandise and auxiliaries of trade, transport, banking, etc. However, the concept includes industries, service sectors and non-profit making organizations. The growing popularity and demand can be seen from the number of students opting for business education as a whole. With the growth of management institutes commerce education is facing a lot of problems and challenges from management education being the off-shoots of business education, should co-operate and supplement each other. Similar to management education, commerce education should give specialized knowledge at higher-level *i.e.*, (P.G.). Thus the issue of the economy is highlighted.

The formal teaching of commerce began in 1886 when a commercial school was started at Pachayappa's Charities (Madras). Now we have innumerable institutions of Commerce education.

At +2 level we aim at giving a broad outline of the course based on the elementary conceptual foundation. The aim is to provide the students of commerce a thorough knowledge of Accounting. Cost Accounting, Banking, Taxation, Business Management, Business laws, etc., to enable the students to take up career in banking, insurance, transport, industries or an independent business.

At the postgraduate level the teachers are expected to produce professionals for key job areas like Accounting, Finance, Tax planning and Management, Marketing, etc.

The expansion of commerce education has boosted up over years. Initially only 8.6% of students opted for commerce education which in the span of four decades has shot-up to 22%. There are more than 4000 commerce colleges and more than 125 P.G. Departments in different universities of India, which may be attributed to the growth of industry and trade in India. Thus the educationists must be kept in link with the industrial development and changes at all levels.

India became the major centre of business and management education with the starting of management departments. The following chart shows the statistical data of the number of Management schools in India between 1962 to 1995.

Year	No. of Schools	No. of Seats
1962	06	200
1982	58	Not Available
1992	100	4000
1995	500	8000

(As per IDL Chemicals Endowment Lecture by Dr. D.P. Sinha at Osmania University, Hyderabad 22-11-95.)

In spite of the fact that there has been an enormous increase in the quality of management schools and institutions, qualitatively we have miles to go to boast about them.

Management education should successfully meet the challenges of the ever-growing needs of public and private sector enterprises. Maintaining the quality of the students and the efficiency of the educationists must be taken care of. Modern teaching aids be used while imparting education and the curriculum be planned as per the need of the time.

Thus quantitative expansion of the education without sufficient preparation and basic infrastructure, without an effective linkage between the industry and user organization, professional bodies and largely the government and the society has very adversely affected the Management Education in India.

We must consider if today's Management Education successfully meets the demands of the society and the industrial units along with its compatibility with the nation's socio-economic objectives. We must also see if our manpower is fed with proper management skills as per the requirement.

The economic reforms initiated by the government leading to globalization of business has increased competition at international levels thus making the globalization of business education a must. The business has expanded to the extent of crossing the geographical barriers over the continents thus a world market has come into existence. Thus Darwin's theory of 'the survival of the fittest' holds good for every business today. Therefore, we need the process of globalization of professional management education to form a linkage and net-working among the business schools all over the world. Institutions giving business education should thus time and again take stock of their course curriculum and revise it to the needs of global business requirements.

The management education at top schools level and the rest has a very wide gap of quality. The quality of the staff is not exceptionally good and the facilities offered by these institutions are equally poor barring the top schools of course. The new heights of the top management schools achieve while the general standard of management education has fallen.

The ever-troubling weakness of Indian management education is that there is a great diversity between what is taught and what is actually needed on a job. This is true specially at semi-urban level schools where the staff is very poorly equipped with knowledge and who are appointed through outside (political) influence and not on true merit. M.B.A. schools are not receiving proper response due to lack of a global integrated world view and a lack of a long-term perspective in it. The major deficiencies in the management schools are seen in the areas of leadership, team spirit managerial personality, personal effectiveness and the job knowledge specially.

The teaching methodology in our country is basically of lecture method punctuated with seminars and discussions. The case method is followed at management school level but that too has inadequate information. Creative and effective response to problems are rarely employed in Management schools except at the top of schools. The inadequacies in pedagogy has resulted in the failure of the institution at large in imparting managerial capabilities and competencies.

Though business organizations seem to be looking for instant managers the fact remains that it is a very long journey of trial, hard work and experience that makes one. Another point is if Western education be used in Indian management education, Indian experience can be equally relied upon in Western schools of management. It is a give and take process. We need to update the management education so that it does not become stagnant. It should change with the fast changing management environment. The task lies before us is how to remould management education techniques for its future development.

Management education should comprise to new young generation who are to be prepared, employees in mind career who do not have the organization skills and specialists who time to time need updating and up-grading in their speciality. The management institutes and industrial organizations should jointly develop the managers. Thus career planning needs to be given maximum attention in future.

Students must be given general education at the same time. Every student must be specialized in a particular skill of management. The basic managerial education as per Professor McGrath should involve learning for its own sake, communicate reading, writing, listening, speaking and graphing skills, collection of information, draw inference from opinion and interpretation of it. It should also consist of solving problems, adjustment to changes, working with team spirit.

Management institutes should offer courses on entrepreneurship and also the use of psychology to understand the benefits and losses of risk-taking.

Emphasis should be given on action-oriented and issue-oriented research in the areas such as entrepreneurship social trendsets.

The decision-making skills of the managers must be sharpened to enable them to face the changing, socio-political and economic conditions. Moreover, there should be a smooth flow of information exchange.

Courses in international business have to be started for which competency and fluency over a foreign language is a must along with the culture of the foreign countries.

Non-cognitive attributes like leadership, administration skills, oral communication skills should not be overlooked or underestimated. They can be encouraged through informal and formal discussions, games, seminars, mocktrials, yoga exercises, etc.

Last, but not the least, the management students ought to be less materialistic and should be taught values of life. Values such as honesty, sincerity and integrity be inculcated in them which ultimately along with their skills and knowledge will make them successful personalities in the sphere of management and commerce. They must be taught that honesty is the policy the easiest way to success which is long-lasting and fruit-bearing if not immediately but for sure in the long-run.

27 Business Education Needs Change

—B. VIJAYA AND BHEEMANAGOUDA

Education is the backbone of development of every economy. Moreover, Business Education, in particular, plays pioneering role in moving the cycles of economic development. It seems, Indian business education, at present is suffering from technical disease and hence, needs some changes to meet the challenges put before it.

In the wave of sweeping changes, there is a miraculous change at the economic front in India. We have already spent four decades of independent life under veiled economy with the generous aid of state and under the protective shelter of Government against the fierce competitions. Indian economy suffered a setback; Public sector enterprises failed to fulfil the needs of nation rather proved a burden on economy.

With the inefficient performance of public sector enterprises, low productivity of labour, use of outdated techniques, labour unrest, bulging population, unequal distribution of wealth India is looking at the ocean of fierce competition where the fittest will survive. The various policies and programmes are to be formulated for bringing a change in the existing education system to meet the requirements of the future. Therefore, the present business education system needs a careful surgery to enter into the twenty-first century.

The present paper is prepared with the objectives of highlighting the existing flaws in the business education system and to suggest some tailor-made measures to meet the challenges put before the business education.

RETROSPECTIVE VIEW

The Business education is a sophisticated name for commerce education which is just like an old product in a new attractive package. History of business education can be traced back to the establishment of Sydenham College of Commerce and Economics, Mumbai in 1913; Postgraduate department of studies in Lucknow in 1921. Special Committee on Commerce Education headed by Prof. V.K.R.V. Rao in 1961 identified commerce as a distinct educational course and thereafter various Indian Universities have adopted commerce education in their education system. Over the years business education is being expanded. Enrolment of the students for the commerce higher education increased tremendously in four decades of independent India's planning period. There are now more than 4000 colleges and more than 125 universities which impart education. Besides that, there are many professionalised management institutes established to cater to the needs of business-India. Keeping the model of American management schools Indian Government started Indian Institutes of Management (IIMs) in 1962 at Ahmedabad and Calcutta and also in Bangalore and Lucknow in 1972 and 1984 respectively. XLR Institute at Jamshedpur, Jamanalal Bajaj Institute at Mumbai and Administrative Staff College at Hyderabad are some of the other management Institutes whose main business is to spread the sophisticated management-cult in India.

Present Scenario

Though a lot of improvement is made in the field of business education in these days of modernisation, it is unfortunate to witness some flaws in it.

1. Fossilized Syllabi : Business schools (colleges, institutes and universities, except some exceptional institutes) in the name of commerce education have commercialized the education system resulting in poor quality of education. The ill-designed curricula of the business schools have rendered no purpose in the present situation. Subjects are descriptive and textbook oriented which do not make the students hungry for practical knowledge that makes the creative thinking of students nullity. As a result they have become shibboleths.

2. Theoretical Approach : Blossoming buds in the business schools get bored by parrot-like teaching and the same teaching in midst of four walls kept the students off the practical world.

3. Selection and Evaluation Procedure : The system of admission to evaluation is not good which does not measure the intrinsic intellects of students. Products of business schools once enter the practical field utterly failed to meet the stress of trade world.

4. Financial Crunch : Most of the state-owned educational institutes — colleges and universities — which also impart business education are suffering from financial crunch. These institutions totally depend upon the Government for their fund-needs without creating their own financial sources. Consequently they failed to equip basic infrastructural facilities. This, in turn, spoils basic purpose — quality of business education.

5. Research Project Selection : There is a dearth of action-oriented research projects undertaken by the business education institutions. This leads the institutions and faculty members to the rust-road. In some of the institution where research is undertaken the students are not allowed to choose their interested areas instead the research area is imposed on the students in which research supervisor is interested. This topples the student at the first step of the research. This system of research has deteriorated the quality of teaching and research.

Now-a-days the business education system is being called as manufacturer of unemployment youth. Fortunately if they get job, there is a greater possibility of mismatch between education and employment. Hence, alumni are afraid of their future. This is because there is no specific area recognised where only commerce people fit.

The above discussion has clearly brought some of the weak spots in the present education system. The policy makers and others who are directly involved in the improvement of the education system should look into these areas and act accordingly.

Foreview Measures

Due to science and technology the pace of progress has been amazingly accelerated during the twentieth century. Now man has left his footprints on the face of the moon. He has almost conquered the time and space. Industrialisation has given a material culture unprecedented.

We are now at the threshold of twenty-first century. Developed countries are now experiencing stagnation in industrial and economic growth and looking for lucrative markets like India for their investments and market. Therefore, it seems that the present process of liberalisation-privatisation-globilisation (LPG) will find tremendous momentum in the future leading to fierce competition in every sphere of world. There is no out-of-way for India also but accept and face the challenge.

During the last few decades one can witness the unprecedented explosion of knowledge. In a traditional society the quantum of knowledge is very limited but in a modern society, the quantum of knowledge is too vast and the rate of growth is too fast. Therefore, one of the important tasks of education is to keep pace with this change and teach the students to acquire such knowledge 'how' rather than 'what'. An attempt is being made here to suggest some policy measures to keep the education on par with the changes in the modern days.

1. Well-designed Curricula : In this complex society of fierce competitive world designing a course curricula is not an easy task. While designing, forecasting should be made to know the demands of market. Some professionals and practically experienced personalities should be included in the body to prepare a curricula. Semester system of education may yield rich dividends by providing for regular assessment of students. The development wheel given below best explains the focus areas while designing the curricula and development of human resource.

2. Two-Way Approach : Action and reaction are the best tools for listening and learning. Hence, discussions may be arranged and seminars would be conducted to encourage the students to take active part in such activities. This participative system of learning is result-oriented and best suited for business schools. Therefore, the system of thinking and learning is to be adopted to replace listening and examination.

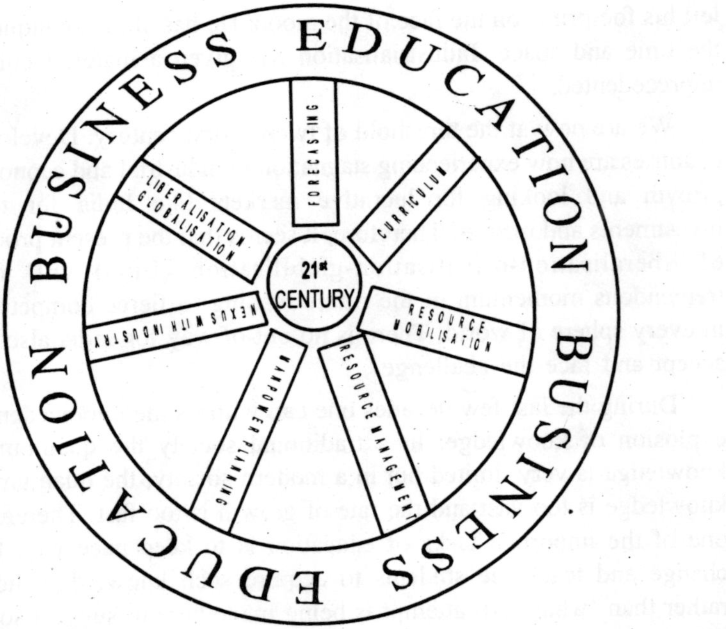

3. Teaching Aids : Parrot-like teaching will not impress the students. Therefore, it has now been realised that our pedagogic skills have to be developed and knowledge of latest developments in our chosen disciplines has to be continuously updated. Educational institution shall have to equip with modern teaching aids. Micro-computers will be widely used for arithmetical calculations. Word processors, overhead projector (OHP), slide projector, and other audio-visuals can also be used for effective teaching.

4. Training to would-be Teachers : Effective teaching is a technique which needs training. A postgraduate cannot become a good teacher unless he is trained. Seminar and internal assessment should be made compulsory to mould the would-be teacher. Special training courses for 3-6 months should be conducted for those who are interested in teaching profession.

5. Nexus between Institute-Industry : Learning in the midst of four walls will not yield better results. Therefore, off-wall learning is the need of hour. Before giving finishing touch-up to the product of institute, it should be given practical touch-up. In the light of this institute should develop a rapport with industry. Students may be deputed in summer for 'in-plant' training. Simultaneously, industry should also respond to the institutes to get the best products to suit their needs. Mutual exchange of teachers of institutes and professional experts of industry will be more helpful to update their knowledge. Teachers would get the practical knowledge and professionals may taste the teaching. Effective participation of practitioner and professionals would solve the problem of inadequate faculty.

7. Common Network : Common network should be established at the national as well as at the international levels among the business schools. This would be useful for sharing the knowledge, library books, etc., available at different and far-off schools.

8. Action-Oriented Research : Business education institutes should undertake the research project which will have a practical value. The selection of the research project should be based on the needs of the industry. Industries should also come forward to sponsor the projects in order to get the help of academic intellectuals. This will not only be helpful to industry but also to those who are involved in such projects of getting the jobs in the industry.

9. Update the Knowledge : Commerce community should meet off and on to update their knowledge to keep pace with the latest developments to face the challenge. Conferences, seminars, symposia must be organized to discuss the burning issues and to chalk out future course of action.

10. Find the Fund-Source : To serve, survive and thrive in 21st century educational institutions will have to find their own sources of funds. Steps should be taken to minimize the university campus by hiring out university space to outsiders, leasing out university buildings and lands to get their own funds. This will not only increase the income but also reduce the up-keep costs.

Institutions must maintain cordial relationship with regional industries and education-loving people to obtain the financial help from them. Government should give tax concessions to industries and persons who contribute to the educational institutions. Institutes should also keep good relationships with old students of the institute. They may also provide financial assistance to their alma mater.

11. Rating : To avoid mushrooming of business schools without having necessary infrastructural facilities, rating system will have to be evolved. This system provides necessary information to the students to enter into well-equipped institutes. This also lessens the burden on students in opting out institutes for their education.

12. Mother-tongue Media : Howsoever we have developed, our rural area based students are still suffering from language barriers. Higher business education is available only in English medium and books, study materials, etc., are also in English. Language should not be a barrier for knowledge and learning. Hence, academicians of high calibre should think over the matter and try to reconstruct the business education in mother-tongue. In fact, education would be effective if it is provided through their own language; for the same reason Christian Missionaries like Kittel, Rev. Ziegler, etc., had learnt Kannada and impressed ideas of their religion on the people of land.

Tomorrows ought to be trimmed today for better returns. It is eleventh-hour for our academicians, researchers, and industrial experts to think over the system and frame a suitable and constructional method of education to face the challenge of twenty-first century.

REFERENCES

1. Mohanty, J., *Indian Education in the Emerging Society*, Sterling Publishers Private Ltd., Bangalore, 1982.
2. Joshi, M.M., "Economic Liberalization and Higher Education", *University News*, Oct. 17, 1994, pp. 5 & 15.
3. Ghosh, D.K., "Higher Education in the 21st Century meeting the Challenge", *University News*, March 4, 1996, pp. 4-7.
4. Sharma, S.K., "Globalisation of Indian Business Education to be or not to be, That's the Question", *University News*, Vol. 35, No. 17, Apr. 28, 1997, pp. 5-8 and 14.
5. Stewart, Frances, "Globalisation and Education", *DPEP Calling* — A DPEP Newsletter, No. 12, Nov. 1995, pp. 20-25.
6. *The Hindu — National Daily*, Open Page, Various Issues.

28 TQM in Management Education : Restructuring Paradigm

—A.P. KALKUNDRI

MANAGEMENT EDUCATION AND ITS NEED

Meaning

"Management education may be called the specific preparation of an individual for a position of responsibility, for the work of others in an organization. It must also undertake the task of equipping the manager to carry out continuing the changing responsibility for the use of manpower and other resources" by Deborah Jones, Kay Ball & Micheal Shallens.

It can be defined as "Courses for practising or intending managers, the purpose of which is to help the student to carry out management activities".

Need

Management is an important catalyst in the economic development and progress of a country. Therefore, it can be directly stated that the development of a country is virtually dependent on the quality of its resources and management. It can be said an efficient management is key to the growth of the economy of any country.

Developing countries like India, suffer from a critical shortage of competent ad experienced managers, persons who not only meet the necessary professional standards but who are committed to their country's advancement and are prepared to act as agents of economic and social change. This shortage is frequently referred to as a "*Management Gap*". This gap is one of the major hindrances for economic growth, promotion of productive employment and social progress in any developing nation.

ASPECT OF TOTAL QUALITY MANAGEMENT (TQM)

Total quality management is a system which involves everyone in the organization from the chief executive to the most humble everknown to improve the effectiveness and efficiency of organization. It encompasses all departments and all functions in the organization. As a system, the procedures and the techniques of TQM used in achieving objectives of organization were first practised in the quality function, then they spread to other management functions. This practice was known as "*Total Quality Management*".

Total Quality Management is a broad-based philosophy that can be applied to the service sector, manufacturing sector, private sector, public sector, health care, education, etc. In fact it can be applied to every sphere of activity and to every walk of life.

TQM IN MANAGEMENT EDUCATION

Need for Total Quality in Management Education

With the words LPG (Liberalisation, Privatisation and Globalisation) gaining more emphasis and importance, no nation can any longer ignore them, as the consequences of ignorance may be disastrous. National independence now depends more on economic strength through institutional growth rather than Military. Japan which failed to conquer the world by war, has now conquered the world by means of quality management.

It is universal truth that, "Management" is an important catalyst in the economic and social progress of any country. So management education has got a good boost in India. Management education acts as resource base for managers. Would-be managers *i.e.*, students need to be educated, equipped and trained in such a way that they fit into any organization they join (after they leave the institution) in the shortest possible time, with least additional inputs, become worthy citizens, and are in a position to take care of their own well-being and that of their families in the competitive world.

Total Quality Management is a synonym of Company Wide Quality Control (CWQC) or Total Quality Control (TQC) as used in Japan. It is interesting to note that Dr. Kaoni Ishikawa and Prof. Hitoshi Kume, both quality gurus and many others like them, who have contributed to quality education in every field in Japan, were from academic fraternity.

When we apply the concept of Total Quality Management to business schools we get a concept as Total Quality Business School. In India, the role of Management institutions in propagation of the discipline of quality management has still to crystallise.

An important aspect which needs to be considered while applying TQM concept and principles for transformation of business schools to TQBS is the fact that TQM principles have evolved over a period of time, keeping the industry atmosphere in view. While applying TQM from industry to management educational institutions it is not a straightforward and simple process but it will require changes in instructional process, the role of faculty, non-faculty personnel and the evaluation process.

This has sparked off a debate in USA, whether students are more than customers in the classroom, as TQM model of the customer in industry falls short in describing the complex relationship between the student, faculty and the institution. Consider the following comparisons :

(a) Students must be actively engaged in learning process just as employees must be actively engaged in their jobs.

(b) Students must be motivated to perform much as employees must be motivated.

(c) Student are concerned with getting their money's worth, employees are not.

In India too they have started initiating the aspect of total quality in select management schools/institutions. This includes training of staff in the basic tenets of TQM as also the education model, evolving vision and issuing statements, forming quality management teams, involving students, parents and suppliers of knowledge *i.e.*, teaching staff as team members, interaction and benchmarking with other institutes, employees and customers' survey, result-oriented process, etc.

MODELS FOR QUALITY EDUCATION

I. Baldridge Model of Education

In this context it would be worth-while to quote the Baldridge model of education (which could be adopted in Management education too). The essence of Baldridge model is brought out by *Fig. 1*. The Core values of this model are :

→ Learning centered education
→ Leadership
→ Continuous improvement
→ Faculty & Staff participation
→ Fast response
→ Partnership development
→ Design quality & Prevention
→ Management by fact
→ Public responsibility and citizenship.
→ Result orientation.

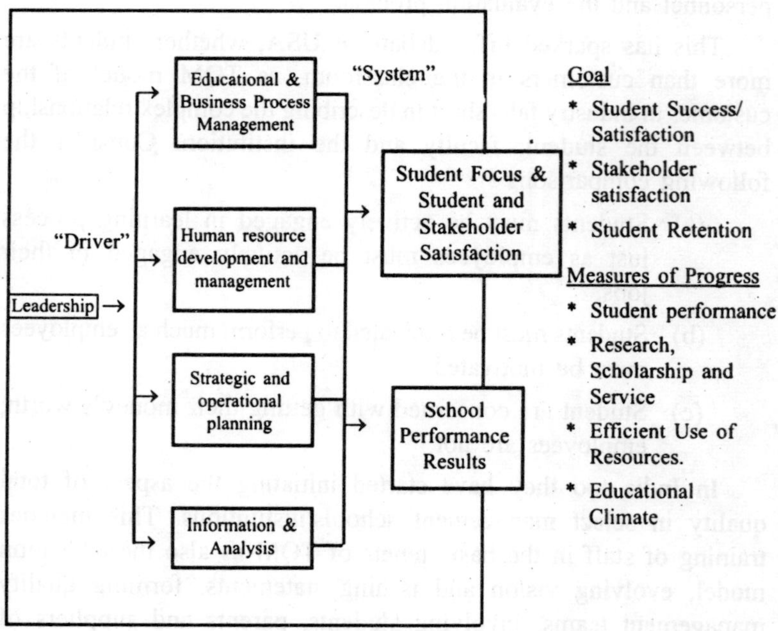

Fig. 1

The *objectives* of the education programme were spelt out as follows :

1. To help improve school performance.
2. To facilitate communications and sharing of best practices information.
3. To foster the development of partnership.
4. To serve as a working tool.

The Baldridge framework *i.e.*, Fig. 1 for education has four basic elements :

(1) *Drivers* : Senior leadership set directions, creates shared values,. goals and systems and guides the pursuit of student and school performance improvement.

(2) *System* : The system comprises the set of well-defined process for improving school performance.

(3) *Measure of Progress* : Measures of progress provide a result-oriented basis for channeling actions to deliver ever-improving student and school performance.

(4) *Goal* : The basic aims of the system are the delivery of ever-improving educational services, leading, to success and satisfaction.

II. European Foundation for Quality Management

European Foundation for Quality Management (EFQM) has adopted the EFQM model for Business excellence to suit education which can be adopted for Management education too.

The customers in the school context are the beneficiaries of the activities of the school namely the students, the parents and eventually industry. The model has already been adopted by several universities in Europe. Some of them are in the self-assessment mode while others are using this model for continuous improvement. Both in USA and Europe many companies have "adopted" School and Colleges and are supporting the TQ movement. The model is represented in *Fig. 2*.

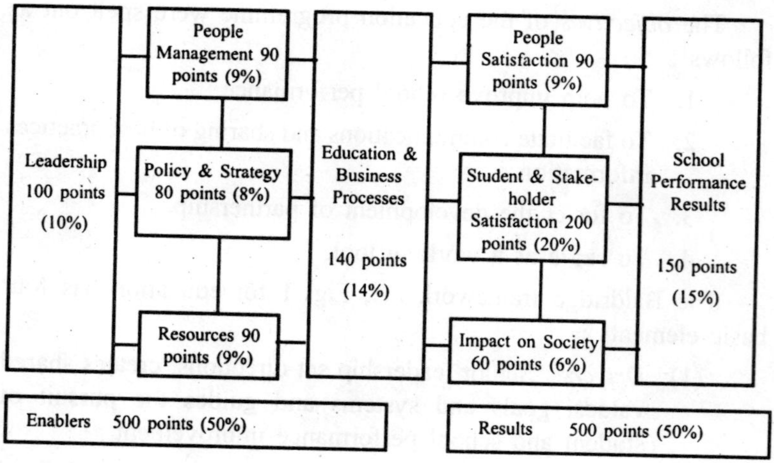

Fig. 2

III. Dr. P.H. Waghodekar's Model

A model proposed by Dr. P.H. Waghodekar for an education system — The main component of an education system primarily is the human resource which can generate, by applying its thinking faculty, other secondary infrastructural type resources like equipments, building, etc.

Through the total quality conscious people (TQP), the working environment can act as a latent motivating force to all concerned for systems quality output than that what it was earlier. The following is the proposed approach to promote this :

→ Consider institute as service industry and

→ Apply TQM base leadership style at all levels of institute functioning.

This model can be easily understood with the help of a figure given below *i.e., Fig. 3*.

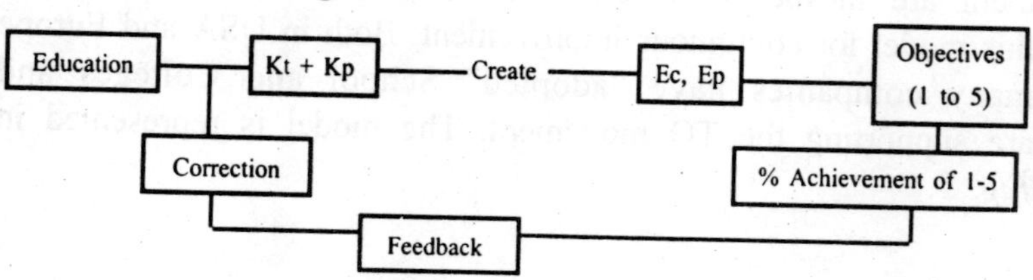

Fig. 3

Where

Kt = Theoretical knowledge (of teachers)

Kp = Practical knowledge (of teachers)

Ec = Conceptual environment

Ep = Physical environment

O1 = Student objectives

O2 = Teachers

O3 = Institute (Managements)

O4 = Industry objectives

O5 = Nation objectives.

Quality can be defined as the totality of features and characteristics of student (*i.e.*, the by-product) / that be on their ability to satisfy the stated or implied need pertaining to themselves and society at large. For example some of the desirable tracts identified for managers are :

* Basic tracts like integrity, punctuality, will to work and aim.
* Ability to plan, control, co-ordinate, organize and take decision.
* Communication skill, both oral and written.
* Physical and mental fitness.
* Knowledge of behavioural sciences.

Obviously, for developing and inculcating such and similar desirable tracts amongst students and staff, each and every institute must have its own defined statement and objectives.

Realisation of individuals both staff and students unrealised potential is, therefore, advocated for achieving institutes objectives, set implementation of quality control within the institute would help to achieve the ultimate objective of *education*, *happiness and prosperity of humankind*.

IV. Quality Circle Model proposed for an Institute

Quality Circles (QC) are small voluntary groups from the same department enabling this group to help handle personal as well as group issues, however these may be.

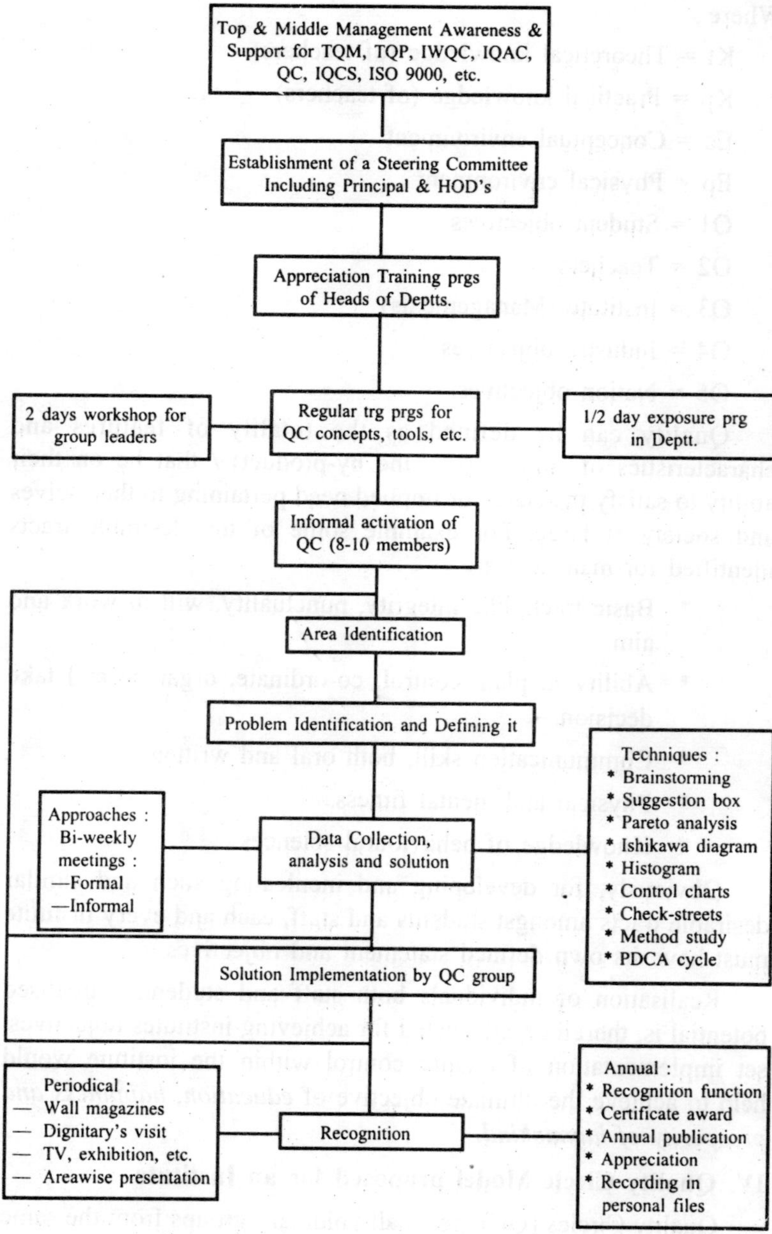
Top & Middle Management Awareness & Support for TQM, TQP, IWQC, IQAC, QC, IQCS, ISO 9000, etc.
Establishment of a Steering Committee Including Principal & HOD's
Appreciation Training prgs of Heads of Deptts.
2 days workshop for group leaders
Regular trg prgs for QC concepts, tools, etc.
1/2 day exposure prg in Deptt.
Informal activation of QC (8-10 members)
Area Identification
Problem Identification and Defining it
Techniques :
* Brainstorming
* Suggestion box
* Pareto analysis
* Ishikawa diagram
* Histogram
* Control charts
* Check-streets
* Method study
* PDCA cycle
Approaches :
Bi-weekly meetings :
—Formal
—Informal
Data Collection, analysis and solution
Solution Implementation by QC group
Periodical :
— Wall magazines
— Dignitary's visit
— TV, exhibition, etc.
— Areawise presentation
Recognition
Annual :
* Recognition function
* Certificate award
* Annual publication
* Appreciation
* Recording in personal files

Fig. 4

The aspect of quality circle can be very well applied to business schools but the support of top management is very much essential and vital for the efficient and effective functioning of quality circles. A steering committee consisting of all the heads of departments need to be established and to be well-trained in all aspects of QC functioning. For each quality circle, a leader is selected by rotation by the members group and facilitators shall be made available for integrating the working of quality circle. With these prerequisite met staff and students can be motivated for voluntary formation of QC at several levels. Ex : Batchwise in a class, departmentwise, interdepartmentwise, inter-institute, etc., involving one or two members of staff and 8 to 10 student members. *Fig. 4* (given on the previous page) gives the holistic view of the exact idea.

CONCLUSION

Today we Indians must become more quality conscious in all fields including education. For this again there must be a hand in hand relation between the industry and the business schools.

As is happening in the west, with support of industry, not only can Total Quality be implemented in our business schools but a long-lasting partnership can be forged between industry and educational institution for mutual benefits.

REFERENCES

1. Venkat, R., Total Quality in Education, *Proceedings of the National Seminar on Total Quality Management & Technical Education* at Tatyasaheb Kore Institute of Engineering and Technology, Warnanagar, Kolhapur, Feb. 27-28, 1997.
2. Dr. Waghodkar, P.H., Total Quality People : The Soul of TQM, *Proceedings of the National Seminar on Total Quality Management & Technical Education at Tatyasaheb* Kore Institute of Engineering and Technology, Warnanagar, Kolhapur, Feb. 27-28, 1997.
3. Konnur, B.A. & Biraydev, B.V., Total Quality Management, A Perspective View, *Proceedings of the National Seminar on Total Quality Management & Technical Education* at Tatyasaheb Kore Institute of Engineering and Technology, Warnanagar, Kolhapur, Feb. 27-28, 1997.
4. Maj. Gen. Gulati, B.R., TQM in Technical Education — An Overview, *Proceedings of the National Seminar on Total Quality Management & Technical Education* at Tatyasaheb Kore Institute of Engineering and Technology, Warnanagar, Kolhapur, Feb. 27-28, 1997.

5. Khan, A.M. & Yadav, K., Management Education in India — Emergency Issues, *University News*, Vol. 35, No. 15, April 14, 1997.

6. Chaudhary, H.C., *Management Education in India — Past, Present & Future*, 1993 ed., Deep & Deep Publications, New Delhi.

29 Emerging Trends in Business Education — A Critical Review

—A.G. PRASAD AND M.R. CHANDAWARKAR

Our Indian tradition is not an ostrich like attitude, refusing to see and absorb the light of learning — around us — from different parts of the world. At the same time, the acid-test of rational discrimination of what is right and what is wrong should be applied; or in other words, the students ought to learn it from the master, how to apply it. In the words of Kalidasa, "Puranamithyeva - Na Saadhu Sarvam....etc." In short, Kalidasa says, "All that is old, is not gold and all that mod, is not bad." He concluded for a healthy and happy system of education, a blending of both the old and the new is a must.[1]

The essence and the role of education in the words of National Policy on Education is : Educations has an acculturating role. It refines sensitivities and perceptions that contribute to national cohesion, a scientific temper and independence of mind and spirit. Education develops manpower for different levels of economy. In sum, education is a unique investment in the present and future.[2] This cardinal principle is the key for the success of any country.

The Business education will be meaningful and realistic if proper linkage is developed between the education and business houses. "Through proper education, the achievement of economic and social development can be facilitated and expedited. Human resource development has a multiplier effect on the utilization of all other resources. That is why the concept of education as an investment in development has been increasingly accepted, and, that is why in 1966, the Report of the Education Commission referred to education as the only instrument of peaceful social change."[3]

The early years of the 21st century are going to be no different from the times we are currently going through. What we mean is that the year 2000 A.D. is not the emergence of an altogether different era, but only a landmark in time at which we must judge the past and plan for the future. The dawn of a new age is going to throw open new challenges and also present us new opportunities. The society of the 21st century will be a society of organizations and corporate citizens. In the years to come, the role of organizations is going to become much more comprehensive and powerful. They will provide an umbrella of services and security for every individual. "If the future society collapses, it will be due to the failure of its organizations, *i.e.*, it will be due to the failure of the people who manage them."[4] Hence for survival, organizations are under increasing pressure to achieve excellence in production of goods and services and at the same time fulfil the socio-economic compulsions of the country.

Changing economic scene is wrought with newer challenges and threats to the practising managers of business and industry. In contrast to the past, Indian economy now is market-oriented as against socialism-directed; result-seeking as against procedure-sticking; and outward looking as against inward looking. As a result, "Management education system enjoys no protected market status and as such is operating in a highly competitive situation."[5] Further it is no longer subsidised and has to be self-supported through a policy of full pricing for its services. Under the prevailing conditions, whether or not Indian Management Education is responsive to these changes is, therefore, a pertinent issue.

OBJECTIVES OF THE STUDY

— To understand the efficacy of commerce education as an effective means of business education.

— To examine the significant role played by management education in the ever-changing business environment.

First let us examine the role of commerce education as an effective tool in business environment.

By 1960 there were 35 universities offering commerce as a special subject and at the school level there were 15 Secondary Education Boards in India dealing with commerce education. With an increase in trade and commerce in the country, the commerce education has also spread rapidly. In India there were about 17900 students in B.Com. courses in 1950. This number increased to about 10 lakhs in 1992.[6]

TABLE 1

Enrolment of Students in Commerce

Year	Enrolment in Commerce	Total Enrolment	Share of Comm. in percentage
1972-73	3,18,888	21,68,107	14.7
1977-78	4,63,957	25,64,972	17.0
1982-83	6,69,813	31,33,093	21.4
1987-88	8,57,971	39,10,828	21.9
1991-92	10,09,832	46,11,107	21.9

Source : U.G.C. Reports.

It is clear from the Table 1 that the enrolment in commerce has increased considerably in the earlier period. However in the later period it has maintained the same level of percentage with total enrolment. Since the Government of India adopted the policy of liberalization and globalisation of business, there has been radical changes in business environment. In this process the business needs are being changed over a period of time. These business concerns need skilled and qualified staff to look after global business activities by making use of modern equipment techniques and means of communication, etc. There has been extensive use of computers and other machines in the fast changing environment.

Though commerce education provides the students with information to enable them to understand the various business occupations and transactions found in the commercial world, it has traditional and conceptual approach. It lacks in practical orientation and fulfilment of job requirements in changing business environment, hence it is unable to solve the industrial and social problems. It is also contended that the present system and courses of commerce education in general do not correlate with the job potential provided by industry, commerce and financial institutions or other occupational courses.

To overcome these limitations first of all the course must be restructured and reprinted to suit the ever-changing demands of the industry. There should be a good number of orientation programmes for teachers to update the information and latest knowledge about changes that are taking place. Of course the Govt. take its agency U.G.C. and also state governments must come forward. The students must be made specialist even at U.G. level if not at P.G. level. Unfortunately, lot many things are taught to the students whether relevant or otherwise and in the process the main curriculum with areas of importance and requirements are pushed to loopline and back seat. Hence, job oriented, task oriented commerce education supported by Computer skills, beside imparting practical training will enable them to get the maximum gain out of this commerce education. Commerce and management being two branches of business education, they should maintain a close contact and act in a cohesive manner rather than conflict and rivalry amongst themselves. Commerce syllabus should be modified on need-based system.

Let us examine Management education as a discipline of business education. Management education in India has grown phenomenally during the last three decades and now it has become an important feature in our economic and cultural life. There is hardly any important organized industry which does not employ professional managers. The number of academic institutions imparting management education and their intakes are progressively increasing. It has grown rapidly to cover a number of sectors, disciplines and functions.

The importance of professional management is now recognised not only in business and industrial sector where the role of manager is self-evident but also in other sectors of development including financial, commercial and social services, health, education and Government administration. Over the years the contents and techniques of management have undergone a tremendous change.[7]

While enterprises today need the professionally educated and trained managers, the questions and doubts about the relevance of the trained professionals for immediate local needs, may progressively become more complex and aggressive. The crucial challenge, though for the management school of tomorrow is how to match the emerging perspective of the global MBA with the urgent managerial agenda of local community.

The emerging scenario of management education in India is as follows :

— "Professional" management education/training is now widely perceived to be useful not only in managing business, but also in managing organizations in a variety of sectors.

— Although initially confined to government sponsored institutions and universities, management education is rapidly getting privatised. As in 1989, less than 15% were sponsored by the central and/or state government, about 60% were university departments, about 20% were affiliated to or recognised by universities, and the balance were private institutions recognised by the Government of India. But this mix may change rapidly in the nineties. Dozens of private sector management institutions have come into being. Hundreds more are in the offing.

— There is a strong trend towards increasing the company management training programmes. Some of the larger business houses and public enterprises, as the Tatas, Hindustan Lever, State Bank of India and Bharat Heavy Electricals Limited have set up substantial in-house management colleges/academies for managerial training purposes.

— Distance education in management is beginning to take root. At least two major institutions — the Indira Gandhi National Open University and the All India Management Association — offer distance education programmes.

A major weakness of Indian Management education is the lack of quality depth. There is a wide divide between the top schools and the rest. Even in the top ten the quality divide is wide. For instance, in a recent poll of campus recruiters the top school got a rating of 9.71; the tenth a rating of 5.14. The quality divide is likely to widen in the next few years as scores perhaps hundreds of new poorly staffed and facilities poor institutions enter this sector. Accreditation process is weak in the sense of ensuring minimum facilities and standards and the entry is currently more or less free.

A second major weakness of Indian management education appears to be the wide gap between what is needed on the job and what is taught in the management schools. For example, in a recent study of the responses of nearly 170 managers, students and faculty members of management institutions, the major deficiencies appeared to be in the area of leadership, team spirit, managerial personality (broad-mindedness, independence, self-control, enthusiasm, etc.), personal effectiveness/job knowledge and personal gratification (excitement, prosperity and freedom etc.).[8]

The failure in imparting the needed managerial competencies, is in part due to inadequacies in pedagogy. It is common experience that MBAs particularly from well-known institutions are not interested in teaching and in research. They find industrial jobs more lucrative and satisfactory. A career in teaching does not meet their expectations.

CONCLUSION AND SUGGESTIONS

Excellence in management is always in great demand although it is in short supply. There are no magic powers at work that make managers excellent. The good thing in excellence is that the right thing that brings success involves the basics and learnable. No one born with it. People can become exceptional in one or more key areas of their lives, regardless of their upbringing, education or previous level of accomplishment. This cannot be taken as a golden rule. Perhaps, everyone is looking for instant managers. Let us examine the management education in India and the steps to be taken for the better performance of the same.

The following are the suggestions offered by the Association of Indian Management Schools (AIMS) (in 1988) at the National Conference of the Heads of Management Institutions that was held at IIM, Bangalore during 28-30 April, 1988. Some of the major objectives of AIMS identified are :

(a) To provide a dynamic network of institutions engaged in Management Education, Training and Research is must.

(b) To contribute to the development of Management Education, in all its aspects, both qualitatively and quantitatively and to help maintain and improve standards of teaching, research and examinations.

(c) To help in the accreditation process of management educational institutions by suggesting specified criteria and evaluation standards of institutions and their programmes.

(d) To take steps for development of Management literature, case studies, teaching materials, books, etc., relevant to the Indian context.

(e) To actively promote linkages between management education institutions and industry, business and the Government.

(f) To strengthen institutional capabilities through faculty development, faculty exchanges, and enable better use of infrastructural facilities.

In the year 1988-89 a study was conducted to redefine the role of management education and business schools in India wherein the heads of leading management schools were interviewed with the help of questionnaire. The result of the study brought following aims and roles of business schools to the fore :

(a) It should identify the needs of industry and shape the education to meet such needs.

(b) It should develop the attitudes, concepts, skills, and tools to suit the prevailing business environment in our country.

(c) It should sharpen the students' analytical and decision-making skills and provide them conceptual inputs coupled with real life Indian case studies. As such, it should relate to the education norms of Indian conditions; and

(d) It would prepare students to contribute to National Economy through efficient management.

(i) To lead or innovate in management education or in some part of management education.

(ii) To give a rigorous training or education in a discipline on group of subjects.

(iii) To provide practical training aimed directly at making the student a more effective manager.

(iv) To solve the problems of the organizations employing the students.

(v) To inform managers of new development and new techniques in management.

Let us now examine what are the practical problems encountered by these institutions which impart management education.

1. Management environment is ever changing. Multinationals are more and more powerful. Globalisation and liberalisation has further strengthened the need to update and adapt the management education to match the reality of national and international requirements. Therefore, the course should be made more meaningful and need-based.
2. There is a mushrooming growth of business schools. Since the Government either being a silent spectator or deliberately interested in promoting new institution a good number of private colleges started offering MBA programme without adequate infrastructure. In 1992 there were as many as 100 institutions, in 1997 there were 550, besides 150 university departments. The total number of business schools — both AICTE approved and others — as on today is estimated to be around 1,000.[9]
3. Regulatory body (AICTE) should be regulated. The nodal agency created by Government to monitor and regulate these institutions is not effective in its functions. Therefore, unless and until this body is made more powerful there is always a conflict between the regulatory body and universities and colleges which are undertaking these MBA programmes.

4. There is no uniform and standardised curriculum. Different universities and institutes follow different curriculum. Hence, there should be an apex body which should take a lead in framing the syllabus taking into consideration, the realistic approach by making the end users also as party to this. Academicians, industrialists, workers' unions, and all other parties who are directly affected by this education should be included in this task.
5. Selection process of students should be on altogether different lines and procedures. These common entrance tests and other interview techniques adopted by different Universities (due to more aspirants and less seats there may not be any other way out) may not be in a position to identify and select the suitable candidates. In the Indian context, this may be the only suitable alternative (Entrance test system).
6. The quality of teachers should be evaluated regularly and adequate provisions must be made to continuously update their skills by sending them to some orientation courses and also by allowing them to take practical training in industries. In addition to this there should be exchange programmes from one university/institution to another and also some of these teachers must be sent to world's best management institutions. They in turn must educate the other teachers through extension lectures and other means.
7. There should be at least one year practical training *i.e.*, management students are supposed to work with an organization during their studies, so that they will be exposed to the realities of the corporate world.
8. Since the state is spending lot of money, the purpose of Governments spending is lost if the end products are not useful for the society's development. Just as the UPSC conducts tests for Central Services like IAS, IPS etc., it could have an Indian Management Service (IMS) on par with IAS and IPS. Once such status in given most of the

management graduates will opt for IMS who would manage various government, quasi-government organizations, besides state and Central Public Sector Undertakings.[10]

9. In this fast changing world, computers have become part and parcel of corporate world; it would be improper to undermine the role of computers in education. Business education with the aid of computers can see the Indian students face global challenges making them better equipped. Hence, it should be given top priority in the curriculum.

Therefore, it is concluded, in the light of new experience of market economy, India needs well-equipped manpower to face the challenges of management of industries and government organizations and public sector undertakings. Thus, it is suggested that the educationists face these challenges and develop create a better industry-University linkage. The objective should be to integrate academic knowledge and social values to foster individual intellectual excellence, participative capability and enlightened corporate citizenship. The task ahead is challenging. Always remember that "excellence requires an unwavering commitment to be the best".

REFERENCES

1. Shanker Dayal Sharma, 'Indian Tradition in Education', *University News* Published by the Association of Indian Universities, New Delhi, Vol. XXV, No. 49, Dec. 7, 1987.
2. *National Policy on Education*, 'The Essence and Rôle of Education', Professional competency in Higher Education, Centre for Professional Dev. in Higher Education, University of Delhi, 1995, p. 3.
3. Ministry of Education, Govt. of India, New Delhi, 1985.
4. Ratan Reddy, B., 'Educating Future Corporate Citizens', *Indian Economic Panorama*, Vol. 7, No. 3, Oct.-Dec. 1997, p. 8.
5. M.S.G.K. Murthy, "A case for responsive management education in India", *Indian Economic Panorama*, Vol. 7, No. 4, Jan.-Mar. 1998, p. 14.
6. Shitole, G.Y., 'Re-Engineering of Commerce Educational in India in changing Business Environment', *The Indian Journal of Commerce*, Vol. XLIX, No. 189, Dec. 1996, pp. 137, 138.

7. Adarsh Baijal & Suneetha Singh, 'Globalisation of Management Education in India', *The Indian Journal of Commerce*, Vol. XLIX, No. 189, Dec. 1996, p. 120.

8. Hussain Ashraf, 'Emerging Trends of Management Education in India', *The Indian Journal of Commerce*, Vol. XLIX, No. 189, Dec. 1996, pp. 130-32.

9. M.S.G.K. Murthy, "A case for Responsive Management Education in India", *Indian Economic Panorama*, Vol. 7, No. 4, Jan.-Mar. 1998, p. 14.

10. Shekhar, V., 'A case for introducing Indian Management Service', *The A.P. Times (Daily)*, Hyderabad, Jan. 3, 1998, p. 5.

30 Business Education in India — Backward and Forward Linkages

—Y. VRUSHABHENDRAPPA

INTRODUCTION

The Indians were the pioneer in the export business during the earlier years and were well-known to all those who have studied history of ancient India. Indians had the knowledge in the Business with regards to textiles, ship-building, gold ornaments and spices. The Indians were the pioneers in ship-building in the ancient days. This factor alone is a prime indicator that Indians were in Business much earlier than anybody else; so through business the Indians came in contact with the Europeans both through land and sea routes. This business linkage opened the doors of Indian Market to Westerners who came to India for business and finally started ruling us. In earlier days the quality was given, utmost importance in all walks of life which can be seen through products of earlier era. Some monuments and precious articles preserved in Museums and in Palaces speak about the quality products of our country. After the entry of Westerns into business in the Indian market, the Indian business had collapsed and finally taken away the freedom of our country. With this background the new business education concepts has to be evolved.

FORWARD LINKAGES IN BUSINESS EDUCATION

Now, we are living in an era of supersonic age. Decisions have to be taken instantaneously so as to be competitive in this liberalised economy. Hence, there is an urgent need to formulate the business education on the following lines namely :

1. Market Liberalization and Policy Issues.

2. Legal Framework, Foreign Investment and Intellectual Property Rights.
3. Asian Financial Markets and their Linkages with Global Markets.
4. Multinational Corporations : Subsidiaries, Joint Ventures, and Alliances.
5. Technology Parks, Software Industry and Value-Added Exports.
6. Managing Diversity : Issues in Negotiation, Communication and Management Styles.
7. Taxation, Accounting Standards and Disclosure.
8. Marketing in a Multicultural and Multilingual Environment.
9. International Sourcing, Logistics and Physical Distribution.
10. Infrastructure, Technology, and Environmental Issues.
11. Ethical Issues in Business.
12. Other Related Topics.

1. Market Liberalization and Policy Issues

Hitherto Indian Business had the protected market and this was sellers' market with very little choice in the market. Accordingly a concept of business education was taught with that background. So no emphasis was given on how the liberalization will have a bearing on business education at present. To quote an example, in Automobile Industry only three names were heard in Indian Market earlier, *viz.* Ambassador, Premier Padmini Standard and Premier Padmini.

Today we have quite a big list of automobiles which are on the road and still many are on the anvils to be introduced in India. What strategies are adopted for sales in each one of these industries are not explained in business education with Indian business context. Under these circumstances there is a need to revise business education in India.

2. Legal Framework, Foreign Investment and Intellectual Property Rights

Earlier who were experts in business education in India had no knowledge about legal aspects which have to be tackled in business world of India today. Earlier business was purely on ethics. Now, the ethics has gone to the background. The legal battles are common in business, to quote an example the controversy between Maruti and Suzuki. The fight between Pepsi and Coca-Cola is still going on. Proctor and Gamble versus Hindustan Lever is known to all of us. These are few examples where Managers of those companies should have a strong legal background. Hence the curriculum must be restructured to teach this aspect in M.B.A. Programme.

There are certain procedures to be followed while going for agreements on the investments by Foreign Companies as collaborators. These aspects have not been dealt in our business education. Controversy of the 'ENRON' project, Kogentrics projects are examples how delicate the issues are. The intellectual property right is another issue which is to be dealt in the business education. The innovative ideas have to be patented and the students of future business education need to know the patenting procedures and about intellectual property rights.

3. Asian Financial Markets and Their Linkages with Global Markets

Today the finance can be raised within no time through public and banks. Many International banks are providing finance. We have not exposed our students how these International financing systems work. This needs to be understood by our students. Also fluctuation in the conversion rates will have bearing on our business. The rise in the dollar rupee conversion rate resulted in an additional burden to Indian economy to a tune of 25 thousand crores this year alone. Reduction in oil prices in the International market resulted in savings of 8 thousand crores, so this type of concept has to be taught to the students who pursue business education in future. The above example indicates how a profit and loss of any company will be decided not on the sales but, on the fluctuations in the conversion value. In this process a country's business can flourish or perish. The students ought to know this aspects very effectively.

4. Multinational Corporations : Subsidiaries, Joint Ventures, and Alliances

Today Bangalore is called silicon valley of India. Bangalore is one of the centres of Software Development in the world. But, unfortunately few Indian firms are worth naming in a Computer Software marketing. They are all working as joint venture companies with Multinational Corporations of other countries. Here the Indian companies are put to heavy loss due to lack of bargaining power with the Multinational Companies. Many a times it is observed that the Indian Companies are negotiating on rupee basis whereas the Multinational Companies are selling the product on dollar basis. This aspect of pricing in dollars, local currency, etc., need to be understood by the Indian business community. Hence it is necessary to teach this type of relevant information in Indian business schools.

The controversy that arised in the agreement between 'ENRON' company, Government of Maharashtra and Government of India has thrown a new light on the role of Multinational corporations in the Indian industrial scenario.

5. Technology Parks, Software Industry and Value-Added Exports

Earlier Switzerland was the leading country in the export of Wrist Watches, Germans were leaders in Camera. Today these markets are taken away by the Japanese. The reason is very clear, it is purely due to value-added export. Even though Japan has limited natural resources, they are the leaders in the world of exports. This is due to only adding value to the products. This technique was not taught in our business education. We are seeing century old Silk Sarees business remaining same even today. There is no change in the value and style in the products. It leads to losing the business in silk.

6. Total Quality Management and International Competitiveness

Indians were once known as the best exporters of Muslin Cloth which could be folded and packed even in match boxes. Such was the quality level earlier in India. Earlier polishing of Diamonds, export of Gold ornaments were almost exclusively done by the Indians mainly due to superior quality. Later due to greediness we sacrificed the quality, consequently lost the business. All of us are using Calculators which are made in Japan having no maintenance problems at all. This shows the quality concept of Japan. In order to be competitive in the international market we must have the goal to achieve excellence in quality. Quality alone can open up the doors of the export market. This aspect has to be taught in the curriculum in business education.

7. Taxation, Accounting Standards and Disclosure

In India we have got Central Taxes and State Taxes. The taxes differ in different states. The tax structure of any State shifts the business from one state to another state within no time. I know many Karnataka people prefer to buy cars from Goa, because of the reduction of taxes on cars in Goa. Likewise in many other products the differential taxation has significantly shifted the business from one state to another. To avoid taxes, earlier dual system of accounting was followed. The business world in India are trying to show loss on papers on the contrary, the real picture is different. The concealed taxes resulted in accumulated black money which had a direct bearing on the Indian economy. The people who have black money hoard the products and create artificial scarcity. A rational taxation can only help the growth of business. Earlier manual accounting procedures were followed. Today the Computers have entered the business arena which need to be taught in business education. The transaction used to take place in cash earlier. Today transaction is taking place through cheques. Shortly it may be through internet. Hence the dynamic accounting procedure need to be taught to the students of business education of tomorrow.

8. Ethical Issues in Business

There is a competition among the business communities both in India as well as in the global business. Ethics have gone to the backdrop. Earlier any promise either oral or written was fulfilled by the promisers. Today people change their business name plates to deceive the general public. Therefore, there is an urgent need to maintain ethics in business so as to have a safer and happier society. Murders among the business giants have become common due to jealousy among the businessman.

CONCLUDING REMARKS

We have to build a strong foundation for the future business education in India based on the International business scenario. A new concept of business education is to be framed through curriculum with an intention of bringing this country to the forefront in international business. More emphasis should be given to the quality, ethics and legal aspects in our business education with a due weightage on taxation, accounting and economics. Emphasis on the above factors should be given in the 21st century business education.

31 New Dimensions of Business Education in India

—E.B. BRAHMANKAR

GLOBAL ECONOMY

With the globalisation of market and open economy around, the concept of relevance of commerce education has changed. Accordingly, it is imperative that the present course content and the mode of education is to be changed as per needs and requirements of the changing social and economic scenario. In a country like ours the policy towards higher education is generally a product of power and persuasiveness of individual bureaucrats and politicians rather than manpower requirements and relevance. The present system has not shown substantial qualitative improvement over a period of time and continues as such without any accountability. It has not been able to generate employment opportunities. However, higher education has a significant role in the context of social change.

It has been felt for a very long time by the Government planners and educationists that the educational system in our country should be oriented towards need-based employment. Mere formal education may result into more and more job seekers. That is why the educational system must coincide with the economic needs of the country. Education and vocational training should be given priority in the human resource development programme. It is necessary to evolve a mechanism which will integrate service training programme with education. While the recognized objective of education is overall development, it would also include a component of vocational training that is relevant locally for need-based skills. One of the ideas is to involve industry in the educational process keeping in view the needs that would arise in the long-term.

This paper deals with the present scenario and the prospects of the problem relating to New Dimensions of Commerce Education.

NEED FOR VOCATIONALISATION

Vocationalisation is neither new nor so different. Relevance and applicability it offers a new dimension. It tries to explore opportunities for employment in the organized sector and self-employment as an individual initiative.

Vocational education is essential for providing manpower for economic growth of the country. It provides the link between the production function, employment and educational process.

The only way to correct the situation is to vocationalise higher secondary education which will help to divert large number of students in the age group of 14 to 18 and prepare them for useful careers in industry, business, government and even for self-employment. Majority of students have accepted the idea of vocationalisation. Karnataka, West Bengal, Delhi, Gujarat, Maharashtra and Tamil Nadu are trying to experiment in their own ways.

Tamil Nadu did not restrict on numbers for vocational training at +2 stage. After vocational training at +2 stage, most parents want their children to go in for general education. In Karnataka, the scheme was related to the actual needs of the industry. The number thus trained was very less. The social attitude to vocational training is being identified with manual training. It would have to undergo a change through a process of education.

NEW EDUCATION POLICY

If the education policy adopted by the Parliament in 1968 had been implemented, 50% of the students at 10+2 level of secondary education should have developed employment-oriented vocational skills. By the year 1982-83 students intake in vocational courses at +2 stage had reached just 60,000 per annum (Challenge of education 2.5).

Vocationalisation in the higher secondary stage was a major plan of the education policy of 1968. 50% of the students at +2 stage were to go into the education stream. The actual figure is too insignificant to deserve mention. This is largely because neither the physical facilities nor a detailed plan of action complete with details of employment opportunities, nature of investigation required appropriate course curriculum and teachers trained for vocational training are available at present. In addition, social values when designate even skilled manual work also stand in the way of vocationalisation (Challenge of education 3.11).

UGC PLAN OF VOCATIONAL EDUCATION

The expert committee appointed by the University Grants Commission has recently suggested 35 vocational courses to be introduced at the Undergraduate Level in 100 selected colleges and universities of the country from the academic year 1994-95 (*Indian Express*, 4th October, 1993).

Thirty-five vocational courses in four areas of discipline (i) science (14), (ii) engineering and technology (9), (iii) arts, humanities and social science (4), (iv) commerce, economics and management (12) have been worked out. The subjects proposed range from archaeology and museology to tax procedure and practices, computer maintenance, seed technology, food science and quality control, rural technology to maintenance of automobiles, refrigerators and airconditioners. For each of these courses, experts have worked out detailed syllabi and indicated structural needs as well as modes of implementation.

However, the major problem of UGC will be providing the funds for these courses. The expert group has said Rs. 111 crore would be needed in the remaining four years of the Eighth plan for providing infrastructure for the courses as well as upgrading the skills of the teachers to be involved in the programme.

NEW DIMENSIONS

It is collegiate education which is always put to test in the context of emerging challenges of the society. The emphasis on Cognative skills, applied field situations, social exploitation, and environment is important. Higher education has an important role in the context of social change. The courses can be modified to suit the requirements of the area. Modifications are required to enrich the course content. It is necessary that the Universities should be activated sensitized and made responsible for the rightful implementation of the vocational scheme. The UGC has extended the scheme to 381 colleges and 26 Universities within first two years of its introduction *i.e.*, 1994-95 and 1995-96. Employment is a socio-economic imperative. It is related to acquiring various skills necessary for business and industry. It means entrepreneurial instinctive and competence in an area of competition. Industry is for production of consumable and non-consumable goods. In the course of production process, it offers employment opportunities. All activities are oriented towards social gains. Education is the most relevant input which contributes to the development of human resource. It promotes employment, social gains and helps to improve quality and standard of life. Industrial linkages are the pre-requisites of the vocational scheme. However, in a competitive economy industry will absorb only such products as contribute to its efficiency and productivity. So the courses also require to be suitably designed and redesigned to meet needs and requirements of Industry. For this participation of teachers, field experts and representatives of industry is needed. Agriculture is the main thrust of our country. Agro-services, water management, horticulture, dry-farming, forest and wildlife management, rural handicrafts are to be considered in this context.

Short duration courses have also been designed by the University of Pune. The Universities are also trying to provide such vocational courses at undergraduate and postgraduate level. Accordingly, Pune University has started thirteen courses of one year duration under the Faculty of Commerce and Management after XII standard and after graduation to meet the needs of business and industry.

The present college curriculum be designed in such way as to meet the challenges of the present society. It should be able to generate employment and it is to be seen that product becomes self-employable. The students must be able to earn their bread on the strength of their education. As such education needs to be useful and meaningful.

While designing the new courses following points need serious consideration :

(1) Social Needs.

(2) Infrastructural and Environmental Needs.

(3) Needs of Nearby Business and Industry.

(4) Need for meaningful education considering economic development of the country.

(5) Skills required for existing business units and industry.

(6) Need for involvement of students in practical application of knowledge.

(7) Need for exposure to students :

(i) World of work

(ii) interaction with business and industry, and

(iii) dealing with case studies/problems.

(8) New Education Policy.

(9) Guidelines issued by University Grants Commission.

32 The Role of Academicians and Practising Managers in Today's Business Education

—SANDEEP SHANDILYA

1. INTRODUCTION

The age of management thinking and learning coincides with that of mankind. It is perhaps, as old as the human civilization. In fact, management techniques and efforts of ancient men, after a journey of many centuries and numerous transformations and changes have translated into present form of management techniques. Management is hidden in almost every activity of the universe. It ranges from the revolution of electrons around the nucleus of an atom to the revolution of planets around the Sun. In modern times, management techniques have found their wide applications in Business Education. This article is an effort to understand the basic pattern of Business Education and highlight the role of academicians and practising managers in its growth and development.

2. BUSINESS EDUCATION : ITS NEED

In the words of 'Peter Drucker' : "An institution that cannot produce its own managers will die. Hence the ability of an institution to produce managers is more important than its ability to produce goods efficiently and cheaply."[1]

In an era of global competition and growing industrialization world over, the need for Business Education is self-explanatory. The wave of liberalization has further catalysed the need for effective and efficient Business Education. New technological developments in almost all fields of knowledge needs to be successfully managed and handled because its improper management can reverse the direction of developments.

3. BUSINESS EDUCATION : ITS DEVELOPMENT IN INDIA AND PRESENT SCENARIO

The first management school to offer Business Management Education in India was the 'Indian Institute of Social Welfare and Business Management' in 1954. There were only six institutions imparting management education in the beginning of the 60's. Now we have approximately 500 Institutions which impart management education in India.[2]

Following table shows the growth of number of management schools in India :

TABLE 1

Year	No. of Schools	No. of Seats
1962	06	200
1982	58	NA
1992	100	4,000
1995	500*	20,000

* Approximately.

Source : Text of IDL, Chemical Endowment lecture delivered by Dr. D.P. Sinha at Osmania University, Hyderabad on 22-11-95.

4. BUSINESS EDUCATION : ITS GENERAL PATTERN

It would be an appropriate and logical sequence to discuss the role of academicians and practising managers in today's Business Education in the light of its general pattern.

A Master of Business Administration (M.B.A.) programme of two years duration consists of four semesters. Each semester consists of 5-6 courses on Business Management and other areas related to Business Education. Exams are generally conducted after each semester. After second semester students go for summer training of approximately two months in an industrial or service organization. After completion of summer training students submit training report. In final semester students submit Dissertation on the area of their interest.

5. ROLE OF BUSINESS MANAGEMENT TEACHERS : ACADEMICIANS *v/s* PRACTISING MANAGERS

The dimensions of today's Business Education are so vast and diversified that it is not easy to clearly distinguish the roles of academicians and practising managers. A clear understanding of their roles is an utmost requirement of today's Business Education; otherwise Business Education will turn out to be a confusing glamourous puzzle for its aspirants. A deep insight into the underlying patterns of today's Business Education can serve the purpose of effectively allocating the roles between the two vital components of Business Education *i.e.*, academicians and practising managers.

A well-balanced M.B.A. programme must be structured in such a manner that student's understanding of business management flows smoothly from understanding of basic concepts to applications and specialised areas/issues of business. A student's learning of various aspects of modern business must pass through the following sequence or stages :

Ist Stage : Learning of basic concepts of business.

IInd Stage : Broad learning of the applications and theory of business.

IIIrd Stage : Learning of operational and technical aspects of business.

IVth Stage : Learning of specialization offered.

To make the discussion more simpler and interesting let us consider the following examples :

TABLE 2

Stages	Ist stage	IInd stage	IIIrd stage	IVth stage
Subjects (Example No. 1)	Financial & Management Accounting	Financial Management	Investment Analysis	International Finance, Bank Funds, Insurance, etc.
Subjects (Example No. 2)	Quantitative Techniques	Research Methodology	Production Mgt. & Operations Research	Production Planning Marketing Research, etc.

In the light of above two examples, let us discuss the subject matter of this article for various stages :

1. Ist Stage : Learning of Basic Concepts of Business

Generally, students pursuing M.B.A. come from various graduation streams. For most of them, 'Management' as a subject happens to be new. So to make students understand and grasp basics of business is the core issue of this stage. At this stage the role of academicians is extremely important. This basic understanding of concepts will lie in the roots of student's further learning of complex business concepts. For example, 'Financial & Management Accounting' subject, which is new for most of the graduates starting their M.B.A. requires its clear cut conceptual understanding, otherwise students would find it difficult to understand 'Financial Management' later on. At this stage little assistance from practising managers might be taken to develop interest among students towards learning of business concepts. We can consider another example of 'Quantitative Techniques' subject, whose conceptual understanding at this stage is a must because it is going to form the basis of learning of core and technical business subjects like 'Research Methodology', 'Operations & Production Management', 'Production Planning' and 'Marketing Research', etc.

2. IInd Stage : Broad Learning of the Applications and Theory of the Business

After students have gone through the understanding of basic concepts, they are in a position to be taught applications and theory of the business. At this stage, the role of practising managers in 'Business Education' becomes comparatively more intensified than that in first stage. A suitable blending of academicians and practising managers in Business Education learning at this stage will make it more purpose serving. At this stage students learn the applications and theory of business from a broader prospective. For example, 'Financial Management' which involves the solution of three major decisions of business, *i.e.*, Financing, Investing and Dividend can be taught at this stage. A peculiar feature of this stage of Business Education must be a well-diversified practical experience of the practising manager, playing the role of part-time business teacher. For example, a manager delivering lectures on practical applications of 'Financial Management' to M.B.As. must have vast and diversified experience and exposure in the fields of Financing, Investing and Dividend. Moreover, these lectures must be well-supplemented by those of academicians to explain the theoretical aspects (of Financing, Investing and Dividend, for example).

3. IIIrd Stage : Learning of Operational & Technical Aspects of Business

At this stage, students are in a position to decide and sort out the areas of their interest. Moreover, their summer training experiences can guide them to take decisions regarding their interests in major areas of today's business, *i.e.* Production, Marketing, Finance and Personnel. Once they have decided about a particular area, they must be taught about the operational and technical aspects of that area/issue of the business. For example, 'Investment Analysis' is an area in 'Finance' stream which can be taught at this stage. Similarly, 'Operations & Production Management' can be taught after students have already been taught 'Quantitative Techniques' and 'Research Methodology' at first two stages respectively. An interesting fact about this stage is that we move from general to particular. For example 'Financial Management' (Stage 2) describes general Finance Functions (Financing, Investing and Dividend), which in 'Investment Analysis' (Stage 3) becomes a particular issue (Investment). At this stage persons with practical experience can significantly contribute to Business Education. Consider the example of a practising 'Investment Analyst', who can effectively supplement the lectures of an academician on the same issue. Practising managers delivering part-time lectures to M.B.A. students at this stage must have intensive practical experience in a particular field of business.

4. IVth Stage : Learning of the Specialization Offered

At final stage of 'Business Education', the emphasis is more on the specialization offered by the students. Generally students offer specialization in the areas which they are willing to adopt as their career option as a future practising manager. For example he/she may opt for 'International Finance' or 'Marketing Research & Information Systems', etc. At this stage, it is essential that students must be told about the practical aspects of the specialization, they have offered. This requirement can effectively be fulfilled by proper participation of persons with vast experience in these specialised areas of business. In business teachings, however, researchers and academicians must be called to discuss new developments in these specialised areas of business.

We can conclude our discussion in the following two tables :

TABLE 3

Stage*	I	II	III	IV
Academicians' Role	More	Comparatively less than that in Ist Stage	Approximately same as that of Practising Manager	Less
Practising Managers' Role	Less	Comparatively more than that in Ist Stage	Approximately same as that of Academicians	More

*These are general quantitative estimates and they may differ from situation to situation and person to person.

TABLE 4

Stage	I	II	III	IV
Nature of practical experience desired in Practising Manager	General & Conceptual	Vast & Diversified	Intensive & particular	Intensive & specialised

6. CONCLUSION AND SUGGESTIONS

India is facing scarcity of good quality business and management teachers. The reasons for this perhaps are as follows :

— Only three to four years back, the mushrooming of management institutes started in all parts of India.

— Within such a short duration, it was not possible to produce good quality business and management teachers.

— Traditional teachers of disciplines like Commerce, Economics, etc. find it difficult to teach business and management subjects.

— Teaching in India is considered a poor career option, so there are very bleak chances of an M.B.A. opting for business and management teachings as a career goal.

Following data also supports the above view :

The following graph indicates the rapid growth in the number of students participating in Management Aptitude Test (MAT). The number has rapidly grown from poor 550 in 1990 to 70,000 in 1996.[3]

The actual figure of students aspiring for M.B.A. would rise significantly if we consider the fact that various reputed management institutes of the country conduct their own entrance tests.

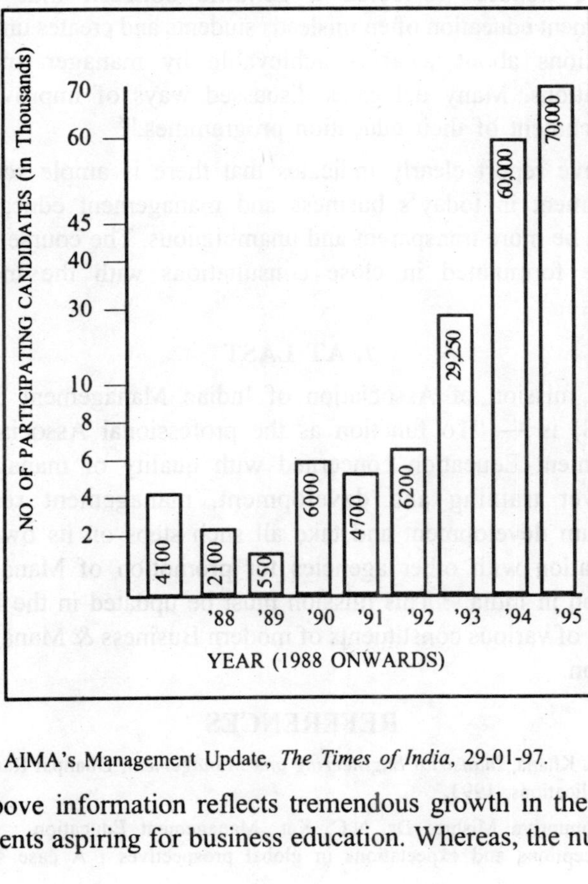

Source : AIMA's Management Update, *The Times of India*, 29-01-97.

Above information reflects tremendous growth in the number of students aspiring for business education. Whereas, the number of

Ph.Ds. in management during last twenty years has only been 1,000 *i.e.*, around 50 per year.[4] This is not at all a pleasant number by any standards. More M.B.A.s as well as practising managers must be encouraged towards research and higher studies in business and management.

Let us consider another example : A number of dissenting academicians met in London to discuss the various management themes fashionable today. Here are some excerpts from the report : "Several delegates admitted to putting dubious things in their text-books, ironically to reduce criticism and help get the book adopted by business schools."

"The debates reflected a genuine concern that current management education often misleads students and creates unrealistic expectations about what is achievable by manager and their organizations. Many delegates discussed ways of improving the critical content of their education programmes."[5]

Above report clearly indicates that there is ample scope for improvement in today's business and management education. It needs to be more transparent and unambiguous. The course content must be formulated in close consultations with the industrial practices.

7. AT LAST

The mission of Association of Indian Management Schools (AIMAS) is — "To function as the professional Association of Management Education concerned with quality of management, manpower training and development, management research, curriculum development and take all such steps on its own or in collaboration with other agencies for promotion of Management Education in India."[6] This mission must be updated in the light of the roles of various constituents of modern Business & Management Education.

REFERENCES

1. O.P. Khana, *Industrial Engineering and Management*, Dhanpat Rai & Sons Publications, 1993.
2. Bishnupriya Mishra; Dr. N.C. Kar, Management Education : Students perceptions and expectations in global prospectives : A case study on

Orissa; *The Indian Journal of Commerce*, Vol. XIX, No. 189, Part IV, December 1996, pp. 156-57.

3. AIMA's Management Update; *The Times of India*, New Delhi, 29 January, 1997.
4. Same as '2'.
5. Steven Henderson, Across the Table II; *The Economic Times*, New Delhi, 21 November, 1995.
6. *Handbook of Management Education*, New Delhi; Association of Indian Universities, 1989.

33 Challenges Before Commerce Education in India

—G.Y. SHITOLE

INTRODUCTION

Business environment in India is passing through the process of globalisation and it has been showing increasing economic integration as well as growing inter-dependence between the countries in the world economy. Business Education has more relevance with changing business environment and commerce is one part of it, which means the knowledge about various business activities like industry, trade, transport, banking, insurance etc. It mainly relates with educating and training the operations of all these business activities.

HISTORY OF COMMERCE EDUCATION IN INDIA

Commerce education was emerged in India in 1886 when the first Commercial School was established in Madras by the Trustees of Pachiappa's Charities. In 1895, the Government of India started the School of Commerce in Calicut and thereafter Presidency College, Culcutta started commerce classes in 1903. The commerce education at University level in India made its beginning in 1913 when Syndenham College of Commerçe and Economics was established by the Government in Mumbai. In this way, the commerce education proliferated in India at the School, College and University levels.

There has been a rapid growth of University Education in India since independence. There were hardly 18 Universities in our country in 1947. Today, this number has gone up to 230 including about 40 deemed Universities. Total enrolment is more than

5 million, of which more than 1 million *i.e.*, about 20 per cent belong to the Commerce Faculty alone. Therefore, Commerce Faculty has become a major faculty in our country. The increasing demand for commerce education was due to the following reasons :

(a) Rapid industrialization all over the country.

(b) Rapid expansion of Banking and Insurance Industries.

(c) Phenomenal growth of public sector.

(d) Growth of demand for scientific approach to management through the absorption of qualified and trained people.

(e) A shift in the attitude of the businessmen.

PRESENT SCENARIO OF COMMERCE EDUCATION IN INDIA

Though the number of students joining commerce faculty has raised substantially after 1970, the situation after 1991 (*i.e.*, in a liberalized economy) has been changed. The number of students enrolled in commerce faculty is not increasing in the pace with other faculties.

It is clear from Table 1 that the enrolment in commerce has been increased considerably in the earlier period. However in the later period, it has shown decrease in percentage with total enrolment. Hence, this study has been undertaken with the following objectives :

(1) To study the adequacy and effectiveness of commerce education in India.

(2) To identify the drawbacks of the present structure of commerce education.

(3) To find out the significance of commerce education in changing business environment and making suitable suggestions for re-engineering the same.

METHODOLOGY

A survey of 50 commerce teachers, 58 commerce students and 15 of their parents revealed numerous views and suggestions. The questionnaires were analysed to find out the effectiveness of commerce education in India in present circumstances and suggestions for its re-engineering in changing business environment.

A detailed questionnaire was prepared and sent to the commerce teachers (more than 120) all over India out of which 50 teachers responded. In addition, 58 commerce students and 15 of their parents were approached with questionnaire to collect their views on certain points.

ANALYSIS OF DATA AND FINDINGS

Analysis of 122 samples covered 41 per cent commerce teachers, 58 per cent commerce students and 11 per cent parents of those students. Out of 50 commerce teachers, 42 per cent were between the age group between 40 and 50 years having teaching experience of more than 10 years. Forty per cent of the commerce teachers had Ph.D. degree in commerce gave valuable suggestions.

Since the Government of India adopted the policy of liberalization and globalisation of business, there has been radical changes in business environment. Large number of multinations and foreign collaborations have emerged in India by which the business activities have become global. In this process, the business needs are being changed over a period of time. These business concerns need skilled and qualified staff to look after global business activities by making use of modern equipments, techniques and means of communications, etc. There has been extensive use of computers and other machines in the fast changing environment.

Though commerce education provides the students with information to enable them to understand the various business occupations and transactions found in the commercial world, it has traditional and conceptual approach. It lacks in practical orientation and fulfilment of job requirements in changing business environment. 48 out of 50 (*i.e.* 96 per cent) commerce teachers who responded in the survey have stated that the commerce education today is unable to cater to the needs of industries and other sectors. It is also contended that the present system and courses of commerce education in general do not correlate with the job potential provided by industry, commercial and financial institutions or other occupational courses.

In 1987, M.V. Mathur Committee Report observed that the commerce teachers have failed to develop expertise and scholarship comparable to that in the sister disciplines like Economics and others. The other problems of commerce education revealed in the survey are as under :

— No linkage with professional bodies.

— Absence of practical approach while determining the curriculum.

— Apathy of Government and U.G.C. towards commerce education.

— In some states of the country, the commerce graduates are not given admissions to B.Ed courses.

— No job opportunities are available to commerce graduates in rural areas.

Another major factor which was pointed by 13 (*i.e.*, 26 per cent) respondent teachers regarding reduction in commerce enrolment was the growth of business management education in the country. In India, management education is considered as professional education, though it is an extension of commerce education. This management education is better organized conceptually and its teaching methods are more refined as well as clear than commerce education. Also, in changing business environment, several new job related areas have been evolved in it like computer, etc.

IMPROVEMENT IN COMMERCE EDUCATION

(A) Task Before the Government

Improvement in commerce education and making it more suitable to the changing environment is present-day need due to its importance to industry and commerce. In this connection, the Government (both State and Central) can play an important role. The survey of commerce teachers, students and their parents suggested some measures which the Government can take to improve the scope of commerce education. 48 of the 50 (*i.e.* 96 per cent) teachers suggested to provide increasing financial support by the government for practical commerce education and to redesign the commerce courses by introducing practical areas such as vocational or career oriented courses. 43 of the teachers (86 per cent), 24 of the students (41 per cent) and 5 of the parents (33 per cent) suggested to increase specialization gradually from first year to third year B.Com. classes. This specialization may be by revising the present syllabus and make it parallel to professional courses like C.A., I.C.W.A., etc. Further more suggestions were given as under :

* Redesign the commerce courses at par with requirement of modern industries and other organizations.
* Reduce the classroom strength.
* Provide regular training to commerce teachers to update their knowledge.
* Selection of the commerce teachers on the basis of their performance.
* Defence services should recognize commerce courses as qualification.
* Introduce commerce subjects at secondary school stage.

(B) Task Before Universities

During the recent period the profile of commerce education has changed. With the shifting of outlines at par with business and industries, the total visual impression of commerce education has become different. This demands the alteration of commerce education in its concept, contents and consideration. This job can be easily performed by Universities, U.G.C., and Ministry of Human Resource Development, Government of India. The report of the Curriculum Development Centre, 1989 indicates that, commerce discipline is not properly understood by administrators, common men and even by educationists. This is being equated with one subject like Physics, Chemistry, Mathematics or History, etc. There is an urgent need to treat commerce discipline at par with Science or Arts for its proper development and growth.

At the University level, many number of measures can be undertaken to improve the scope of commerce education. In the survey of commerce teachers as well as commerce students, the major suggestion was to revise the syllabus of commerce courses from time to time and make it up-to-date with changing business environment. In addition, some more suggestions were given as under :

- — Enforce the inspection of commerce colleges by the team of experts in commerce.
- — Scrap A.T.K.T. which is in some of the Universities.
- — Universities should conduct all examinations on time and declare results on time.
- — Universities to organize Seminars and Workshops for commerce teachers and update their knowledge.
- — Promote vocational courses providing practical guidance.

(C) Task Before Commerce Colleges

Commerce Colleges are engaged in imparting commerce education to the student community. They should formulate the uniform structure of commerce education with gradual specialization in various areas such as Management, Marketing, Production, H.R.D. etc. Further, there can be extensive specialization in different areas such as Financial Management, Portfolio Management, Equity Research Analysis, Treasury and Forex Management, etc.

The survey of commerce teachers, students and their parents revealed a number of suggestions at college level to improve the scope of commerce education in changing business environment. Some of the suggestions are as under :

- — Enforce strict discipline among the commerce teachers.
- — Enforce knowledge oriented teaching rather than examination oriented coaching.
- — Enforce enrichment of commerce teachers by reading books and magazines.
- — Develop Libraries with rich collection of books and periodicals.
- — Conduct examinations under strict supervision and control.
- — Organize industrial visits for commerce students.
- — Introduce Job Placement Cells for commerce graduates.
- — Provide audio-visual aids to the teachers.
- — Enforce internal examinations for commerce students.

— Introduce case studies and project work for commerce students.

— Organize Seminars and Workshops for teachers and students.

— Enforce compulsory 75 per cent attendance of students.

— Introduce teacher evaluation scheme for every year.

(D) Task Before Commerce Teachers

Commerce teachers play an important role for increasing the scope of commerce education in changing business environment. They can provide latest knowledge about changes taking place in the field of Industry and Commerce and help the students to understand this changing environment. These students can be encouraged for self-employment with practical training in Industries, Offices, Banks, Stock Exchanges, etc. The commerce teachers would stress on specialization in certain areas of knowledge in commerce and improve the standard of commerce education. There is a need to undertake extensive research in different areas of commerce and link it with changing business environment.

CONCLUSION

Due to fast changing business environment, there are several challenges before commerce education in India. There is a dare need for its re-engineering to increase the effectiveness and to keep pace with changing economic and business environment. The measures are required to be taken at different levels and develop commerce education as it is desired by business and industry.

REFERENCES

1. Dr. B. Narayan, *Commerce Education in India*, Devdas Bhorali (Ed.), Deep and Deep Publications, New Delhi (1987).
2. Mathur, M.V., *Report of the Special Committee on Commerce Education*, New Delhi (1981).
3. *Report of the Curriculum Development Centre in Commerce*, New Delhi (1989).

Statistical Tables

Table 1

Share of Enrolment in Commerce Faculty

Year	Enrolment in Commerce	Total Enrolment	Share of Commerce in percentage
1972-73	3,18,888	21,68,107	14.7
1977-78	4,63,957	25,64,972	17.0
1982-83	6,69,813	31,33,093	21.4
1987-88	8,57,971	39,10,828	21.9
1991-92	10,09,832	46,11,107	21.8
1993-94	10,96,438	50,06,575	21.8

Source : (1) U.G.C. Reports.
(2) *University News,* March 11, 1996.

Table 2

Classification of Respondents

Sl. No.	Type	Gender: Male	Gender: Female	Total
1.	Commerce Teachers	40	10	50
2.	Commerce Students	4	54	58
3.	Parents	14	1	15
	Total	58	65	123

TABLE 3

Age Groups of Teacher Respondents

Age Group (Years)	No. of Respondents Male	Female	Total
25-30	3	2	5
30-35	2	1	3
35-40	8	4	12
40-45	9	2	11
45-50	10	—	10
50-55	4	—	4
55-60	4	1	5
Total	40	10	50

TABLE 4

Experience of Teacher Respondents

Years	Male	Female	Total
0-5	5	1	6
5-10	3	2	5
10-15	6	3	9
15-20	10	2	12
20-25	5	1	6
25-30	6	-	6
30-35	5	1	6
Total	40	10	50

TABLE 5

Education of Teacher Respondents

Degree	Male	Female	Total
M.Com.	40	10	50
M.Phil.	8	5	13
Ph.D.	17	3	20
Total	65	18	83

TABLE 6

Suggestions Analysis

Sl. No.	Suggestion	No. of Respondents	Percentage
1.	Agreed for decrease in the strength of Commerce students	32	64
2.	Suggested strong specialization in commerce	43	86
3.	Recommended practical training to students	48	86
4.	Recommended 75% attendance	35	70
5.	Recommended teacher evaluation	21	42
6.	Recommended Computer Education to Commerce students	18	36

34

Commerce Education in Indian Universities : A Study of Students Enrolment

—S.S. AINAPUR AND C.S. BASAVARAJ

Education is a powerful instrument of social change. In an individual it is a process of development from birth to death. The system of education is meant to achieve the social, economic, political, cultural and spiritual goals of the nation. Education is certainly the most important input for improvement of the quality of manpower and a very significant factor in achieving rapid economic development and technological progress.

Commerce education has a vital role in relation to the management of Industries, Trade and Commerce, Transportation, Insurance houses, Government departments such as Commercial Taxes, Income Taxation, Auditing, etc. Commerce education prepares students for business and business related activities.

NEED FOR THE STUDY

It is felt by the most of the commerce teachers and students that there is a sharp decline in the enrolment of students to traditional Commerce courses like B.Com. and M.Com. Hence, to see whether it is really happening at all-India level the study has been undertaken. It covers the enrolment of students to Commerce, Arts and Science Degree and postgraduation from the year 1989-90 to 1993-94 and for the year 1995-96.

THE STUDY

Table 1 exhibits faculty-wise enrolment of students in Indian Universities. It is apparently noticed from the table that faculty of Commerce stands second in all the five years of data covered.

TABLE 1

Students' Enrolment in the Universities : Faculty-wise from 1989-90 to 1993-94

Courses of Study	YEAR				
	1989-90 Enrolment	1990-91 Enrolment	1991-92 Enrolment	1992-93 Enrolment	1993-94 Enrolment
Commerce	9,31,765 (21.94)	9,69,882 (21.92)	10,09,832 (21.90)	10,52,244 (21.90)	10,96,438 (21.90)
Arts	17,17,437 (40.44)	17,89,480 (40.44)	18,65,605 (40.46)	19,43,960 (40.46)	20,25,606 (40.46)
Science	8,34,087 (19.64)	8,69,119 (19.64)	9,03,776 (19.60)	9,41,734 (19.60)	9,81,287 (19.60)
Others	7,63,589 (17.98)	7,96,766 (18.00)	8,31,894 (18.04)	8,66,835 (18.04)	9,03,244 (18.04)
Total	42,46,878 (100.00)	44,25,247 (100.00)	46,11,107 (100.00)	48,04,773 (100.00)	50,06,575 (100.00)

Notes : 1. Arts section also includes the Oriental learning courses.
2. Other sections include Engineering, Medical, Education, Agriculture, etc.
3. The figures in the bracket indicate the percentage of students enrolment to the corresponding total enrolment.

Source : Compiled from *Annual Report of U.G.C.* for the year 1993-94, New Delhi, 101.

The share of commerce education in the total enrolment of students in Indian Universities for the different years is 21.94% in 1989-90, 21.92% in 1990-91 and 21.90% in 1991-92, 1992-93 and 1993-94 respectively. The table also notices that, there is a very meagre decline in the enrollment of commerce students in the year 1991-92, 1992-93 and 1993-94 when compared to the respective preceding years. It is interesting to note that the percentage of students' enrolments is almost constant in all the years under consideration.

Table 2 highlights sex composition of students for different Bachelor and Master Degree Courses in Indian Universities. The total enrolment of students during the year 1995-96 is 49,83,329. Out of this the enrolment of boys is 31,30,240 and girls enrolment is 18,53,089.

TABLE 2

Students' Enrolment in the University : Faculty-wise during the Year 1995-96

Course of Study	Boys	Girls	Total
1	2	3	4
B.Com.	7,92,456 (70.60)	3,30,017 (29.40)	11,22,473 (100.00)
M.Com.	60,635 (76.74)	18,377 (23.26)	79,012 (100.00)
B.A.	14,18,200 (58.22)	10,17,784 (41.78)	24,35,984 (100.00)
M.A.	1,64,884 (61.22)	1,04,439 (38.78)	2,69,323 (100.00)
B.Sc.	6,30,830 (64.53)	3,46,683 (35.47)	9,77,513 (100.00)
M.Sc.	63,235 (63.86)	35,789 (36.14)	99,024 (100.00)
Total	31,30,240 (62.81)	18,53,089 (37.19)	49,83,329 (100.00)

Note : The figures in the bracket indicate the percentage of students enrolment to the corresponding total enrolment.

Source : 1. Compiled from the *University News,* Vol. 35, Nos. 48, 50 & 52, dt. Ist, 15th & 29th Dec. 1997, pp. 16, 17, 20 & 21.

2. *Selected Educational Statistics* 1995-96.

The enrolment of students for B.Com. and M.Com. Degree courses in the year 1995-96 happens to be 11,22,473 and 79,012 respectively which in aggregate stands at 24.11% of the total enrolment of students in the year. The share of Arts and Science students in the total enrolment works out to 54.29% and 21.60% respectively.

The table 2 also exhibits that, the enrolment in the faculty of Commerce stands second. Though, overall enrolment of students in commerce education stands second, we are lagging behind in the enrolment of girls. The enrolment of girls for B.Com. Degree course is only 29.40% whereas boys is 70.60% and for M.Com. Degree course it is 23.26% and 76.74% respectively.

TABLE 3

State-wise Enrolment of Students for B.Com. Degree Course in the Universities during the Year 1995-96

State/Union Territory	Boys	Girls	Total
1	2	3	4
Bihar	1,97,952	43,424	2,41,376
Maharashtra	1,24,344	93,041	2,17,385
Gujarat	71,450	47,000	1,18,450
Andhra Pradesh	59,746	32,884	92,630
Karnataka	42,132	32,608	74,740
West Bengal	62,915	6,712	69,627
Tamil Nadu	31,467	22,156	53,623
Uttar Pradesh	49,964	3,208	53,172
Madhya Pradesh	44,288	4,264	48,552
Delhi	26,901	8,611	35,512
Rajasthan	13,777	3,493	17,270
Kerala	8,095	8,770	16,865
Punjab	9,394	6,433	15,827
Haryana	9,134	5,926	15,060
Orissa	13,246	1,806	15,052
Assam	11,760	1,960	13,720
Goa	3,473	3,308	6,781
Himachal Pradesh	4,407	1,345	5,752
Jammu & Kashmir	2,927	1,003	3,930
Other States/U. Territory	5,084	2,065	7,149
India (Total)	7,92,456	3,30,017	11,22,473

Note : The total column of the table has been compiled in descending order.

Source : *University News*, Vol. 35, No. 52 dt. 29th Dec. 1997, pp. 16.

Table 3 reveals state-wise sex composition of students for B.Com. Degree course. Bihar stands first and Jammu and Kashmir finds last place in the total enrolment. The enrolment of girls is less than 50% when compared with boys in almost all states except Kerala. In Kerala girls are more interested in Commerce education than boys. Girls enrolment is 52% of the total enrolment in the state. It is interesting to note that girls are turning towards Commerce education in Kerala where hundred per cent literacy is achieved. Though Bihar stands first in total enrolment it finds 14th place when compared to the percentage of Girls with boys. And Uttar Pradesh is in first place *i.e.*, 94% in Boys' enrolment for B.Com. Degree course.

TABLE 4

State-wise Enrolment of Students for M.Com. Degree Course in the Universities during the Year 1995-96

State/Union Territory	Boys	Girls	Total
Bihar	10,826	3,372	14,198
Maharashtra	9,924	3,954	13,878
Uttar Pradesh	13,112	458	13,570
Madhya Pradesh	8,770	1,638	10,408
Gujarat	4,500	3,500	8,000
Tamil Nadu	2,304	1,112	3,416
Andhra Pradesh	2,434	409	2,843
West Bengal	2,145	205	2,350
Karnataka	1,054	787	1,841
Delhi	820	805	1,625
Rajasthan	1,153	387	1,540
Orissa	1,265	87	1,352
Kerala	540	681	1,221
Other States/U. Territory	1,788	982	2,770
India (Total)	60,635	18,377	79,012

Note : The total column of the table has been compiled in descending order.

Source : *University News,* Vol. 35, No. 48 dt. Ist Dec. 1997, p. 21.

Table 4 displays state-wise sex composition of students for M.Com. Degree course. The total enrolment of students for M.Com. Degree course during the year 1995-96 is 76,012. Out of this the enrolment of Boys and Girls is 60,635 and 18,377 respectively.

The table 4 brings to light that, Bihar state stands first and Kerala stands last in total enrolment. Though the Kerala state finds last place in enrolment of students, the Girls enrolment is highest with 56% when compared to other states. Delhi stands in the second place having 50% for both boys and girls. And Uttar Pradesh stands first *i.e.*, 96% in boys enrolment for M.Com. Degree course.

Table 5 deals with enrolment of SC/ST students for B.Com. and M.Com. Degree courses in Indian Universities. During 1993-94 SC/ST students enrolment is 7.35%, *i.e.* 75,235 out of 10,25,000 of the total enrolment for B.Com. Degree course and it is 11.10%, *i.e.* 7,934 out of 71,438 for M.Com. Degree course. During the year 1995-96 the enrolment of SC/ST students is 6.91% and 9.85% for B.Com. and M.Com. courses respectively.

TABLE 5

Enrolment of SC/ST Students for B.Com./M.Com. Degree Courses in Indian Universities during the Years 1993-94 and 1995-96

Courses of the Study	1993-94				1995-96			
	Overall Enrolment	Sheduled Castes & Scheduled Tribes			Overall Enrolment	Sheduled Castes & Scheduled Tribes		
		Boys	Girls	Total		Boys	Girls	Total
B.Com.	10,25,000 (100.00)	58,200 (5.69)	17,035 (1.66)	75,235 (7.35)	11,22,473 (100.00)	58,532 (5.21)	19,126 (1.70)	77,658 (6.91)
M.Com.	71,438 (100.00)	6,659 (9.32)	1,275 (1.78)	7,934 (11.10)	79,012 (100.00)	6,181 (7.82)	1,605 (2.03)	7,786 (9.85)
Total	10,96,438 (100.00)	64,859 (5.91)	18,310 (1.67)	83,169 (7.58)	12,01,485 (100.00)	64,713 (5.39)	20,731 (1.72)	85,444 (7.11)

Note : The figures in the bracket indicate the percentage of SC/ST students' enrolment to the corresponding overall enrolment column.

Sources : 1. *Selected Educational Statistics* for the year 1993-94.

2. *University News,* Vol. 35, No. 48 & 52, dt. Ist & 29th Dec. 1997, pp. 21 & 16.

By observing table 5 we find that there is a decrease in the enrolment of SC/ST students for B.Com. Degree course by 0.44% in the year 1995-96 when compared to 1993-94. The decrease is 1.25% for M.Com. Degree course.

Table 6 reveals faculty-wise award of the Doctorate Degrees in India. The Doctorate Degree award in Commerce faculty is only 346, 409 and 453 whereas in Arts faculty it is 3,327, 3,489 and 3,621 and in Science faculty it is 3,002, 3,226 and 3,386 during the years 1990-91, 1991-92 and 1992-93 respectively.

TABLE 6

Faculty-wise Award of Doctorate Degrees in India during the Years 1990-91 to 1992-93

Faculty	1990-91	1991-92	1992-93
Commerce	346 (5.18)	409 (5.74)	453 (6.07)
Arts	3,327 (49.85)	3,489 (48.98)	3,621 (48.54)
Science	3,002 (44.97)	3,226 (45.28)	3,386 (45.39)
Total	6,675 (100.00)	7,124 (100.00)	7,460 (100.00)

Note : The figures in the bracket indicate the percentage of students' enrolment to the corresponding total enrolment.

Source : *Annual Report of the U.G.C.* 1992-93 & 1993-94, New Delhi, pp. 69 & 106.

The table highlights the meagre number of Doctorate degrees awarded in commerce faculty when compared to the other two faculties. The award of Doctorate Degree in Commerce works out to 5.18% in 1990-91, 5.74% in 1991-92 and 6.07% in 1992-93 when compared with the total number of Doctorate Degrees awarded in Arts. Science and Commerce faculties taken together.

FINDINGS OF THE STUDY

1. The analysis of the data reveals that the enrolment of students in Indian Universities for B.Com. and M.Com. courses

from the year 1989-90 to 1993-94 remains almost constant when per cent share of enrolment with Arts and Science students is considered. But in 1995-96 there is an increase of 2.21% in the enrolment when compared to 1993-94. No significant decline in the enrolment of the students is found in the study period.

2. In all the years under consideration the enrolment of students to Commerce courses is more than Science students but less than Arts students.

3. Except Kerala in all other states boys are more in number when compared to girls for B.Com. and M.Com. courses during the year 1995-96.

4. There is a slight decline in the enrollment of SC/ST students in the year 1995-96 when compared to 1993-94.

5. Award of Doctorate Degrees in Commerce is much less in number when compared to Science and Arts faculty. It highlights the fact that research activity is to be encouraged in the field of Commerce.

SUGGESTIONS

1. As the enrolment of students for B.Com. and M.Com. Degrees is almost constant when compared to the share of Arts and Science students' enrolment, the students are to be motivated to take up Commerce courses.

2. Girls are to be encouraged more to pursue Commerce education as their share is less in the total enrolment (except in Kerala).

3. SC/ST students' enrolment shows a slight decline in the year 1995-96. The students from SC/ST community are to be attracted to the Commerce courses by providing the support needed to them.

4. Research orientation is to be provided to the cream of the Commerce Graduates as the existing research activity seems to be inadequate.

35 Action Plan for 21st Century Business Education

—P.N. UDAYACHANDRA

1. PRELUDE

(Learned speakers who presented their papers earlier have dissected the present body of Commerce education *vis-a-vis* business education and identified the ailments. I thank them for their depth of knowledge and the surgical insight of analysis. Now I am looking for the tasks ahead.)

The future generation to which we are going to enter, will be totally different from the present scenario. We will be witnessing the unbound expansions in the field of science and technology with its business applications. So there is a need and urgency to cope up ourselves with the changing situations.

Total dismantling of the existing systems, institutions of higher learning and administrative set-up may not be feasible and a Practical way-out. What best can be done, will be a complete re-orientation, restructuring and re-designing so that least disturbance can be caused to the existing body, which can absorb the future shocks.[1]

The next generation will be of those organizations, institutions and enterprises which will have cost and quality consciousness, with passion for excellence and a high degree of precision. That is what is envisaged and that will be the society we are entering.

The aim of future business education, to quote Peter F. Drucker, should be "to equip the students the elementary skills that should make them effective as members of an organization, the ability to present ideas orally and in writing, the ability to work with people, the ability to shape and direct one's own work, contribution and "It should provide a kind of 'Mobile security' " where geographical boundaries are not the limit.

Viewed from this background, a high degree of responsibility is vested on the teachers and lecturers. In the changed environment it seems to me, we the lecturers will have a greater role to play.

2. ACTION PLAN

A. Redesigning of Higher Learning Centres

The existing higher learning centres have transformed into a Monolithic structure with high degree of bureaucratic rules and regulations. In the just changing situations there is a need for debureaucratisation. Autonomy should be given to higher learning centres. To have accountability and quality standards, there must be a separate Assessment and Accredition centres, which will go through the procedures of admission, recruitment, and the relevance of quality inputs. This Accredition and Assessment Centre will act like ISI marking which provides a guarantee for quality. Members from the faculty of present Commerce teachers should become the panel experts in the Assessment and Accredition centres so that they can better understand the ins and outs of business education. At present there is undue influence of non-commerce academicians in the Policy decisions pertaining to Commerce education.[3] Accredition and assessment centres may contact business, Industry and Govt. sources for fixing parameters of quality requirements. Once these benchmarkings are done, higher learning centres should be given autonomy to carry on with their Scheme of education.

B. Consolidation and Continuation in the Curriculum

The curriculum to be taught should consider the following. The study package should include core optionals and specialization papers so that the curriculum should provide for

(a) Employment opportunities.

(b) Professional consultancy and research.

(c) Self-employment possibilities.

It should begin at +2 level and should be continued after +3 level also.

So the need is consolidating and adopting a continuing study package for business education. The process should be merging +2,

+3 and +2. The syllabus should be in Unit form with part I elementary level, part II advanced level, part III specialization for consultancy, and research.

C. Innovation in Teaching Methodology : Assessment

New study package needs innovative methods of imparting knowledge. This should include case studies and field visits, where the student will gather the information and present a detailed report. Practical orientation with application of what is learnt can be correlated by the student. Here the role of the teacher will be to guide and help the students to acquire the skills of analysis, written communication and presentation.

While assessing the students, objective type of questions with practical components should be combined; based on this grades should be given.

To have uniformity and objectivity in assessment, broad guidelines should be given to the teachers. Depending upon the local situations within the broad parameters, student assessment will be made.

D. Industry/Business Unit Contact and Placement Schemes

The guidelines should be framed in liaison with the available industry/business units, it assures the users (employers) the quality inputs provided in the education and it also makes the students to learn what is expected by the end users. Contact programmes will familiarise the students, what exactly is going on at the practical level, and he learns the techniques to survive in the field. Later if his performance is to the level of the expectations of the employer final placements can be made.

In this model, learning centres will be a bridge between the learner and the employer where each knows about what is going on and what is expected and how best the knowledge can be acquired and utilized.

E. Creative Administrative Set-up

These ideas at best can become a reality only if there is a creative unconventional administrative set-up.

Business Education Administration set-up should consider the whole education pattern in totality. There is a need for a paradigm shift. Today we find Government funds for the teachers, University prescribes the syllabus and the teachers teach. Paying master's view the system from a different angle whereas University looks from another dimension. So, the existing dichotomy should be removed by establishing a separate system which takes care of both personnel administration and quality input.

F. Training for Teachers and Educational Administrators

There must be a Scheme of continuous training programme for both teachers and educational administrators.[4] Innovation in teaching is best possible only when there is conducive administrative and academic environment. This is possible only when both are trained. In the training programmes the need for the change and the changing roles should be stressed. Because both teaching and administration are dynamic forces which requires constant updating.

Teacher training should be for teacher development. When the teacher is motivated a student can be motivated to learn. Innovative teaching methods will take more energy and time of the teacher, so it should be balanced with proper opportunities for career development and career advancement.[5]

This can be created by imparting proper and timely training programmes for teachers and educational administrators.

G. Teacher Partnership and Involvement in Educational Policy Decisions

Not only as a principle but as a practice teachers' role in policy decision-making should be considered.[6] At present teachers' involvement is marginal and at worse those who are involved are not the real representatives. This tendency has created a sort of detachment on the part of teachers towards the education system in general and what is taught in particular. Here the main culprit is the system — which is not an evolved one but a borrowed one which is in majority of the cases, is thrust upon.

This trend can be solved by legitimising the teacher involvement by creating suitable standing committees and governance by consensus. If this is done changes will be accepted with less or no resistance. It will be accepted because of the fact that the whole creation is teachers' making. Those who involve in the policy making will see that it will be implemented *in toto*.

H. Fund Matching

Once proper linkages are established with business and industry and as they are involved in the process funds can be collected through proper corporate sponsorships and study financial aids.

Teacher consultancy should be allowed with a proper ratio, wherein teachers are also contributing for the cause of education.

Business education should really mean business.

I. Nomenclature

The new study package should be properly marketed with a proper brand name. The existing nomenclature gives a traditional, conventional outlook. So it is proper as it was deliberated earlier in various seminars and in conferences that 'B.Com. degree' should be changed to B.B.S. This changed 'nomenclature' will create a definite impact as far as 'end users' are concerned. It really means business. In the same nomenclature if modifications and alterations are made it seems like an altered or modified one. Once the whole study package is completely redesigned and restructured, there is a need for a name which will assure or guarantee the input quality. So in my opinion B.B.S. and at P.G., level M.B.S. is a better title for the holders.

3. END WORD

All aspirations with good intentions will become a part of the reality. It may be a matter of time only. Now a beginning is made here and I am sure the message will be carried on to see that some changes will definitely take place in the field of business education. With the rapid changes taking place in and around one has to find certainty in uncertainty. This is possible only through right kind of education which imbibes basic business knowledge, business skills and professional expertise, *i.e.,* Business education which should mean, it is business.

REFERENCES

1. Alwyn Tofler, *Future Shock.*
2. Peter F. Drucker, *Managing for future beyond 1990's.*
3. Dr. S.G. Hundekar, *Reading material Refresher course*, Dharwad, 9-3-1996 to 29-3-1996. Article : Current issues in Commerce Education.

4. Dr. G. Kotrappa, *Reading material — Refresher course*, Mysore 8-9-97 to 30-9-97. Reviving Commerce Education.

5. *Souvenir* published by Federation of Teachers Councils of Commerce and Management in the IInd State level conference in Davangere, 11th & 12th July 1997.

6. Interactions with Prof. Eresi & Dr. B.C. Sanjevayya, Bangalore University.

36 Case Approach for Management Education

—K. SWAMY

Quite oftenly the word management is used in a loose sense. Some people believe that management is managing one's own boss or maintaining good relationship with the subordinate staff. Management is primarily concerned with the allocation of scarce resources to the most productive uses and their effective utilization. It refers to manage men, material, machines and money tactfully. It is a process of creating environment to work and getting done things by people. It is certainly about the people not systems. People get together to achieve the defined objectives of an organization. Management should create the environment to achieve the corporate objectives. In order to realise the corporate objectives right decisions should be made on right time for right results. Thus, the management is expected to meet the changing challenges with confidence and courage. Though management looks very simple, it is complex in nature. Poor and ineffective management will not only hamper the credibility of the organization but also leads to bankruptcy.

The success or failure of any business organization largely depends upon its managerial capabilities. Management consists of team of managers playing different roles in the functional areas. The business firm should select right managers in right time for right positions. Every organization must have a kind of career planning *i.e.*, after lapse of time where do an employee stands, what will be his future prospects. The organization should train and develop managers properly to suit the organizational requirements.

A good manager is one who forecasts the things well in advance. He should be clever enough to understand the business situation, and convert it in favour of the management. He is expected to create the environment so as to extract the best possible from the employees of an organization.

A good manager is also an effective communicator. Good managers are not born, they are made. They are fashioned by experience of business exposure to day-to-day problems and realities of the workplace. They grow in stature and managerial skill largely from their encounters with people and problems, but not from mere studying the notes and theories catalogued in textbooks.

Once it was believed that to become a manager one had to learn how to plan, organise, coordinate, command and control. But now it is widely accepted that the systems view is simplistic. The environment keeps changing, the target keeps moving, events and people do not always conform long enough to be planned and controlled. The ways and means of management, therefore, involve continual experimentation with new approaches to old and new problems.

Always a better manager may learn and grow by practising, thinking, rethinking, observing, experimenting and continuously questioning. Worthful alternatives may be generated from the heat of action, from dealing with the course of real business events, from the problems and the personalities involved in them.

The Business schools play vital role in growing the managers to suit the requirements of an organization. The incumbent managers should be trained both theoretically as well as practically in such a way that they will be able to meet all the possible challenges which will arise in the course of conduct of business.

There are growing opportunities for young management graduates in various industrial sectors, provided they are well-versed with the subject and capable of facing the changing challenges. The increasing size of business organizations and the establishment of multinational companies created the demand for more number of managers and has the potentiality to absorb the talented managers.

In the recent past large number of business schools are coming up to offer business management programmes. Barring aside few institutions, many have failed in delivering the goods. The standards imparted by these business schools could not rise to the expectations of the prospective employers. These business schools are becoming commercial rather than service. They are not training the students to understand the business situation and merely awarding degrees without imparting the required managerial skills.

The degrees awarded by some business schools have high saleability in the market and the degrees awarded by other business schools have lower or no saleability at all. For instance there is a lot of visible difference between the business schools of Indian Institute of Management and other business schools.

What Makes the Difference?

The possible reasons could be the 'quality' of the product, exposure to the real business situations and industrial linkages. The quality depends on several factors such as the inputs that are being provided in grooming the students. It is a continuous process of involving them in classroom teaching, group discussion, interacting with the teachers and groups, role playing, combining industrial experience by using cases, etc.

The second one is very vital for imparting any professional education *i.e.*, exposing the students to real business situation by using the case method. This is being widely used in business schools of IIM and other reputed institutions, but the other business schools are not giving much importance to this kind of method. Hence, in the absence of case method students are lagging behind and handicapped.

In the words of Charles I. Gragg "Wisdom can't be told", mere listening to lectures, wise statements and sound advice does little for anyone. In the process of learning, the learners' active participation, and total immersion is required, which does not arise automatically, however, it has to be provided for and continually encouraged.

Thus, the key to understand business situation case plan of teaching has to be introduced which dignifies, and dramatises student life by opening the way for students to make positive contribution to thought and by doing so to prepare themselves for action.

Instead of textbooks, traditional lecture methods, the case method uses description of specific business situations. Instead of giving lectures, the teacher under the case method leads a discussion of these business situations. A case is a real situation where partial data is given and the problem requires to be identified by the students relating to a situation. The students are exposed to variety of situations. A case is a typical connecting link which draws together the experience of executives and prospective executives, management development programme and researchers to understand the process of management.

A case may be written so that the student is faced with a decision to make, or they may recount what happened and how it was decided. The teacher may lead the discussion or let the class lead it, he may try to work toward a school solution, or point up the many solutions that can be arrived. All these variations will be made in accordance with the instructor's evaluation of what he wishes to present, of what he hopes to achieve, and of himself.

A case is a description of a real situation faced by an organization. It clearly states the conditions and circumstances surrounding a particular managerial situation or series of events faced by an organization.

A good case will help students to actually experience in the class a variety of situations which might take them years to experience in the real business. Cases are the training devices for students participating what manager would do if confronted with same circumstances. Exposure to more and more number of cases will help students to take up managerial positions without having a worry about their practical inexperience. It is a method which helps to learn while doing. The cases will develop the following set of skills :

* problem identification
* data analysis
* analytical and critical thinking
* challenging assumptions
* making judgements
* predicting outcomes

* making decisions
* communicating findings and ideas
* promoting evaluation of decision processes and outcomes.

The impact of case method may be divided into four stages (1) an initial reaction of frustration (2) an arousal of curiosity (3) a development of insight and (4) a final achievement of power.

With the case method, all the members of the academic group are in possession of the same material in the light of which analysis is to be made and decision arrived at. Each, therefore, has an identical opportunity to make contributions to body of principles governing business practice and policy. Business is not an exact science, hence, there is no single, demonstrably right answer to the business problems. In every business situation, there is always a reasonable possibility that the best answer has not yet been found. It is the common consciousness arrived at the majority of the participants.

The role of the teacher who assigns the cases for discussion is to act as a responsible member of the group delegated to provoke argumentative thinking, to guide discussion by his own experience and questions towards points of major importance, and if he chooses, to take a final position on the viewpoints which have been threshed out before him. The more powerful are the student arguments, the heavier is the burden on the teacher, he has to understand and evaluate each contribution, out of which many are new to him, regardless of how thoroughly he studies the cases or how many times he used them in the earlier classes. Every class meeting to the teacher is a new problem and new opportunity both to learn and help others to learn.

— Its primary purpose of the training of men for positions of actual business responsibility, all its activities stem from, and are beamed at, the problems of current business to make him understand about the material, men, machine and money.

— The Businessman is interested in decision building not in theory construction, the skill in making decisions comes from practice, emphasis is placed on the case situation, as such rather than on compiling theories from a number of cases.

— The individual courses and curriculum should be designed not simply to convey knowledge but to require the students to assimilate useful ways of thinking and the data they demand in a meaningful manner.

The business schools should aim at imparting the qualities needed by a businessman. Management educational institutions must be directed to developing in students the qualities of understanding, judgement and communication leading to actions. These institutions should aim to accelerate the students' ability to act in mature fashion under conditions of responsibility.

The case method instills confidence, develops interpersonal communication skills and helps to acquire leadership qualities among students. This method helps to understand and apply the managerial skills relating to a particular situation.

REFERENCES

1. Stephen P. Robins, *Organizational Behaviour*, Prentice Hall of India.
2. Koontz, Harold and Donnell, *Principles of Management*. McGraw Hill.
3. Makolm P.M.C. Nair, ed., *The Case Method at the Harward Business School.*

37 Progress and Problems of Business Education During 50 Years of Post-Independence Period

—S.H. TEKKANNAVAR

Education system has become common both in sense of finding fault with every aspect of education and regarding the implementation of education reforms. We express dissatisfaction with the structure of education, with the functioning of the educational institutions, about the students' as well as teachers' behaviour. Some go so far as to blame education even whose focus lies outside education. The positive contribution of education, especially higher education, to our national development is so obvious that it were not for the prevalent self-enunciation on our part. No other developing country achieved such tremendous resources of training and education, since the sixties. We will not depend on foreign higher education for almost any branch of learning. Now even advanced countries welcome and employ highly educated personnel, from India.

One of the most prominent feature of our educational system has been its tremendous expansion by a factor of almost 15 in a span of 34 years since independence. Such a rate of expansion is perhaps unparalleled in the history of any country and system designed in such a way to meet the manpower needs at the highest level. The broad objectives of the higher education are liberal education with the aim of understanding the society and social changes of the human relationship. And the human and social implications of technological change, and developing a capacity to appreciate the finer value of life, etc. These broad objectives are taken as implied in the case of business education also.

COMMERCE EDUCATION/BUSINESS EDUCATION

Commerce education is called to be business education also. But in tune with the needs of the business and society, independent professions have started as such chartered accountant, cost and works accountant, company secretary and business administrators. Thus, commerce education has now remained as an academic discipline giving general and liberal education.

Commerce education is an integral part of total education system. The term 'commerce' originally refers to and includes all those activities which create time, place and ownership-utilities for the individual and social ends. It is a living discipline and it is totally different from other disciplines. For the economic development of the country and to meet the growing needs of the society, there is a greater need for development of commerce education in India.

What is Business Education? Author Leverett S. Lyon defined business education as "Any education which a businessman has which makes him a better businessman is for him business education, no matter whether it was obtained within the walls of a school or not".

Another author Fredrick G. Nichols defined commerce education in the following words : "Commerce education is a type of training which while playing its part in the achievement of the general aim of education on any given level has for its primary objectives the preparation of people to enter upon a business career or having upon such career to render more efficient service therein and to advance from there present levels of employment to higher levels."

Thus, business education is that area of education which develops the required knowledge, skills and attitudes for the successful handling of trade, commerce and industry.

PROGRESS OF BUSINESS EDUCATION/COMMERCE EDUCATION

Business/commerce education in India was started in 1886 over a hundred years ago. Business education has become an integral part of the social change. It continues to occupy an important place in the country's educational system. Business education began in a haphazard way and on a very small scale. The beginning of commerce education was made in 1913 by starting graduate course in commerce in Sydenham College, Bombay. By 1940 only five Universities in the country had the Departments of Studies in Commerce.

The growth of commerce education took rapid development after 1947. There was an increase in the number of students and the institutions, offering commerce education after the independence. Since Independence, the administrative set up of the university also changed. The Government of India passed an Act and established Boards, etc. In 1932 established Indian Accountancy Board, Chartered Accountant Act, 1949. Another new area emerged on the professional education in commerce is cost accounting. The Government of India established in 1959 the Institute of Cost and Works Accountants to train Cost Accountants. Since then it has experienced tremendous growth. Commerce faculties are established in about 140 universities, out of a total 226 universities including deemed universities.

In recent days, due to the Government policy on liberalization, privatisation and globalisation, the business faculty is fetching more importance.

Enrolment of commerce students in 1950-51 is 0.36 lakh, whereas in 1995-96 it is 14.10 lakhs. Thus, there is an increase of 3,780 per cent.

Presently the enrolment in graduation and postgraduation in business education increased during last one and half decades. Another feature is number of girl students increased in graduation and postgraduation also.

Number of commerce students in state-wise, Bihar stands First Rank in 1995-96 and Maharashtra Second Rank and Gujarat Third Rank, Karnataka state ranks Fifth in the said list. Commerce is popular in urban areas rather than in rural areas. It has spread throughout the country. Now it has taken roots in all the States and Union Territories. Commerce's share in total enrolment has increased from 17.1 per cent in 1975-76 to 21.9 per cent in 1995-96.

TABLE 1

Number of Commerce Students : State-wise

Sl. No.	State	1970-71	Rank	1995-96	Rank
1.	Andhra Pradesh	24,690	4	95,473	4
2.	Arunachal Pradesh	—	—	225	28
3.	Assam	4,240	13	12,462	16
4.	Bihar	12,554	8	2,55,574	1
5.	Goa	469	19	6,938	17
6.	Gujarat	42,010	3	1,26,450	3
7.	Haryana	1,642	14	15,690	15
8.	Himachal Pradesh	186	21	5,972	18
9.	Jammu & Kashmir	919	18	4,188	19
10.	Karnataka	14,535	5	76,581	5
11.	Kerala	11,794	9	18,086	12
12.	Madhya Pradesh	17,810	6	58,960	8
13.	Maharashtra	87,143	1	2,31,263	2
14.	Manipur	112	23	608	24
15.	Meghalaya	—	—	728	23
16.	Mizoram	—	—	260	26
17.	Nagaland	—	—	367	25
18.	Orissa	1,160	16	16,404	13
19.	Punjab	1,447	15	16,091	14
20.	Rajasthan	14,156	7	18,810	11
21.	Sikkim	—	—	148	30
22.	Tamil Nadu	7,282	11	57,039	9
23.	Tripura	1,152	17	1,926	20
24.	Uttar Pradesh	11,679	10	66,742	7
25.	West Bengal	81,950	2	71,977	6
26.	Andman & Nicobar Islands	—	—	198	29
27.	Chandigarh	419	20	1,615	21
28.	Dadra and Nagar Haveli	—	—	—	—
29.	Daman & Diu	—	—	248	27
30.	Delhi	7,107	12	37,137	10
31.	Lakshadweep	—	—	—	—
32.	Pondicherry	168	22	1,325	22

TABLE 2

Distribution of Students Enrolled in Higher Education By Field of Studies — All India

Faculty	1975-76 percentage	1995-96 percentage
Arts	44.5	40.4
Science	19.1	19.6
Commerce	17.1	21.9
Education	3.2	2.3
Engineering & Technology	4.0	4.9
Medicine	4.3	3.4
Agriculture	1.2	1.1
Veterinary Science	0.3	0.3
Law	5.8	5.3
Others	0.5	0.8
Total	100.0	100.0

Thus, a single discipline — commerce, accounts for about 22 per cent of the total enrolment in higher education. Unfortunately, it is not getting adequate attention to its needs from the Government and UGC.

PROBLEMS OF BUSINESS EDUCATION

(1) *Lack of Practical Knowledge of Business Education*

The commerce products are not accepted by the business or industry because they find that there is lack of practical knowledge.

(2) *Poor Communication Skill*

Industrialists and businessmen are not ready to accept the commerce students due to their weakness in communication skill, both oral and written.

(3) *The Course Content is Unchanged*

In the business education course contents remain unchanged since a long time. The changes in some areas are also not equal to fast changing conditions.

(4) *Lack of Training to Teaching Faculty*

The teaching faculty is not adequately trained or oriented to the new changes in the field of business education.

(5) *Examination System is not in Testing Real Ability of the Students*

The examination system is also faulty enough to test the real abilities of the students.

(6) *Absence of Specification of Job Areas*

It is unfortunate to find other faculty graduates being preferred to commerce graduates for those jobs which are basically meant for commerce graduates. Thus other faculty graduates make an encroachment in the job markets.

(7) *There is no Opportunity to B.Com. Graduates to B.Ed.*

There is no opportunity to commerce graduates to B.Ed. which fetches more job opportunities in teaching.

(8) There is a lot of damage that is being done as regards the medium of instruction and examination in regional language. We talk of globalisation of business but we do not want to serve the cause of globalisation of Indian business. There is no point in producing large number of graduates and postgraduates without acceptability in the job market.

(9) *There is no Wide Publicity and Acceptability of Business Education in Rural Area*

There is a good response to business education in urban areas and cities, but there is a very poor response in rural areas.

(10) *Lack of Proper Infrastructure*

It is sometimes remarked that many colleges are not having minimum requirements of infrastructural facility.

(11) *There is no Wide Opportunity for Selecting Subjects in Competitive Examination in State as well as Centre*

The other faculty graduates have more subjects in choosing for competitive examinations but in commerce syllabi at competitive examination it is not attracting even the meritorious commerce students.

(12) *Improper Admissions*

In many cases students who are not able to get seats in other courses are opting for commerce. In such a case it is not possible to get good results.

(13) *Commerce Teacher is a Jack of All Trades*

Perhaps he is the only person who is expected to teach all the subjects.

Thus, since Independence, commerce education is facing innumerable problems today. These problems have a direct bearing on the course objectives, course content and course conduct. These problems need serious attention. It is high time for giving a better deal to commerce education in the years to come. "As the economy becomes more industrialised and society becomes more complex the knowledge and skills required to deal with the situations also changed. Hence, for enabling students to acquire the desired capabilities content of course and their combinations need to be revised, diversified and made more flexible."

REFERENCES

1. *Journal of Commerce Conference*, July, 1994.
2. *Presidential Address of All India Commerce Conference*, December, 1997.
3. *Report of the Curriculum Development Centre*, Published by UGC.

38 Challenges Before Business Education

—V.M. BHANDARI

INTRODUCTION

As compared to other branches of education, business education which is technically called Commerce Education as a separate branch of education developed very recently. Though its origin in India can be traced back to 1886 when Trustees of Pachiyappa's Charities started a commercial school in Madras. Later in 1895 provision of teaching commerce was made in Calicut and in Calcutta in 1903 by Government of India. Since 1903 and onwards number of management institutions started to develop slowly offering business education in different parts of the country. Growth of trade and commerce widened the opportunity for business education and necessitated the establishment of institutions which can offer business or commerce education. The establishment of Sydenham College of Commerce and Economics in Bombay during 1913 began commerce education at the University level and laid the foundation stone for the development business education in India.

This paper is prepared to give the brief highlight of objectives of business education, its challenges and measures or remedies and divided into three parts as Part I Objectives, Part II Challenges and Part III Remedies.

PART-I

OBJECTIVES OF BUSINESS EDUCATION

Economic development of any country strictly depends upon development of trade, commerce and industry of that country. Accordingly Government of India also gave importance to the development of trade, industry and commerce and as such trade, industry and commerce started to develop slowly. The developing trade, industry, commerce, banking and insurance business both in private sector and public sector were in need of persons with commerce or business education background and offered a big challenge to business education. To meet the requirement of growing needs and demands of business, industry and banking, several institutions which can offer business education were started in different parts of the country. Today more than 500 institutions offer business and management education all over the country. Some of the premier management institutions which offer higher business education in India are Institutes of Management funded by the Central Government : (1) IIM at Ahmedabad, Calcutta, Bangalore and Lucknow (2) Institutes of Management funded and promoted by other agencies like XLRI, XIM, IRMA, Manipal and Bajaj (3) University departments of management and institutions affiliated to them.

The main aims and objectives of business education were to educate and develop such skills, attitudes and knowledge in students as are essential for the successful conduct of business, trade, profession and services. The objectives of business education are specific and of different nature than those of general education. They are :

(1) To promote the general education of business and commerce and to equip students for understanding and appreciation of business.

(2) To prepare students for executive and non-executive positions in business and service sector.

(3) To promote entrepreneurial skill for self-employment.

(4) To develop skills in teaching and research in various areas of commerce.

Thus, business education has been developed in our country to support growing manpower needs of business enterprises that come up after the advent of British rule. In the initial stage, business education had limited objectives of providing, clerical and accounting personnel with emphasis on training in typing, shorthand, letter writing and business methods. But with the expansion and growth of trade, commerce and industry, the objectives of business education were widened. In this connection the report of the *Special Committee for Commerce Education* (V.K.R.V. Rao Committee) is noteworthy.

"Commerce education is not merely a liberal education. Commerce education has to give graduate some special attitudes, which is not likely to accompany the imparting of education in other fields."

PART-II

CHALLENGES

Though aims and objectives of business education as noted above were to fulfil the growing needs of developing business, industry, commerce, and banking, to what extent business education has achieved these objectives is a debatable question. Is business education capable of accommodating its students in banks, insurance companies, Indian railways, investment trusts, industry, factory and other business establishments? Is business education providing employment to its students like B.Com., B.B.A., B.B.M., M.Com., MBA students? Has business education motivated the students to learn business education unlike science and other technical education? Is business education really providing employment opportunities to its students and attracting them towards it? Is business education giving competition to other branches of education? Is the syllabus of business education has any relevance in changing business environment? The answer to the above noted questions is no. Indeed business education has failed in achieving its objectives and there is a big challenge before business education of providing employment to its students and to its dependents. As observed by Dr. B. Narayan "The commerce education even today provides narrow traditional and conceptual education. It lacks practical orientation and hence is unable to solve the industrial and social problems." There are many other ills in the commerce education like lack of uniformity in the curriculum, indiscriminate admissions, no linkage with professional bodies, apathy of Government and UGC towards commerce education. Thus, *Business education as it stands today is completely insulated from the realities of industrial environment*. The most practical course has become highly theoretical over the years. Banks, insurance companies private industries, government organizations often clamour for recruiting science and engineering graduates even in the areas where commercial acumenship is most wanted. Even at the school level commerce is not taught as a serious course. Naturally the students and parents look towards science and engineering education neglecting business education. There is also a strong case for strengthening the research facilities in commerce. There are hundreds of research institutions for developing science but for commerce there are very few. Another area which needs immediate attention of educationists in commerce is to develop an attitude for consultancy in commerce.

The strong reasons for this sorry state of affairs are lack of dynamism in the course content to meet the changing business environment, lack of adequate accommodation, lack of practical training facilities and above all absence of reservation of jobs to commerce graduates in banks, insurance companies, government and private enterprises, etc. The very aim of commerce graduates getting absorbed in banks have been discouraged particularly after the nationalization of major commercial banks. After the nationalization of major commercial banks, recruitment in banks is made through bank test which is open to graduates of all disciplines. As banks test consists of reasoning aptitude, general English and mathematics, the commerce syllabus in many institutions and states does not include mathematics as one of the subjects though included, it is optional. Hence commerce graduates fail in mathematics in bank test while science and arts graduates who have studied mathematics will pass and get absorbed in banks. Commerce students will experience the same problem while getting absorbed in Insurance companies, Investment trusts, Railway Recruitment, Armed forces, Defence, Staff Selection Commission examination. In view of this attitude of BSRB and Government, business education has failed to give employment to its students in banks, insurance companies, etc.

As business education is not taught at primary school level, unlike science and arts students, business education students have no scope to become teachers at primary school (This is with reference to Karnataka State).

B.Com. graduates are not considered while allotting seats for B.Ed. course, commerce graduates cannot hope for becoming high school teachers. (This is also with reference to Karnataka.) It is to be noted that business education is also not taught at high school level also. Thus the semifinished products of business education school like B.Com., B.B.A., B.B.M. and other students who complete diploma in business management are neither preferred nor reserved in jobs in banks, insurance companies, government and private enterprises, primary schools and high schools who are treated at par with other discipline students. Subjects included in the syllabus of business education are not included in the syllabus of banks and insurance tests to be conducted to recruit their personnel. Thus, those who study business education have no employment opportunities in banking field and insurance companies. Employment opportunity in primary school and high school is virtually nil as business education is not taught at both the levels. Thus, provision of employment opportunities for the students of business education itself is the big challenge for business education. Nowadays it has become the practice of appointing graduates of any discipline in industry and factory and not necessarily the graduates from business education and commerce facility. Higher education in the field of business and commerce like MBA, CA, ICWA, company secretary course are made open to all graduates of different discipline and, therefore, commerce and business education graduates have to compete with the graduates of science, arts, engineering and other disciplines while seeking admission for above said higher education courses. This is also one of the reasons why business education has failed in attracting the students towards it. Thus, from the point of view of employment opportunities, students of business education have no future.

Now globalisation, liberalisation and computerisation are the talks of the hour. Nation is moving towards 21st century. The whole world of business is getting computerised. Banking field, Insurance companies, major industries and factories, railway systems have already adopted the computer system. The system of computerisation itself is a big challenge to business education. There is a necessity of including the subject relating to computer in the syllabus of business education without which business education is going to prepare more un-employed graduates rather than creating employment opportunities.

Therefore, to face the above challenges of business education, the following measures or remedies can be suggested.

PART-III

REMEDIES OR MEASURES

(1) Provision should be made to teach business education from primary and high school levels all over the country.

(2) For teaching business education at primary and high school levels, students of business education only be appointed.

(3) Anyone subject relating to business education should be made compulsory at high school level only.

(4) Business education at college level (including plus two) must include computer as one of the compulsory subjects.

(5) Students of business education must and should be given 50% job reservation in both private and public sector banks, insurance companies, financial institutions, co-operative societies, industries, factories and other business establishments at the time of recruitment.

(6) Subjects like bankings, accountancy and business management should be included in the bank test to be conducted by BSRB and other private sector bank tests at the time of recruitment in banks; so that students of business education can pass the bank test and can get absorbed in banking sector.

(7) Subjects like accountancy, business management, marketing and salesmanship, taxation should be included in the tests to be conducted by insurance companies, investment trusts and financial institutions for recruiting its employees.

(8) The subject business mathematics should be made compulsory to the students of business education at P.U. level only so that students of business education can take any competitive examination with the subject mathematics.

(9) Business education at the college level (from P.U. level only) should be made more practical oriented. For this, students of business education have to undergo practical training in banks, insurance companies, industries and factories before they obtain their degree. 25 marks in each subject in each year should be kept (since P.U. level) for assessing practical knowledge of the students.

(10) Business education should aim at encouraging its students to start self-employment.

(11) Higher educational courses like M.B.A., C.A., I.C.W.A., C.S. are open to the graduates of all disciplines including engineering. Graduates of business education are finding it difficult to compete with engineering and science graduates and are unable to get seat especially for M.B.A. course. Therefore, seat reservation for the graduates of business education in the above said courses should be ensured.

(12) According to changing business environment, the course contents of business education should also be reviewed and if need be changed at least once in 10 years.

Thus it can be concluded that, in the changing business scenario business education is facing severe challenges, if not faced boldly with necessary action, students and dependents of business education have no future or little future.

REFERENCES

1. *University News* : January 10, 1994; June 6, 1994; November 14, 1994; January 16, 1995; July 31, 1995; March 4, 1996; November 11, 1996; June 9, 1997; August 11, 1997; October 20, 1997; February 10, 1997; October 27, 1997; November 31, 1997; December 8, 1997.

2. *Souvenir of 2nd state level conference* published by Federation of Teacher's Councils of Commerce and Management held at Davangere.

39 Challenges Before Business Education

—S.G. KULKARNI

According to Dr. V.K.R.V. Rao, "Commerce Education is a University discipline. It must fulfil the broad liberal requirements of University Education. In other words, Commerce Education should lead to the cultivation of mind, develop the capacity to distinguish between valid and fallacious reasoning, impart sense of social responsibility and lead to the development of the sense of duty and functional integrity."

Commerce Education has come a long way, beginning with producing typists, clerks, and accountants. It has entered into the era of producing managers and entrepreneurs. The basic contents of the course and the approaches, however, have not changed much.

The problems in Commerce Education can be understood through the words of Dr. B. Narayan, "there are many ills in Commerce Education, for example, lack of uniformity in curriculum, indiscriminate admissions, no linkage with professional bodies, apathy of the Government and U.G.C., towards Commerce Education, non-availability of suitable text-books and absence of practical approach."

The challenges in business education can be visualised from the fact that Commerce Education as it stands today is isolated from the realities of industrial environment. The most practical course has become highly theoretical over the years. The main reasons for this state of affairs are lack of dynamism in course content to meet the changing business environment, too much emphasis on theory, lack of coordination among Universities and professional bodies, lack of practical facilities and absence of reservation of jobs to commerce graduates. The bank and other institutions clamour for recruiting science and engineering graduates. Naturally, the students and parents look towards science and engineering education relegating Commerce Education as an after-thought.

PROBLEMS AND CHALLENGES

(1) Parallel Institutions

The greatest challenge in business education is commercialisation of Commerce Education by the 'teaching shops'. A private tuition class is the first choice of the students before they take admission to a college. This disease which started in science course has spread to commerce also. In cities, for subjects like Accountancy, Income-tax and Costing more than 90% of the students join private tuition classes run by their college teachers or others.

While there is nothing objectionable for students learning in a tuition class, there are some serious 'side-effects' of them. Bunking of classes, indiscipline, short-cuts to success in examination and over-emphasis on Accountancy are some of its maladies. This is the greatest challenge for our courses.

(2) One-way Teaching

Commerce courses which are supposed to be highly interesting tend to be boring due to 'one-way' and stereotype lecturing method. Group discussion, role-play, etc., are not adopted in our teaching due to overloading of syllabi, disproportionate strength, lack of necessary apparatus, etc. The passive approach in imparting knowledge does not invoke any enthusiasm.

(3) Lack of Training to the Teachers in Commerce

Mostly, the teachers in this faculty are theoretical, whereas most of the students come from business community with practical ideas. This results in a world of difference because urban students with English medium culture have wide exposure to information, which the teachers lack. Our courses are not challenging to them, because they can 'manage' them at the end of the academic year for passing the examination.

(4) Irrelevant Out-dated Syllabus

The syllabi are not revised in tune with the development in the industry. In most of the subjects the emphasis is on irrelevant and unwanted topics. For example — we teach about liquidation of firms and companies from pre-university to degree in both Accountancy and Commerce as if we want them to be the experts in winding up.

(5) Disproportionate Strength and Indiscriminate Admissions

Due to a large number of students in each class, it is difficult for the teachers to know their students individually. The method adopted in the class resembles more of 'shouting' rather than 'teaching'. Added to this is the problem of indiscriminate admissions which is determined by influence and donation, none of them appearing on the records.

(6) Stereotype Questions and Assurance to Next Class

There is no challenge in commerce courses because of stereotype questions in the examination with ample-choice, which means that a student can get through without studying the syllabus in full. Added to this drawback is the carry-over system of going to the next class, irrespective of the result.

(7) Research in Commerce

It is seen that research in commerce revolves around same titles except with some changes in respect of place or area. They make no significant contribution to the development of knowledge or solution of the problem of the industry. It is difficult to determine what problem the researcher is attempting to solve. There is no relation between what they have learnt or what they teach and the topic of their research. They do teaching in one line but research in another line.

Most of the research is Economics oriented. According to the Special Committee for Commerce Education, "this could be for the fact that professors who were in-charge were mostly men with their university training in Economics".

Those who do their M.Phils and Ph.Ds do not continue their research work except that of signing the thesis prepared by their students. Their research activity is measured in terms of the number of M.Phils and Ph.Ds produced by them, which is superficial.

There is a great scope for consultancy to the business undertakings or what can be termed as 'job research' so that the educational institutions help in solving the problems of business. This approach shall make research pragmatic and not just another bound volume in the library.

(8) Practicals in Commerce

In actual practice it is found that a commerce student does not know how to buy a D.D. or fill up an income-tax return. This most useful faculty can be made pragmatic by including some practicals in commerce. Following is the list of some such practical assignments :

Subject	Assignment
1. Marketing	Conducting of market survey Identifying misleading advertisements. Developing Ad. copy.
2. Taxation	Calculation of tax, filling up of tax-returns.
3. Accountancy	Account writing with computer packages.
4. Office Management	Using word processor, use of filing system, designing office layout, use of fax, pager, internet, etc.
5. Production Management	Visit to factories for studying location, layout, planning, etc.
6. Entrepreneurship	Computer video-games, project report, psycho-motor experiments to estimate risk-taking attitude.

For postgraduation in commerce, there should be internship programme in Industries and offices on the same pattern as that of company secretaryship.

Such an approach of introducing practicals in commerce will bridge the gap between theory and practice. This helps in bringing the students close to the teachers. The teachers get a change from routine lectures. The students will find practicals refreshing and their theoretical concepts become clear. Involving successful managers from local industries for guest lectures also helps in making the course challenging. It helps them in introducing themselves to practical field and self-employment. It is necessary to ensure that practicals help in shaping the personality of students and they do not become a mere show.

(9) Social Responsibility

The teachers and students of commerce should develop social responsibility by associating themselves with local trade associations, consumer associations, productivity councils, etc. For example, in one of the projects our students were involved in detection of duplicate ration cards. Such involvement helps in increasing their horizon of knowledge beyond the four walls of a classroom.

(10) Challenge of Liberalisation, etc.

Commerce courses have to cope up with the new waves of change in the form of liberalisation, privatisation, and globalisation, because they are indispensable. The teachers and students should think global, think big. We have to study Western Culture to match ourselves to the new environment. We may miss the bus, if we do not change from the study of stone age to the challenges of computer age which is faster than jet age.

In conclusion, it can be said in the present scenario of global liberalisation, the challenge for commerce courses is phenomenal. A mere theoretical knowledge without exposure to real life situations or applications will be inadequate to face the challenges of the changing scenario. The demands of skill required for banks, insurance, manufacturing and service are not the same as they were in the last decade due to introduction computers and scientific approach. The changing scenario has provided a great challenge to adopt new practices.

REFERENCES

1. Chand Bidi, *Commerce & Business Thought*, Deep & Deep Pub., New Delhi, 1993.
2. Sharangpani, *et al.*, "Towards a Value-Added Commerce Education", *University News*, Vol. XXXII, No. 2, Jan. 10, 1994, p. 1.

40 The Challenges Before Business Education in India

—G.A. HEGDE

The educational system that we have today is not an indigenously evolved one. It is actually derived from a methodology which was originally developed by the Western rulers. The chief function of this educational system was to produce a work force capable of performing the administrative chores for them. The right kind of education has to aim at empowering the individual, which should take place at the intellectual, emotional, and physical levels. Education with well-defined objectives and goals, imparts skills, inculcates values and helps to shape all-round personality development.

The business education in India, (so called Commerce education in those days) dates back to 1886, when the trustees of Pachiyappa's Charities Chennai (the then Madras) commenced their commercial school. In turn, GOI made a provision for teaching Commerce in Calicut in 1895 and later in Calcutta in 1903. Between 1903 and 1917, good many institutions came into existence in the places like Mumbai and Delhi. It informs us that there has been a historic growth in Business education.

Initially, Commerce education embarked with imparting basic knowledge of commerce and bookkeeping. Necessity is the mother of invention, which is responsible for inventing new things, techniques and practices. No doubt, change is the law of nature. Business by its nature is never constant and accelerating changes are taking place in every sphere. We have been observing that thoughts, assumptions, perceptions and values of human being are not constant, and are changing in tune with changing scenario.

Education system in general, business education in particular is not exception to that.

Business education throughout the world is in a flux. The reason for this is the changing and increasingly paradoxical nature of relationship between the society, state and higher education system. The present challenge before business education can be understood, within these dynamic complex relationships. It is true that quality in the business education is a greater challenge before us. There is an ongoing concern that business education is not able to respond sufficiently to the challenging needs of the Economic and Social challenges. One more undercurrent of thought is over-dependency on Public funds and it needs to be more cost conscious. On the other hand Indian Institutions or Universities will have to absorb the treatment of shock given by the Foreign Universities which are trying to dominate the Indian scene with their reputation. As the concept of Total Quality Management (TQM) is going to govern the future of educational world we cannot undermine the significance of Quality education. Quality is as DOHERY put it, "you cannot define it but you know it when you see it" we all have an instinctive understanding, based on common sense and conventional wisdom of what quality means. In another context, quality is related to the degree of satisfaction experienced from the beneficiary. Therefore, ever-changing and dynamic scene of business education calls for high Quality. How to inject quality is the basic, dominant, serious, pertinent challenge before business education.

Tomorrow's organization will be the knowledge creating organization, which fuels ideas and innovation, as well as the personal and organizational self-renewal. In a knowledge creating organization, every one is a knowledge worker. New knowledge always begins with the individual and the individual's personal knowledge is transformed into organizational knowledge. Forces of global markets, rapidly changing values and tastes among consumer, the new technologies, deteriorating natural resources, etc. will create a different dimension for the search of knowledge while, adjusting with this type of new trend, knowledge creation becomes irrecurable. Hence business education has to accept the fact that it cannot satisfy with the present curriculum. It poses a dull scene.

Therefore, by extending one more productive year a dual degree option may have to be thought of in order to make the potential and marketability of the receiver of business education.

Today's business world has felt that the academic institutions do not produce commerce and management graduates with the right kind of skills needed by them. There is a mismatch between product and demand. Here the challenge before business education is, we cannot produce whatever we can, but we have to produce whatever Society/Consumer wants. In this respect, the business houses are more dynamic to cope with the rapidly changing technology, while the Universities and colleges find it difficult to adopt quickly to the changing needs. Therefore, Universities will have to see that they should be adaptable, flexible and dynamic to meet the changes on a continuous basis. We are rapidly moving to internet, e-mail, multimedia, etc. These techniques breakdown barriers, customize instruction, make education and learning more cost-effective. The information Technology is going to provide us new ways of improved learning with less expense. It may deliver qualitative change in the nature of learning itself. It promotes life-long learning at work and at home. To adopt and absorb change, our teachers and students community is to be prepared mentally. Moreover, we academicians are stuffing the young minds of today with facts and figures of earlier innovations, rather than motivating them to innovate. This system will have to be stopped. Students must be taught in such a way that they can learn for themselves the new things of tomorrow. Curiosity, open-mindedness, objectivity, respect for evidence and capacity to think critically will constitute the mindset of future students. Therefore, institutions' goals and objectives will act as parameters while determining its legitimate entity. Curriculum, teaching, learning, research, consultancy, etc. are going to determine the factors of academic, excellency and health of the institutions of higher learning. At present our educational institutions have proved themselves to be incapable of assuming major responsibilities for the kind of business education necessary for India, to remain competitive in the new economy. Therefore, many of us are already frustrated by the slow pace of reform and feel instinctively that our system is lagging behind. Even the system of conventional department structure resulted in constraints which became confinements and boundaries became barriers. This has stifled growth of effectiveness and efficiency, cross fertilization, free exchange of ideas, innovation and creativity in the system. Therefore a big challenge before business education is necessity of more flexible adoptable healthy academic structure.

Moral, ethical and cultural values are really part of education which have in fact virtually been disappeared from the education text. Education, according to Mahatma Gandhi, was nothing without Character and Character was nothing without elementary personal purity. He attached more significance to character-building than mere literacy. In a dynamic changing environment, an acquired qualification will be tested in the light of personality and personal traits of the concerned. Hence components of personal traits play a golden role in establishing an excellent human personality. Today employment market also demands the personality possessing both excellent qualification with knowledge and strong personal traits. It is, therefore, felt the need to restructure educational institutions to evolve moral values. Moreover, today's urgent need is, we all of us have to learn how to live happily without sacrificing humanity.

Today, having seen the global trend of business, it may be said that "Commerce is the mother of all corruption". Any commercial activity, while awarding contract, issuing licence, have inbuilt potentiality for visible or invisible give and take. More interesting fact here is that maximum people involved in this corruption are the products of our education system, they may be politicians, Senior managers, Industrialists or dealers. Therefore, business ethics must be designed and implemented at all graduation level. Students of business education should be exposed to the fair and unfair dealings of business practices. Documented case studies need to be discussed in classrooms to bring home the message that one should be fair and transparent in business dealings. It must be recalled that fairness, honesty, transparency followed by business ethics were the important hallmarks of the long-lasting business houses.

EPILOGUE

We are knocking at the door of 21st century. When this door opens it will present an altogether different scenario which will overwhelm us, if we do not prepare ourselves to face the challenges. We are standing on the crossroads. Business education system has major responsibility of providing very competent people who can think strategically, comfort with modern technology, able to practise business ethics. Therefore, system of business education will have to face many challenges for its meaningful existence. If we have any stake in the future of this country, we must begin to prepare ourselves to face these challenges. No doubt, forthcoming years will be proved to be full of challenges, opportunities, and question marks to the system of business education, in the multisided changed environment.

41 Business Education : Problems and Solutions

—P.G. DANDIN

Universities are the organs of civilization and the intellectual pioneers of culture and the sanctuaries of the inner life of the nation. In the modern world university has become the main instrument of social change and the main agency for the development of human resources. Like this the business education became the main agency for change in the outlook of the Cos and the business organizations. Education is the core of human development and education is investment in people. No investment is greater than investment in people. The main job of the education is not merely to train the mind, body and soul of our youth but to draw their best to the fulfilment stage, to teach them the art of living harmoniously and graciously with one's own fellow men, to equip them, to face the realities of tomorrow and make them to follow a noble path. Somebody rightly said, that nothing on earth could be equated with knowledge.

As we have different organs to carry out the various functions of body, the education has different branches like Arts, Science, Law, Medicine, Business which include Commerce and Management, etc. As everybody is aware the base for all the activities is money. How to get it? How to use it? How to save it and reutilise it for one's growth and expansion is the knowledge given by business education at different levels like undergraduates, Diplomas and postgraduation. Though management education is a part of business education, it is relatively recent phenomenon, it is now widely used and recognized that it is vital for the process of national development. The change in the coming decade would be to bridge the managerial gaps in the development effort to make optimum use of the human and material resources already developed. Therefore, another challenge would be to extend and strengthen the use of management know-how to non-corporate, unorganised and other socially relevant sectors.

The teaching of Commerce education in India was started in 1886 when the trustees of Pachiyappa's Charities of Madras started their commercial school. In 1895 and 1903 the government of India made provision for teaching Commerce in Calicut and Calcutta respectively. Between 1903-1912 number of schools in the field of business education came into existence in big places like Bombay and Delhi. PG department in Commerce was established in 1921 in Lucknow which was an important milestone in the history of business education.

Formal management education was started in India in 1950. The first Commerce College was established in 1913 in Bombay known as Sydenham College. First MBA was started by Commerce Deptt. in Andhra University. Out of the total 8000 Colleges nearly 50% Colleges are giving education in Business/Commerce.

The leadership of U.S.A., in the field of Business education is well-known in the world. It is the only country which is offering maximum degrees in various subjects of Business education. The U.K. comes second in the list. The Business education people are widely recognized and highly paid in both these countries. In U.K. Commerce deptts. as such are not necessarily in Commerce faculties of University. In Germany almost all Universities have faculties for political economy which in most cases are divided into two branches : (1) Political economics (theoretical and applied economics including statistics, A/c, Law and Sociology), (2) Business administration including Accountancy, Economics, Statistics and Law. Next to U.S.A., India has the largest number of Business education institutions offering B.Com., M.Com., as well as IIM's. Our students are in full demand in other countries. Business education degree is considered a key to success in the corporate world.

The economic reforms initiated by Government of India have had a major impact on Indian industries. So Business education institutes will have to accept this challenge and manage host of changes to ensure their survival and reap the benefits of the global competitiveness. Now the whole world would be a common business field and all domestic, multinational and global players would play together to win the competition. The fittest will survive and rest will vanish. The business education should have linkages with industry in both theory and practice. Sir Walter Mobterly the Chairman, UGC of UK said that the right balance between theory and action is very much essential in the education system. Business education without industrial surrounding is like a fish without water and *vice versa*. There should be strong interface between these two for mutual benefit.

In the wake of liberalisation of Indian economy and involvement of multinational in growth and development of country, the Business education institutes have to rise to the challenge of producing business leaders. The courses being offered have to be modified accordingly with greater focus on service sector, practical management, quality, society services, practical ethics, environment management. The business schools have often been blamed for being slow in responding to changing business needs and, therefore, special effort is required to keep with the development that is taking place in the country as well as outside. The interrelation between academicians and practitioners is the need of the hour.

Globalisation of the society calls for new methods of instruction. The report of the UNESCO, International Commission on Education for the 21st century should have four pillars of foundations :

(1) Hearing to know.

(2) Hearing to live together.

(3) Hearing to do.

(4) Hearing to be.

The above requirements call for new methods of instruction.

BUSINESS EDUCATION PROBLEMS

(1) Large number of students.

(2) No restriction at the entry level.

(3) High ratio between students and teachers.

(4) No practical examination and training.

(5) Too many subjects lead to lack of specialisation in any subject.

(6) Old and outdated classroom teaching.

(7) Lack of practical knowledge on the part of the teachers.

(8) Essay type of answers.

(9) Lack of awareness among the students about courses available after B.Com.

(10) Non-involvement of practical people in the field of business education.

(11) Lack of tutorials and assignment work to the students.

(12) Lack of linkage of business education with requirement of industry.

(13) No apprenticeship training during vacation.

(14) No Job placement system after degree.

(15) Lack of field trips to factories and establishments in places nearby colleges.

(16) No personality development programmes.

(17) Too much dependency on University for syllabi.

POSSIBLE SOLUTIONS

(1) Higher education specially Commerce education should be made only to the students who really deserve it. A student pays just 3.5% of total expense as fees whereas balance amount is paid by the Government in the form of subsidy. It encourages everybody to go for higher education without any quality.

(2) Opening of new Colleges on any base should be stopped.

(3) Entry at the first year level should be made purely on the merit basis. Minimum 45% at higher secondary level for Commerce (Recently it has been introduced by Government of Rajasthan).

(4) Arrangement of field trips to Factories, Industries, Banks and other establishments in places nearby the colleges.

(5) Arrangement can be made for the students to undergo apprenticeship training during vacations.

(6) Solving management case study to take managerial decisions.

(7) Using modern teaching methods like Slides, Projectors, VCP/VCR, TV/Internet.

(8) Providing various facilities to the students and staff for carrying out research projects and understanding the problems of the business world.

(9) Introduction of 2-4 months' practical training to the students of part-time base.

(10) Inviting practical people from industry to give lectures to the students.

(11) Conducting of group discussions and interviews.

(12) Preparation of project report work should be assigned as a separate subject (Recently it was introduced by Goa University).

(13) Internal marks can be awarded to the students who regularly write and submit assignments.

(14) Autonomy should be given to the Commerce/Business schools to frame the syllabi by taking the local requirement of industries into consideration.

(15) Objective type of questions should be introduced to encourage the students to understand all the chapters.

(16) Business education deptt. and industries should work together in identifying areas of research which should be action-oriented.

(17) Teachers should be allowed to take up consultancy services in the field of Project planning, Accounting, Tax planning, Marketing research, etc. So it helps them to expand their knowledge.

42 Business Education for Posterity

—R.V. GANACHARI

Call of the hour is to pause for sometime for introspection regarding negotiability of traditionally trained graduates and post-graduates in commerce with reference to the changing environment in global concepts.

We stand at the dawn of the new era because of the revolution in information technology that is sweeping the competitive world.

The traditional training imparted at Colleges and Universities as per course pattern in the light of syllabi, divorced from professional skills, needed for trade and industry is heading towards extinction because the entire system has failed to deliver the goods which was expected at the time of formulating the courses. Commerce graduates have become outdated with no job opportunities. The present system of education has reduced them incapable of pursuing self-employment. There is a yawning difference between theory and practice, what we are offering and what is needed.

The one and the only panacea to the issue confronting, of late, is to recast and remould the Business Education with practical orientation making it more socially relevant in order to subserve radical changes and complex environment.

Business Education a synonym for Commerce Education is a distinct discipline disseminating business skills and talents on systematic way forging the students to take up a career in business on different levels. Gone are the days when it was confined to type-writing, shorthand, book-keeping, etc. Globalization has created new challenges to the business and industrial world.

Unbridled growth of trade and commerce has increased the need in abundant measure for Business Education in India. There is a change beyond expectation in the attitude of organizational issues and professional approach to business management by trained personnel for various areas in the industry. The University and the Industry must work in cohesion on questions of common concern and come out with appropriate measures. There must be perfect interaction between academicians and industrial sectors.

The introduction of B.B.M. Course is a first step in the right direction where the students are exposed to some kind of practical training, visits to industrial establishments and preparing project reports under instructions of the Executive of industrial establishment with guidance of a faculty member. By this process, the students are made to face the business world with ground realities.

Now-a-days there has been mushroom growth of Institutions with little infrastructure offering management degrees or diplomas. These Institutions pose a serious threat in maintaining high standards and care has to be taken against this pollution by the competent bodies while granting permission to institutions who admit the students on various considerations. Suitable reforms are needed in the examination system for evaluating performance of the students.

In order to do away with the deficiencies and develop Business Education in pace with the present-day requirements, some modest suggestions are placed before this august congregation :

(i) The entry to courses should be based on procedure consisting of written test, group discussion, and interview. The students with apt attitude, right temperament and conducive inclination towards business education should be admitted and trained rigorously which will enhance credibility for the degrees in the business world.

(ii) There is a need to bridge linkages with professional bodies on the one hand and the long-standing management bodies on the other with a view to make it professionally oriented. Professionals, Business Executives and persons with varied experience in the field should be drawn as the guest faculty to reduce the gap between theory and practice.

(iii) Redesigning of courses with relevant subjects to meet the present-day requirement is an important aspect. Security Analysis,

Computer Applications, Business Promotion and Project Planning, Sales Management, Human Resources Development, Financial Analysis have gained momentum overtaking conventional subjects. The process of transformation appears to be difficult task and if not impossible one.

(iv) The research should be encouraged by extending necessary assistance. Chalk and talk method should be reduced giving way for group discussions, case study method, seminar sessions and industry visits.

(v) The indifferent attitude of students stems from lack of involvement in teaching by the teacher who has to inspire the students to learn the subjects. The administration should take lead in deputing teaching staff to attend Seminars, Conferences and Refresher Courses which will improve teaching skill with more information, even if they come in the middle of academic year.

There will be breakdown of the Education system, if the teacher does not motivate himself to discharge responsibilities, since he is the life blood of it.

43 Business Education in India : Renaissance — Need of the Hour

—G.L. NARAYANAPPA,
D. PRADEEP KUMAR AND V. MALLIKARJUNA

A growing economy requires talented resources. Talented resources can be developed only through long-term planning and timely allocation of ingredients. Since independence the Government has concentrated on few institutions and started to look for quality products from those institutes only. The development of at least the secondary level institutions to augment the requirements of the Business/Industry was not given a fair thought. In this back drop many institutions came into existence, started attracting the aspirants to the industry, given them training at a very substandard level which only they could afford to. The industry even had to accommodate this substandard quality as their requirement is huge. The sufferers are the industry, economy and the nation as a whole. If the system continues, India can never enter the 21st century and all the efforts toward Globalization and the dreams of becoming superpower are only superficial. How then can India look forward from the present growth-hindrant education system in its 50th year of independence? Undoubtedly it calls for revolution in the Business Education which can add competence to the managers, industry and the nation.

EXISTING SYSTEM — A DIAGNOSTIC APPROACH

Before a new system is proposed for Business Education present system has to be thoroughly analysed, shortcomings diagnosed. Alongwith the premier institutes Business Education has started in Universities and its affiliated colleges. The recruitment of the staff in the University and the affiliated college could not attract the cream because of inadequate facilities and less remunerations compared to the industry. Even the recruited staff are not able to cope up with the dynamic industry scenario owing to the dearth of faculty development of programmes. In view of the absence of proper support from the Universities and the Managements of the affiliated colleges there exists no Dynamism and Competition in the teaching field and the faculty are becoming stagnant and resorting to conventional teaching methods.

Though the curriculum, syllabus and teaching methodology are adopted from the premier institutes, the Universities and the Affiliated Colleges fall short of bringing in such quality. The M.B.A. Programme is run as just another Department and the specific requirements of the Highly Professional Programme as it should be are not understood by the Universities/Managements.

Initially the requirement of the management graduates was huge and the institutions could not supply the much-needed man-power. The opportunities thus created for the Management Graduates have lured many and the Managements cashed it. The Government gave away the permissions to more than required and quality became secondary.

The fee structure of M.B.A. Programme varies from State to State and Institute to Institute. While some Institutes charge exorbitant fee, still offer the same facilities as of the Institutes charging less. The Institutes charging less in spite of their best efforts could not raise to the level of premier institutes due to the shortage of funds.

Struck with so many problems from varied fronts Business Education in India could still somehow serve the needs of the industry in the closed economy. As now the gates are open for Globalisation and liberalisation the industry is virtually on a hunt for quality managers.

ERA OF GLOBALISATION

Globalisation offers a wide variety of products to the Indian Consumer. MNCs brought along with them the most Advanced Technology, the much differentiated product offers, world class management and with the latest techniques of understanding the consumer behaviour they are much closer to the Indian consumer. Many Indian corporates succumbed — merged, takenover and sold to the MNCs, and those in the market, understanding the need are reengineering and moving towards total quality management. The MNCs are not leaving any opportunity to gain even meagre shares of the market. The financial muscle of MNCs, the experience of Indian companies, the jazzy foreign brands, the trusted Indian names are in the foray. The war is on....

Can an average Indian Management Graduate dare to fight out the battle? If only he adds his skills of analyzing information, perseverance, commitment, persuasion, risk-taking ability, creative and quick strategic decision-making capability under severe stress to his armoury.

Yea... it is certainly a challenge to the B schools in India to inculcate the habit of winning the battles.

TASKS AHEAD

Based on the thorough analysis of the present system the authors present here a modified system of training. It is the need of the hour that the Govt. must now take an active role in planning the business education. The Government must conduct research on quality and quantity of manpower requirement of industry and the output of the B schools. Government should establish the quality standards to the B schools and which fall short should not be allowed.

At the same time the management of B schools should know and understand the nature and scope of the expectations of the Industry and support the programme with increased commitment and better provision of facilities *viz.*, Access to information highway, conducting management meets, Arranging Placements, Guest Faculty, etc. Apart from this every Institute should affiliate with a professionally managed firm which operates in a competitive market. The University authorities must ensure the industry affiliation to all its affiliated colleges. To procure the cream into faculty positions better remuneration and facilities on par with industry are to be provided.

The faculty must identify the changing needs of the industry, inputs required, ways and means of inculcating dynamism and competence through innovative teaching methods. To augment the skills of teachers more Faculty Development Programmes are to be organized. The faculty can learn and contribute to the industry by offering consultancy services.

One such arena, where students can undergo the experience of competitive environment under stress is the project work. The industry must view it seriously and thoroughly train the students under Project Work. Barring a few, most of the B schools are sending their students to project works after second semester and for 8 weeks only. The duration must be extended to at least 90 days, and the students must undertake the project after the third semester, after acquiring a better insight into the subjects to make it a meaningful exercise. In addition to this continuous training is to be given to the students in all the concepts by its affiliated industry.

Theoretical concepts can better be understood if students can take decisions in a simulated environment. The methodology adopted must incorporate such simulations in all the functional areas. For example in Marketing, Simulated Market Experiment can be undertaken. It requires the participation of Super Markets/Companies directly concerned. Number of items of various product lines can be brought in and arranged in the model of a shopping complex. Student can plan the alterations in the product offers and display them whereby decisions on sales promotional measures, retailing, Advertising, Packaging and Labelling, Pricing, etc. can be taken with the help of their theoretical knowledge. In the process they specify the objectives of each decision. A group of consumers can be called in and their behaviour and responses to the offer can be studied, an exercise which can give students a practical understanding of all the marketing concepts. Exercises of this nature being expensive, Universities/Groups of Colleges can undertake, benefiting more number of students.

To impart skills of international level B schools require advanced and expensive facilities. The fee structure accordingly should match. Care must be taken that uniform fee exists throughout the nation as are the facilities.

All said and done, Business Education in India calls for active involvement from Government, Industries, Universities, Managements of Affiliated Colleges, Faculty and Students to strike a balance between the requirements of Industry and the output of B schools.

44 Challenges Before Business Education in India in Open Regime

—B.L. PAWAR

INTRODUCTION

Business education means talent qualities of development of individuals. It can be defined as in the field of business as the development of habits, skills, understanding and ability to adjust to effective living and to make oneself busy with job, work or activity in our society. Business education can be defined as a process of acquiring the Art and Science of a particular subject relating to business *i.e.* Management, Accounting, Banking, Trade and Commerce, etc. When we are talking about Business Education we invariably refer three dimensions of Business Education *viz.* (a) Commerce Education (b) Management Education, (c) Professionalisation in Commerce Education.

PRESENT POSITION OF COMMERCE GRADUATE

Looking at the product of Business Education from the Institutes and Colleges following observations are very commonly noted :

(1) The Commerce Graduates cannot even be efficient Clerks or Accountants.

(2) The M.B.A. Graduates obviously have very high expectation but get lower grade jobs.

(3) The M.B.A. Degree holders fail to be efficient managers even when they get certain opportunities having a few exceptions.

(4) Management Degree seems to be losing sheen. Less number of companies recruit students from college this

year (*Times of India*, dated 15-1-98). This placement problem may be due to the situation particularly bad in the financial sector and even with the economy slowing down and what will be the new economic policy of the new Government.

Therefore, one of the main objectives of Business Education should be to train young students for different jobs in business and Government Enterprises as also to equip them to manage efficiently their own enterprises, if they choose self-employment. Naturally, business education or its curriculum has to take note of different opportunities (jobs as well as self-employment) available in the economy of the country. It has thus to study the specific job requirements, identify the existing gaps and redesign the curriculum from time to time to improve its utility and worth in ever-changing business world. Application of new changes anticipated in business and new concepts of different subjects of Business Education has been significantly influenced by a changing world-wide competitive environment, recent economic and financial sector liberalization and advance in data processing and information technology. These changes mandate shift in business education as well.

NEED OF BUSINESS EDUCATION RELEVANT TO CHANGING PERIOD

To achieve the objective of rapid-growth, opening up of economy, better use of resources, competition and market friendliness both at domestic and global levels is necessary. Eventually, the economy started moving from State to open markets through deregulation and liberalisation.

As we passed the seven years of nineties of the present century and stand on the threshold of the 21st century, automation, extreme specialization and computerization would become common place and the order of the day. "Karnataka Government is all set to create tech-savvy generation, with the intention of making the next generation Computer Literates. The Government will also endeavour to increase number of college students who specialise in information technology to meet the needs of the I.T. Industry" (*Times of India*, dated 24-1-1998).

The hereditary styles of management will fast become outmoded and professional management will dominate the entire management scene. As of today, there are 213 Universities (including deemed Universities) and nearly 8000 colleges in our country. The students enrolment is more than 4 million — nearly 88% offering Graduate courses, 10% Postgraduate courses and 2% research. There is mismatch between education and employment and lack of planning in the setting up of new universities and colleges has led to great degree of frustration. The complexity coupled with pressure to expand, mismatch of supply and demand and limited sources pose a serious challenge to educational planners in India.

In view of the liberalisation, globalisation and privatisation all over the world, we must understand that what the business was 55 years ago, it is no longer today and is going to be further changed in years to come because of the impact of many powerful and many a times conflicting forces, ideologies and development of science and technology.

CHALLENGES BEFORE BUSINESS EDUCATION

Our first degree colleges of Arts, Science and Commerce do not come up to the standard. Our degrees are not considered to be of international comparability. This is because, a large majority of these colleges are engaged in mere teaching. There is very little of self-study. The students are expected just to learn textbooks and not understand the subject. They just rely on dictation of notes and guidebooks or private coaching classes and obtain limited knowledge. Such knowledge is not substantial in the age of "Electronic Commerce and Business". In the context of Electronic Commerce I am furnishing the challenges of business education.

ELECTRONIC COMMERCE

Under this head the following points are covered :

(1) Change due to Internet.

(2) Office Automation — Office Elimination.

(3) Material Management and Technology of Production.

(4) Product Development.

(5) Marketing through Internet.

(6) Multinational Companies.

The Electronic commerce is very speedily emerging as a new phase of commerce shattering the traditional concepts of Home as well as Foreign trade and the aids to trade. The International walls of restrictions on free flow of goods and services are collapsing and the measures taken by various countries to protect their economy from foreign competition are now broken.

The opportunities, the possibilities and the prospect in respect of international trade are far better and greater than they have been in any of our lifetimes, in any time in human history. These are the features that will have an enormous bearing on the way the business is done, all over the world.

CHANGE DUE TO INTERNET

The swift rise in the business use of the internet has created a worldwide communication web that allows network of smart people to collaborate from all points on the globe.

Today more than half of the gross domestic products (GDP) in rich economies is now "Knowledge based", including industries such as telecommunication, education, television, computers, software, pharmaceuticals.

Hi-tech industries have almost doubled their share of manufacturing output over the past two decades to around 25 per cent and knowledge intensive services are growing even faster.

Twenty-five years ago only 5000 computers existed in the whole world. Today these are more than 150 million.

OFFICE AUTOMATION — OFFICE ELIMINATION

We are advancing new technologies, newer jargon and a plethora of application possibilities have only intensified the plans of transition. The early promises of computer era are now becoming a reality and future corporations will either live or die by digital sword. The early promises of office automation can now be seen in action.

(1) E-mail Electronic mail has become a reality.

(2) Apart from conversation one can exchange data, reports, software and information.

(3) Now Teams can work together on the same application at the same time.

This represents the explosion in 'net working' in office automation within software, the fastest growing segments in packaged software.

(4) All this above indicates the new found popularity of office automation.

(5) In the future this trend is likely to accelerate.

IMPACT OF PRODUCTION MATERIAL MANAGEMENT AND TECHNOLOGY OF PRODUCTION

The design and operation of manufacturing systems present and future require a radical change in our approaches outlook and practices.

(a) The manufacturing units in the changing scenario are exposed to rapid and high speed change in technology of production.

(b) Technological change is too high in the areas of communication, transportation and in the use of production of electronics.

(c) The Hi-Tech business will require Hi-Tech materials management. Materials managers will not only have to keep themselves abreast of the latest changes but also learn to anticipate and management changes.

(d) Competition is far greater now requiring companies to be more cost-effective. They have to produce reliable quality goods.

(e) Product life-cycles are becoming shorter. Innovation is the rule of the day.

(f) The revolution in information technology and data communication facilitate the linking of marketing suppliers, distributors and key customers directly to the factory.

PRODUCT DEVELOPMENT

(a) With globalisation the pace of change has accelerated and many new products and service innovations are invading markets.

(b) With the introduction of new product and services in the market new needs and demands have been created.

(c) The need of the Indian Industries is to re-engineer the entire process of manufacturing.

(d) Only re-engineering is not enough but the managers, employees and the workers will have to be motivated to accept the change and support the process.

MARKETING THROUGH INTERNET

(a) The Internet is a tool of empowerment that unleashes creativity and foster greater communication.

(b) The Internet takes your marketing efforts beyond conventional lines.

(c) It is a powerful weapon in your company's arsenal of marketing tools.

MULTINATIONAL COMPANIES

The Indian Industries will need constantly reviewed strategic information system to meet the challenges of multinationals who are gaining the information through the networks.

Multinational companies move quickly to take advantage of the internet transplanting brands to the worldwide web. But they face a major marketing challenge because of public suspicion of multinationals.

Everything changes with the change of the era. Sometimes environment acts as a catalyst to facilitate this change. Commerce and Business Education is also no exception. In the context of changing scenario of India and its consequences on the corporate world, a fresh look over the future expectations from Business Education is required. Hence the development of human resources with high levels of education and skills is necessary. A well-trained, creative and knowledge-rich talented people in the country are the real agent of change to meet the challenges. The educationalists and learned thinkers can give a further thought to this, so that the present education system will be useful and fruitful to the society.

REFERENCES

1. Prof. S.B. Pandit — (i) "Agent of Changes" (ii) "Electronic Commerce". Paper circulated in Refresher Course at Amalner of U.M. University, Jalgaon, Nov. 1997.
2. Dr. S.S. Sahasrabudhe, "Re-orientation of Management and Business Education for Future". Paper of the XXth Conf. of I.A.M.D. & I.U.C. B.E.R, Kolhapur, Jan. 1990.
3. Prin. Dr. R.J. Gujarathi, "Some Issues Relating to Commerce curriculum in changing times". Paper submitted at the XXth Conf. of I.A.M.D. and I.U.C.B.E.R. at Kolhapur, Jan. 1990.
4. Prin. R.G. Sharangpani, "Value-added Commerce Education". Paper prepared for R.C. of North Mah. Uni., Jalgaon, Nov. 1997.
5. Dr. B.B. Ekshinge, "Future Directions of Business Education in India". Paper for XXth Conf. of I.A.M.D. & I.U.C.B.E.R. at Kolhapur, Jan. 1990.
6. N.K. Uberoi (Editor), "UGC Professional Competency in Higher Education". Prepared by CPDHE, Delhi.
7. *The Times of India*, dated 15th & 24th Jan. 1998.

45 Business Education in Retrospect and Prospect

—J.G. NAIK

CONCEPTUAL FRAMEWORK

The concept of Business education, in its wide spectrum, includes commerce education, management education and professional education. The aim of the business education is to develop entrepreneurs, business-oriented employees, professional managers, professional consultants and academicians.

COMMERCE EDUCATION IN RETROSPECT

The commerce education made its beginning in India in unorganised private Commercial Training Institutes, about a century back. The basic objective was to train the students to take up clerical and typing work. With the widening of business horizons and complexities trained account writers were felt. These private Commercial Institutes could not rise up to the occasion. So the real education in commerce at the colleges began in the year 1913 by starting Sydenham College of Commerce and Economics in Bombay.

The commerce education now begins after tenth standard of high school. Prior to the introduction of 10+2 scheme, at high school level commercial subjects were taught.

Our universities adopted commerce education only in 1961 when Special Committee on commerce education headed by V.K.R.V. Rao strongly recommended that commerce education is a distinct field of education and there should be independent departments in the universities. Now there are over 4000 colleges imparting commerce education working under 130 universities.

MANAGEMENT EDUCATION IN RETROSPECT

The growth of management education in India can be traced to the establishment of four Indian Institutes of Management (IIMs). Now two more IIMs are started. The IIMs offer two years' full-time postgraduate diploma courses. These are sought after PGDM courses, for the candidates get handsome salary and enviable positions. Besides, there are about 25 management institutes like IRMA, NIBM, XLR, etc., which conduct management diploma courses. About 85 state universities and six central universities have also set up postgraduate management departments to conduct MBA programmes. In addition, there are over 400 autonomous private management institutes which are known as Business schools, recognized by All India Council for Technical Education (AICTE). Due to liberalisation and globalisation of our economy many foreign universities especially from USA, Australia, UK have come up in joint venture to conduct management education programmes at international standard. Adding to this many financial institutions like UTI and industrial houses like Nirma have started management institutes in the recent times.

PROFESSIONAL EDUCATION IN RETROSPECT

The accounting professional education is regulated by two national level Quasi-Government Institutes. They are : The Institute of Chartered Accountants of India (ICAI) conducting Chartered Accountants examination and regulating financial accounting profession. The Institute of Cost and Works Accountants of India (ICWAI) conducts Cost Accountants examination and regulates the cost accounting profession.

The profession of company secretary is regulated by the Institute of Chartered Secretary of India (ICSI). Besides, the Institute of Chartered Financial Analyst of India conducts professional exam of Chartered Financial Analyst.

SWOT ANALYSIS OF COMMERCE EDUCATION

Though the seminar seeks to probe into Business Education. I wish to confine the SWOT (Strength, Weakness, Opportunities and Threat) Analysis of Commerce Education to throw light on how other wings of the Business education are cutting into its predicaments.

STRENGTH

The strength of commerce education lies in the following :

1. It has a long-standing existence.
2. It costs very low fees affordable by anybody.
3. It is a choice of bright and many mediocre students.
4. It has well set up infrastructure and wide network.
5. It is well regulated by the universities.

WEAKNESS

The commerce education as it prevails now is suffering from the following weaknesses :

1. Indiscriminate admissions.
2. It is narrow, traditional and conceptual education.
3. It lacks practical orientation.
4. It lays more stress on mechanism than thought provocation.
5. Lack of uniformity in syllabi.
6. Poor standard of textbooks, question papers and evaluation.
7. Step-motherly attitude of UGC in funding commerce education and research.
8. Lack of liaison with business, industry, B-Schools and professional bodies.
9. Lack of appropriate trainers' training.
10. Teachers' apathy to changes in curriculum.
11. Lack of rapport with professional bodies.
12. Financial crisis, with UGC and Govt. cutting grants.
13. Lack of teachers, teaching aids, and willingness to work.

OPPORTUNITIES

The commerce graduates are not absorbed in the jobs which really need commercial acumen. Employers are crazy about appointing either engineering or science graduates for such jobs. Commerce graduates lack confidence and entrepreneurship. All these are because of the above cited weaknesses. If efforts are made in the following directions the commerce graduates have very fine opportunities :

1. Make syllabus inter-disciplinary.
2. Develop analytical mind and strong thinking power.
3. More exposure to the practical world through work assignment in industry and business houses.
4. Conduct Business clinical exercises.
5. Holiday assignments of business surveying, report writing, etc.
6. At least once in seven years syllabi should be updated and that after fifth year draft syllabi be brought out for discussion and considerations.
7. Proper teachers motivation and training.
8. Establish good rapport with the business, industry and professional bodies.
9. Self fund-generating activities like consultation, conducting training, surveys, etc. for business and industry.

THREAT

1. Threat to commerce education is not from science or engineering courses. It is the management courses like BBA, BBM, MBA, PGDM, etc. that are going to pose threat. If the weaknesses are not overcome the day is not far off when commerce colleges will have to shut down the B.Com. course and run BBA like courses at a lower scale.

2. Industry sponsored and foreign university courses are also going to eat away commerce students. Even they may pose threat to the B-Schools itself.

3. The professional courses have opened up their courses after 10+2 of any discipline, of course subject to passing of foundation courses. As a result the creamy layer of commerce students, who often prefer these professional courses may discontinue commerce education and directly go for professional course after completing foundation exams of the Institutes.

4. With great stride in the computerization of business houses and industries, accounting function of commerce graduates has substantially reduced. Fast growth in electronic media and information technology is going to pose threat to commerce education.

BUSINESS EDUCATION IN PROSPECT

The Business Education in future is not confined to internal business world but international world. The students must be well-trained in handling international dealings. They must be trained in handling new technologies. The future need is for well-educated, trained and ready-to-work business graduates.

There is going to be dire need for well-qualified business graduates in Hopitality industry, Health care institutes, private establishments, Non-government Organizations, educational institutes and co-operatives.

With drying up of Government employment opportunities, the Business graduates may have to be self-employed. For this they need better training and inculcation of entrepreneurship.

To meet these challenges three wings of Business education must gear up. As far as the professional education is concerned, the professional bodies are well-tuned to the changing environment. The professionals are also well aware that if they are not relevant to the existing situations, they have doomsday.

The B-Schools do face the problem of faculty, infrastructure, funds and foreign universities. They have to go in for faculty exchange programmes, Inter-school students exchange programme and sharing of library facilities through internet.

The commerce colleges should build up on their existing strength and further consolidate. Commerce colleges should come up with computer labs, new instruments of electronic media, clinical labs for business studies. By regulating students teachers ratio and increasing practical training we can see our commerce graduates well-suited for tomorrow's business world. For this we need determination and commitment. The intake of after-taught students must be stopped. Also people coming to teaching profession as a stopgap and stepping stone must be discouraged. There must be freedom to appoint and fill in the vacancies of teachers lying for over a decade. Besides standard fees, there should be provision to collect additional fees for extra facilities in laboratories. If the remedial measures suggested above are not taken at right earnest the commerce colleges will be deserted.

46 University-Industry Interface in Business Education

—M.R. SHOLLAPUR

INTRODUCTION

The system of education through its network of institutions with a well-designed curriculum and predetermined instructional objectives and methods, imparts knowledge, infuses values, promotes an attitude of reason and produces the skilled manpower. The skills so built are to be related to the requirements of the society in general and the developmental needs of the nation in particular.

The system of education is a product of the total system or the overall environment of the nation. Besides the socio-cultural traditions and ethos; the economic needs and the future aspirations thereto, the long range strategies to be pursued and followed etc., have a moulding effect on the educational system. Especially the needs of the nation in terms of the type of manpower required get amply reflected in the curriculum so that the products of the system fit well in different streams of occupation and in different strata of nation building. "Higher education and the intelligentsia nurtured by it have a special role in determining the quality of the overall environment. Higher education also supplies a wide range of increasingly sophisticated and ever-changing variety of manpower needed in industry, agriculture, administration and services."[1] It is equally true that the system of education, at times, influences the overall environment. The educational system through its studies and research attempts to see clearly the problems confronting the society, suggests alternative solutions, makers choices and finalises the course of action for the betterment of the overall environment. Thus, there is an ongoing reciprocity between these two, in the sense that, the educational system being influenced by the total system attempts to meet the desired expectations of the sectoral needs of the overall system and the overall system being realigned on the suggestions of the educational system.

Against this background, the present paper attempts to examine the possibility of establishing interface between the University and the Industry, in so far as the commerce discipline is concerned and tries to identify the strong areas where a meaningful interface can be established between the two.

The paper is divided into four sections. The first section presents in brief, a backdrop of Commerce Education in India. The second section prepares a case for interface in Commerce Education. The third section deals with the nature and ramifications of interface highlighting the areas of interface between the University and Industry. The last section concerns itself with the future course of action in making the 'Interface' a meaningful exercise.

The term 'University' when read in this paper in the context of interface/interaction/linkage signifies the Schools of Commerce and the Postgraduate Departments of the Universities which are engaged in imparting the Business Studies, also called as Commerce Education. Similarly, the term 'teacher' in this context means the teachers of commerce. Besides, the term 'industry' that is referred to in the present paper is looked upon as an entity or a system concerned with production and supply of goods and services to the community at large with a network of sub-systems *viz.*, production, marketing, financing, personnel, etc. It is tied up with the environment where a wide variety of forces like competitors, suppliers, government consumers, workers, financiers, etc. operate.

I

COMMERCE EDUCATION : A BACKDROP

The formal teaching of Commerce in India can be traced back to 1886 when the Trustees of Pachyappa's Charities (Madras) started their commercial school. The Government of India made provision for teaching Commerce in Calicut in 1895 and later in Calcutta in 1903. Between 1903 to 1912, good many institutions came into existence in the places like Bombay and Delhi. The Sydenham College of Commerce and Economics, Bombay (1913) and the Postgraduate Department of Studies in Commerce in Lucknow (1921) laid foundation stones at different strata of Commerce education.

Commerce education takes a formal beginning at +2 stage, though some stray issues related to Commerce field are dealt with at the secondary level. The main thrust at +2 stage is to present a broad outline of the course based on the elementary conceptual foundation. The course aims at preparing the students either for undergraduate stream in Commerce or for the professional stream through Foundation Courses. At the undergraduate level, a thorough knowledge regarding a wide ranging areas like Accounting (Financial accounting, Cost accounting, Management accounting, etc.), Banking, Taxation, Business Management, Business laws etc. is given. Besides these subjects of general background education, specializations are also offered preferably in the final year. The course prepares the students either to take up careers in banking, insurance, transport industries or to launch an independent business on a small scale or to pursue studies in professional or academic lines. At the postgraduate level, the emphasis is on preparation of specialists as required by industry in its key job-areas like Accounting, Finance, Tax Planning and Management, Marketing, HRD, etc. and accordingly a vast majority of the postgraduates eventually get employed in industry both in private and public sectors. A few may launch an independent business or professional unit based on the specialized knowledge gained; some may find employment in government organizations and still a few may continue their education further (M.Phil. or Ph.D.) with the objective of taking up career in academia as teachers and researchers.

Over the years, there has been an expansion in Commerce education both quantitatively and qualitatively. The total strength of the students in higher education and of the commerce education therein was 3.97 lakhs and 0.34 lakh respectively in 1950-51. It has increased to 44.25 lakhs and 9.70 lakhs in 1990-91. The proportionate share of commerce students to the total of the students' community has shot up from 8.6% to 22.0% during the span of four decades. There are at present more than 4,000 commerce colleges and more than 125 postgraduate departments of commerce in different Indian universities. The commerce education with its incipient focus on book-keeping, typing, shorthand, commercial correspondence, etc. has now branched out into more than one hundred specialisations.[2] The expansion of this kind may be attributed to factors like growth of trade and industry, increasing emphasis on organizational problems, growth in demand for scientific approach to business management, and above all, qualification in commerce being considered as a desirable condition for different job areas in the industry. Thus, the industry has an enormous stake in commerce education because the output of the universities are the inputs in the industry. Hence, 'the academicians in the institutes should not be totally isolated from the industry and other customers of their educational system. They should teach what the market wants and not what they know.'[3]

II

PREPARING A CASE FOR INTERFACE

The four decades (1950-1990) of Indian industrial scenario is characterized by the predominance of public sector with social welfare orientation, policy of protection from foreign competition, granting of generous subsidies, less foreign interactions, entry barriers to MNCs, etc. Accordingly, industry required the manpower which had a general exposure to all the functional areas of business and this need was largely met by the institutions imparting commerce education. Consequent on adopting the new economic policy since 1991, vast changes have taken place both in the policy and orientation concerning the industrial sector. These include delicensing of industry, permission for foreign investments, elimination of export-import restrictions, abolition of export subsidies, equitisation of public sector, etc. The resultant phenomena of such a strategic shift from regulation to liberalization and from protection to integration with international markets are free and fierce competition, wider applicability of theory of competitive advantage, survival of the fittest. This necessitates the Indian industries to evolve new thinking, new approaches and new skills to acquire a greater competitive ability, cost effectiveness, quality consciousness so that they can make an effective inroad into the fiercely competitive markets. The personnel requirements of the industry, therefore, are the 'specialists', unlike the erstwhile 'generalists'. It needs specialists in the areas like Finance, Accounting, Production, Marketing, Human Resources Development, Information Technology, Computer Applications, etc. The specialization has become so intensive that even in these broad spectra of functional areas, further specializations have emerged. Highly specialized, thoroughly professional and globally efficient personnel are the needs of the hour. In this context, 'the universities and institutes of higher learning cannot keep toying with producing unmarketable ware, but have to get on to produce the best of technical and intellectual human capital to meet the global competition.'[4] It is, therefore, imperative on the part of the University and the Industry as well, to sit together and discuss the issues which are of mutual interest. The plausible issues of common interest are :

(a) What are the needs of the industry?

(b) What type of personnel does the industry require?

(c) What the industry expects from the products of the University?

(d) Is the commerce curriculum designed according to the needs of the industry?

(e) Is the University competent enough both academically and financially to produce the products as desired?

(f) Is the University undertaking research studies on those issues which are directly concerned to the industry?

(g) Is the industry willing to extend the facility of industrial training to the students?

Hence it is felt that an interaction between the University and Industry is the need of the hour to rid of the issues which have been the cause of their concern. The case of interfacing is based on the assumption that both the University and Industry possess things which can be gainfully exchanged on the basis of mutual benefits. The University can extend to the Industry the benefits of knowledge, the fruits of their research findings, the academic infrastructure, etc. On the other hand, Industry can provide a platform to the University to testify whether the theoretical knowledge of the latter stands the test of the time, besides supporting the activities of the University in varied ways.

III

NATURE AND RAMIFICATIONS OF INTERFACE

The term 'interface' signifies a situation where the University and Industry seek a common meeting ground, coordinate the theoretical knowledge and practical experiences into a common pool, assist each other in understanding the problems and seeking solutions to the best advantage of both. "A link can be established provided a polarity is established where we propose to bring about a linkage. It must be understood that a link is not lassoing of an unwilling party. Linkage, therefore, is a two-way understanding which alone can bring to fruition the objective of such a linkage."[5] Thus, interface is an ongoing willing interaction or linkage, yielding gains to both the participating entities.

. The University and the Industry can establish interface at varying levels with different degrees. Following are the areas where the strong linkage can be forged between the University and Industry :

1. Curriculum Design and Development

The future of the industry depends upon the availability of highly skilled graduates, hence the industry should make it clear the type of students that it needs for its requirements. Accordingly, the University can start tailor-making its educational programmes to suit the specific requirements of the industry. To make the curriculum more effective, the industrialists may be co-opted as the members of the academic bodies of the University who can provide significant inputs to the designing and developing the curriculum.

2. Action-Oriented Research

Universities are the basic sources of ideas and techniques, which through their research studies can have a profound impact on the operational efficiency and the financial viability of the industry. It has, however, been felt that the research studies are more academic than being based on the needs of the industry. Hence, the University and the Industry together should join hands in identifying areas of research and the University to carry on the research on behalf of the Industry. Thus, greater empiricism can be ensured in the research studies undertaken by the University.

3. Financial Support

Industries get benefited from the University by way of educated/ professional manpower and of new, innovative ideas relevant to industries. Industry can think of reciprocating by making voluntary contributions out of the profits earned. Such funding may also be encouraged by extending the benefit of tax exemptions to such contributions made by the industry. Besides, the industry may also support seminars, symposia, conferences etc., organised by the University where the interests of the former are involved. Further, Industry can set up Chairs in the University which would benefit both the academicians and industrialists.

4. Platform for Practical Training

The skills as required by the modern industry cannot be taught in the classrooms but on the jobs. Hence, the students should be sent to Industry for 'Inplant Training' in different job areas according to their specializations. "Industry can train more effectively, more economically and with greater skill than can a University or School of Business."[6] Thus, by providing platform for practical training, Industry makes the graduates readily acceptable and thereby solve the problem faced by the University in turning out the erstwhile unemployable graduates.

5. Consultancy Services

The University possesses the necessary expertise to offer consultancy services to the Industry on the critical areas like entrepreneurship, product design, modification/development, cost management, tax planning, financial engineering, personnel development packages' etc. Such consultancy services not only add to the income of the teachers but also improve their quality of teaching because of their involvement into the live issues of industry. It also gives new insights into probable areas of further research.

6. Faculty Improvement

In order to make the teaching and research more effective and result-oriented, arrangement for teachers to spend sometime in industry and work there on its problems may be thought over. Besides, the senior level executives in the Industry may be invited to the University as the parttime/visiting Faculty. This arrangement fusions an effective linkage between theory and practice in imparting instructions.

7. Management Development

The University on the request of the Industry, can develop programmes and systems for its employees of managerial cadre according to the contemporary needs. Arrangement of such programmes and the participation therein, facilitate the continuity of education, updation of knowledge, and the upgradation of skills of the personnel. Besides, the teachers of the University may be invited as the Visiting Faculty to the In-House Training Cells of the Industry.

From the preceding discussion, it is clear that there are so many overlapping areas of activity and concern between the University and Industry. The benefits that each can derive from the other are fairly well-identified and ascertained. Hence, the dynamics of close interaction between the University and Industry is strongly recommended.

IV

PREREQUISITES OF MEANINGFUL INTERFACE

The programme of linkage being a bipolar process, expects from both the University and the Industry to fulfil the following prerequisites :

1. Responsiveness and dynamism on the part of University and Industry,
2. Identification of common areas,
3. Openness in making each other know about their expectations and limitations,
4. Willingness to forge linkages,
5. Statutory/institutional sanctions,
6. Financial viability and academic feasibility, and
7. Inclusion of other functionaries like Practising Accountants, Bankers, Engineers, Lawyers, etc. in the linkage programme.

These prerequisites go a long way in fusing the linkage between the University and the Industry for the common good. If the interface programme is implemented as envisaged, the universities will be fit to be called as institutions imparting, innovating, creating the knowledge of universal application.

REFERENCES

1. *The Challenge of Education*, Ministry of Education, Government of India, New Delhi, (1985), p. 6.
2. *The Report of the Curriculum Development Centre*, published by U.G.C., has identified totally 115 papers for undergraduate and postgraduate studies in commerce.
3. Industry Academia Interaction, *Chartered Financial Analyst,* November, 1996, p. 25.
4. K.L. Johar, Economic Reforms and Management Education, *University News*, August 12, 1996, p. 2.
5. Madhuri Shah, Universities and National Development, *University News*, April 15, 1979, pp. 2-7.
6. Gordan and Hawell, *Higher Education for Business,* Ford Foundation, (1959), p. 112.

47 Management of University B-Schools

—R.L. HYDERABAD

INTRODUCTION

With the advent of LPG policies in India, the industrial scenario has undergone a dramatic change. The entry of MNCs with funds and technology has forced the Indian corporates to rise from their deep slumber. The family-managed Indian corporates are craving for professional approach to keep themselves fit and free to face the onslaught unleashed by competition. Business mergers, amalgamation, demergers, restructuring, environmental and societal concerns, etc. are not only discussed in Indian corporates' board rooms but a spate of such changes has also been observed in recent times. The competition bug has not spared even the Public Sector Enterprises and restructuring and divestment policies have already been unfurled to make them 'competition fit'. The financial sector is also witnessing tremendous changes both in the form of contents and quality. Innovative instruments are employed to quench the hunger for funds by corporates and means of holding money by 'ever-unhappy investor' in the capital market.

STRUCTURE OF MANAGEMENT EDUCATION

In the midst of such fluid and hazy business environment, the industries require professional touch. There has been a burgeoning demand for B-school graduates to guide and lead corporates profitably and productively. Industrialists are vying with each other in attracting the best talents to their corporates by offering the attractive pay packages.

To catch this clamour for B-school graduates, the number of management institutes are on the rise in India in the last one-decade. There are basically five varieties of B-schools, which offer full-time postgraduate courses. The structure can be depicted in the form of a pyramid, adopting quality of education imparted as the basis :

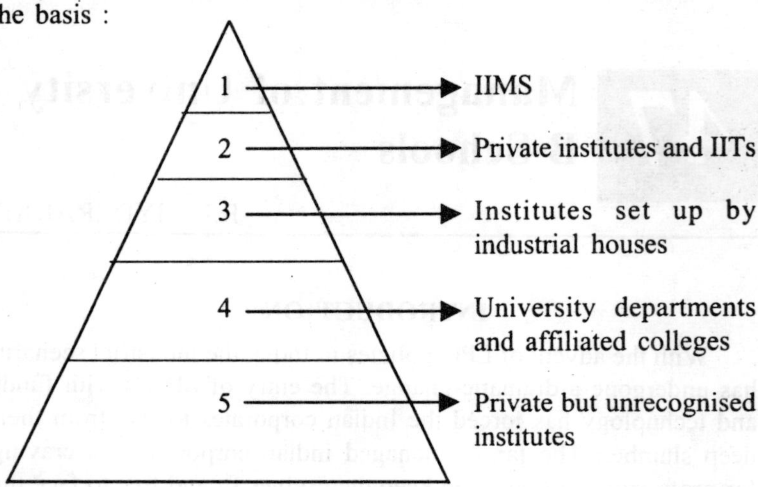

Fig. 1 : Structure of Management education in India.

The top layer is dominated by Indian Institutes of Management [IIMs] established at different places. These are the premier institutes and are singled out as the established centres of academic excellence.

The second layer consists of exceptionally sound and competitive B-schools under private management and management departments of Indian Institutes of Technology [IITs]. Symbiosis [Pune], S.P. Jain Institute of Management and Education [Mumbai], Bharatidasan Institute of Management [Thiruvantapuram], etc. are some of the private B-schools, which have achieved excellence in management education.

The B-schools established by industrial houses take third position in terms of quality of education. Nirma Institute of Management [Ahmedabad], Prestige Institute of Management [Indore], Kirloskar Institute of Management [Harihar], etc., are some of the examples. The financial resources and manpower at their command prod them to produce equally competent management graduates.

Barring a few well-managed university departments and affiliated colleges, by and large institutes in the university system take fourth layer. Finally, there are the 'fly-by-nights' institutes that had better remain unnamed, that also indulge in academics. These are those 'also rans' who continually look at the bottom line and have an attitude of 'what is in it for me'. Usually, these do not have any full-time faculty to back their programmes and are managed by administrators having an 'interest' in education or some bureaucratic work experience that fits the bill.[1]

OBJECTIVES OF THE STUDY

The top three layers are the best managed and efficient B-schools while the fifth layer consists of those schools about whom 'the less said, the better it is'. No amount of efforts would be sufficient to improve their performance.

It is in this backdrop, the quality of management education provided by the university departments and affiliated colleges, which are mushrooming now-a-days, assumes importance and are the real cause for worry. The universities are extending affiliation benefits to many institutes throwing to the wind their own rules and regulations. The management education has become a general education and the number of MBAs to the list of unemployed is growing. Big business houses shun these graduates as 'half-baked' for the job of managing corporates. These B-schools have dual affiliating agencies, namely the AICTE and the respective area universities. The authority wielded by these agencies has not yielded the desired result in stemming the rot in management education. The gullible students are continued to be lured by their advertisements, affiliation information and grand announcements.

Except for the Jamanlal Bajaj Institute of Management Studies [JBIMS] and the Faculty of Management Studies [FMS], which are affiliated to Mumbai University and Delhi University respectively, the top-10 B-schools in India are dominated by IIMs, IITs, private and industrial houses' management institutes.

Table 1 gives information of top-10 B-schools in India.

TABLE 1

Top-Ten B-schools

1.	IIM, Ahmedabad
2.	IIM, Calcutta
3.	IIM, Bangalore
4.	IMT, Ghaziabad
5.	NITIE, Mumbai
6.	FMS, Delhi
7.	IIM, Lucknow
8.	XLRI, Jamshedpur
9.	Jamnalal Bajaj, Mumbai
10.	S.P. Jain, Mumbai

Source : *The Economic Times*, 5 March, 2000, Bangalore, p. 1.

The present paper traces the problems/difficulties encountered by university run B-schools in imparting quality education. Further, the paper aims to provide plausible remedies to arrest the rot in the education.

WHAT AILS UNIVERSITY MANAGEMENT DEPARTMENTS AND AFFILIATED MANAGEMENT INSTITUTES?

Inadequate Infrastructure Facilities

The majority of management institutes in the university system are ill-equipped as far as infrastructure facilities are concerned like well-furnished buildings, libraries, computer facilities, etc. Further, some are located in places where there are hardly any industrial unit worth the name, thus depriving the students of the first-hand experience of industrial working.

Poor Curriculum

The institutes suffer from the common malaise of teaching outdated/obsolete curriculum. No efforts are made to tune the syllabi according to changing environment. This is basically because of strenuous procedure involved at university level in getting new curriculum drafted and approved.

Management is an inter-disciplinary science. However, curriculum lacks this basic requirement. Strategic planning in curriculum development is also conspicuous by its absence. Use of outdated case studies is also another menace among these institutes. Traditional areas of business functioning, namely, finance and marketing are given undue importance much to the negligence of other spheres of management.

Ill-equipped Faculty

Another important grouse of university management institutes is ill-equipped and insufficient faculty. Many times the rules of the AICTE are flouted with impunity in faculty recruitment. Guest faculty, visiting faculty, part-time faculty, etc. are the means adopted to run through the academic year. Further, the faculty has been found to lack abundantly inter-disciplinary approach. Too much emphasis is laid on specialisation. Training and faculty development programmes are found to be grossly inadequate or sometimes not available to equip oneself of the continuous changes in business environment.

Administrative Laxity

Administrative lack-lustre is another contributing factor for the present malady of management education in the university system. The leaders of the institutes lack dynamism and suffer from bureaucratic syndrome. Opportunities for improvements are overlooked and preference is accorded to the traditional way of doing things. Cases of indiscipline and misbehaviour are not used to assert top man's powers and are used to settle private scores.

Laxity in Enforcement

Besides problems indigenous to the institutes, the AICTE and the universities are to be blamed for poor governance of such institutes. Affiliation is accorded with scant respect to the basic infrastructure facilities and faculty. Industrial map of the area is also ignored in granting permission for opening up of the management institutes. Delayed revision of syllabi, infrequent inspection of institutes, incompetent inspection team, preference for collecting affiliation fees than proper functioning, etc. are some of the reasons contributing for the downfall of MBA institutes.

FUTURE OUTLOOK OF UNIVERSITY MANAGEMENT EDUCATION

The LPG policies have come to stay. India cannot remain immune to technological and informational changes sweeping across the world over and has to gear up its wherewithal to meet the challenges. The LPG policies would give equal credence to both large and SSI sectors. Both the sectors have to employ strategic methods and contribute to the industrial progress. Professional approach is the need of the hour in injecting strategic concerns in both the sectors. This calls for large number of MBAs or business graduates, who are fit enough to guide entities to sail smoothly through the roughshod business environment.

The products of IIMs, IITs and other industrial houses' business schools are not adequate in numbers to fully meet the demand for professional experts. Many times such graduates are lured by lucrative offers from the western world. This leaves the ground to the graduates from the university system. Institutes in the university system should recognise the vacuum and should make allout efforts in trimming their institutes, faculty, infrastructure, etc. to satisfy the demand for B-schools graduates. Quality of management education of IIMs, IITs, etc. could be replicated by the universities without much difficulty. In fact, the universities are the traditional schools of business education. From the universities, the B-schools of western type have grown and flourished.

The university management institutes can become centres of innovation and creativity. New direction and orientation are necessary in generating new knowledge and ideas. Management education is a dynamic process and the corporate management always expects newer and improved ways of doing things. A constant search for better things is always the objective of corporates. Change is the eternal truth of business. Management institutes have to fulfil this objective by constantly generating new knowledge and its dissemination to business sector. A knowledge created is wealth created. New knowledge enables a business to optimise resource utilisation and to achieve goals set for. Men, money, materials, machinery, etc. are extinguishable resources. A better use of these resources saves cost and optimises profit. A new orientation is all what management institutes of universities require to germinate and disseminate new frontiers of knowledge. Strategic thinking, liberal financing, academic autonomy, better curriculum, etc. can all change the facelift of university management education.

SUGGESTED MEASURES

The paper aims to provide the following dictum for the better management of university management institutions in particular and for the resurrection of management education in general. The dictum is "Quality, Cost-effectiveness, Autonomy and Innovation [QCAI]". The detailed strategies to be adopted in the dictum are outlined below.

Quality

The success of any enterprise, be it industrial or educational, is always decided by the quality of the outturn of that particular institution. User-made product is always saleable in the market. This can be adopted in building curriculum, infrastructure facilities and faculty development.

(a) Available funds collected through capitation fees should be deployed to streamline information facilities. Adequate number of computers, networking, well-equipped libraries, etc. ensures process quality.

(b) Qualified and trained manpower should always be preferred. Ample opportunities for faculty development, industrial visits, consultancy, foreign trips, academic exercises like research, conferences, workshops, etc., should be provided, encouraged and financed.

The faculty should have men with practical experience. For this purpose industrial executives, management consultants, practising CAs, CWAs, LWAs, CSs, etc. should be drafted for the noble cause of management education. Continuous interface should also be ensured between permanent management faculty and visiting industrial executives whereby theory could be thrashed to suit facts and practices or an ill-advised practice could be rectified.

These measures ensure manpower quality.

(c) Prospective candidates should be selected thoroughly and selection should be made through tests, group discussion, etc. Interaction, participation in academic exercise, working of case studies, completion of assignments, visits to industrial units, preparation of project reports, etc., should be strictly enforced. An independent group should evaluate the completion of all these requirements. This ensures input and output quality.

(d) Continuous comparison between what is taught and what is required by users should be done with a view to make curriculum more user-friendly. All pedagogical issues should be recognised. People from industries should be drafted in curriculum development.

The case study method, which is increasingly being used, is indeed a two-edged sword. It is an excellent pedagogical tool, but only if handled well. If it is not used to develop theory, it degenerates into story-telling exercises.[2]

Thus, an improved process, manpower input and output qualities guarantee business success and rebuild confidence.

Cost-effectiveness

Cost and quality do not always move in tandem. Higher quality is achievable at higher cost. Cost-effectiveness is concerned with the maintenance of best quality at the lowest minimum cost. The cost-effectiveness ensures that management education is available to all classes of people and will not be a distant dream for meritorious but belonging to poorer sections of the society. An institution, which has cost-consciousness as a philosophy would inculcate the similar values in its outturn.

Autonomy

The management institutions, both departments and affiliated colleges, should enjoy absolute academic leeway in framing as well as in revising the course contents. Industrial map must also be considered in granting affiliation and autonomy. Frequent review of academic performance should be done by the universities and the AICTE for renewal of affiliation or autonomy.

Innovation

A paradigm shift is very much necessary in course contents. Rather than a meek follower of Japanese and western style of management philosophies, these institutes should evolve India's own management philosophy by looking at their own backyards. The world has not seen a greater manager of resources than Lord Shri Rama, who fought a war with the Ravana and his henchmen with the help of monkeys. There is no greater strategic thinker and planner the world has seen than Lord Shri Krishna in Dwaparayuga. To reestablish the 'Righteousness', he used just Five men and got rid of the world all the evil doers. Thus, 'Ramayana' and 'Mahabharata' are repositories of great management principles. A well-thought reorientation will churn out all that can be termed as 'Indian Management Philosophy'. Besides, Indian family values, culture, ethos, etc. provide rich management principles. For the future of their existence, the institutes under university system should rethink, reorient and modify their approach on these lines.

EPILOGUE

All these steps, if adhered to and followed, would prove beneficial to management institutes in the university system and put them on the recovery path and in the long run products would be as competitive and acceptable as any other management institutes in India.

REFERENCES

1. Sorab Sadri, Placement Time in B-schools, *Indian Management*, Vol. 38, No. 7, July, 1999, p. 22.
2. Sorab Sadri, *op. cit.*, p. 24.

48 Re-Designing of Commerce Education in India in the Context of Changing Business Environment

—D. OBUL REDDY

PURPOSE OF EDUCATION

The broad objectives of the University education are liberal education with the aim of fostering in the students an attitude of objective enquiry and some understanding of the society and social change, of the problems of human relationships and the human and social implications of technological change, and developing a capacity to appreciate the finer values of life *et cetera*. These broad objectives are taken as implied in the case of business education also.

Education should be a three-fold process of imparting knowledge, developing skills, and inculcating proper attitudes and values towards life and society in general. It must enable the individual to develop the activity and skill to earn and carry on reasonable standard of living and it must also enable him to develop his creative faculties to the utmost so that intellectually, morally, physically and spiritually he is in a position to enrich his personality.

BUSINESS EDUCATION

What is Business/Commerce Education? Leverett S. Lyon defined Business Education as "any education which a businessman has which makes him a better businessman, is for him business education, no matter whether it was obtained within the walls of a school or not".

Fredrick G. Nichols defined commerce education in the following words : "Commerce education is a type of training which while playing its part in the achievement of the general aim of education on any given level has for its primary objectives the preparation of people to enter upon a business career or having entered upon such career to render more efficient service therein and to advance from their present levels of employment to higher levels."

Thus, Business Education is that area of education which develops the required knowledge, skills and attitudes for the successful handling of trade, commerce and industry.

COMMERCE EDUCATION

Till yester years, commerce education is business education. But, in tune with the needs of the business and society, independent professions have emerged in the form of chartered accountant, cost and works accountant, company secretary and business administrator (M.B.A.). Thus the cream of commerce has gone and it remained now as an academic discipline giving general and liberal education. Hereafter, I will concentrate on commerce education.

Commerce education is an integral part of total education system. The term commerce originally refers to and includes all those activities which create time, place, form and person utilities, for individual and social ends. It is a living discipline and is totally different from other disciplines. Hence, it must charter new routes to service the aspirations of the nation. To man the economic development of the country and to meet the growing needs of the society, there is greater demand for sound development of commerce education in Indian Universities. But, what has been going in the name of Commerce education is only liberal and general education. Is that the objective of commerce education? In the process of catering to everybody, we are not able to cater the needs of anybody.

STATE AND STATUS OF COMMERCE EDUCATION IN INDIA

Commerce Education in India was started in 1886, over a hundred years ago. Since then it has experienced tremendous growth. Commerce faculties are established in about 140 Universities out of a total of 226 Universities including deemed Universities.

In order to understand the progress of commerce education in India since Independence and its present position, we have to rely on statistics. But adequate and up-to-date data are not easily available and the available data also are not consistent. However, to give a broad idea, some available data are collected from different sources and presented in Tables 1 to 5.

Table 1 presents the increasing number of commerce students since 1950-51. The increase in enrolment is substantial from 0.36 lakh in 1950-51 to 14.10 lakhs in 1995-96. Thus there is an increase of 3,780 per cent.

Table 2 presents the enrolment in M.Com. and B.Com. courses in India during last one and a half decades. One important feature of it is that the number of girl students in commerce is on increase in absolute and relative terms both at M.Com. and B.Com. levels.

Table 3 presents the proportion of enrolment at B.Com. and M.Com. levels. It is clear from the table 3 that about 8% only are going for M.Com./higher education. About 92% stop with graduation. Therefore, there is a need to make commerce graduation courses more meaningful and purposeful.

Table 4 presents the number of commerce students state-wise and Table 5 presents the distribution of students in higher education (in percentage terms). From these data certain broad conclusions can be drawn :

(i) Commerce is popular in industrialised states.

(ii) Commerce is more popular in urban areas rather than in rural areas.

(iii) It has spread throughout the country. Now it has taken roots in all the States and Union Territories, even though started late.

(iv) If we analyse the enrolment during the last two decades (see Table 5) in percentage terms, commerce share in total enrolment has increased from 17.1% in 1975-76 to 21.9% in 1995-96, whereas all other faculties exhibited either a marginal decline or *status quo*.

TABLE 1

Number of Commerce Students in Recognised Institutions — All India

Year	No. of Students	% Increase 1950-51 = 100
1950-51	36,347	100
1955-56	58,918	162
1960-61	78,312	215
1965-66	1,57,996	435
1968-69	2,75,385	758
1969-70	3,27,722	902
1970-71	3,54,615	976
1975-76	6,16,983	1,697
1983-84	6,46,654	1,779
1991-92	11,54,804	3,177
1995-96	14,10,119	3,880

Sources:
1. 1950-71 : *Statistical Abstract of India*, 1975, C.S.O., Deptt. of Statistics, Ministry of Planning, G.O.I., p. 505.
2. 1975-76 : *Statistical Abstract of India*, 1982, p. 507.
3. 1983-84 : *Educational Statistics at a Glance*, Association of Indian Universities, New Delhi, 1987, pp. 184-85.
4. 1991-96 : *U.G.C. Annual Report*, 1995-96.

Thus, a single discipline commerce, which accounts for about 22% of the total enrolment in higher education, unlike Arts or Sciences consisting of many departments, unfortunately is not getting adequate attention to its needs from the Government and UGC. Further, it is not properly understood by the administrators also. This is being equated with one subject such as Physics, Mathematics or Public Administration. This is a Faculty by itself and should be recognized so. In this regard, the Indian Commerce Association should play a vital role.

TABLE 2

Commerce Enrolment in Educational Institutions by Stages and Sex in India

Stage	Sex	1980-81	%	1883-84	%	1995-96	%
1	2	3	4	5	6	7	8
M.Com.	Boys	36,464	92.4	47,370	86.7	60,635	76.7
	Girls	3,013	7.6	7,251	13.3	18.377	23.3
	Total	**39,477**	**100.0**	**54,621**	**100.0**	**79,012**	**100.0**
B.Com.	Boys	4,13,081	86.0	4,77,367	80,6	7,92,456	70.6
	Girls	67,361	14.0	1,14,666	19.4	3,30,017	29.4
	Total	**4,80,442**	**100.0**	**5,92,033**	**100.0**	**11,22,473**	**100.0**
M.Com. & B.Com.	Boys	4,49,545	86.5	5,24,737	81.1	8,53,091	71.0
	Girls	70,374	13.5	1,21,917	18.9	3,48,394	29.0
Grand Total		**5,19,919**	**100.0**	**6,46,654**	**100.0**	**12,01,485**	**100.0**

Sources : 1. 1980-84 : *Educational Statistics at a Glance*, Association of Indian Universities, New Delhi, 1987, pp. 184-85.

2. 1995-96 : *Selected Educational Statistics*, 1995-96, Ministry of HRD, GOI, New Delhi, pp. 16-18.

TABLE 3

Commerce Enrolment in Educational Institutions By Stages In India

Stages	1980-81	1983-84	1995-96
M.Com.	39,477 (7.6)	54,621 (8.4)	79,012 (6.6)
B.Com.	4,80,442 (92.4)	5,92,033 (91.6)	11,22,473 (93.4)
Total	**5,19,919 (100.0)**	**6,46,654 (100.0)**	**12,01,485 (100.0)**

Sources: 1. 1980-84 : *Educational Statistics at a Glance*, Association of Indian Universities, New Delhi, 1987, pp. 184-85.

2. 1995-96 : *Selected Educational Statistics*, 1995-96, Ministry of HRD, GOI, New Delhi, pp. 16-18.

TABLE 4

Number of Commerce Students : State-wise

Sl. No.	State	1970-71	Rank	1995-96	Rank
1	2	3	4	5	6
1.	Andhra Pradesh	24,690	4	95,473	4
2.	Arunachal Pradesh	—	—	225	28
3.	Assam	4,240	13	12,462	16
4.	Bihar	12,545	8	2,55,574	1
5.	Goa	469	19	6,938	17
6.	Gujarat	42,010	3	1,26,450	3
7.	Haryana	1,642	14	15,690	15
8.	Himachal Pradesh	186	21	5,972	18
9.	Jammu & Kashmir	919	18	4,188	19
10.	Karnataka	24,535	5	76,581	5
11.	Kerala	11,794	9	18,086	12
12.	Madhya Pradesh	17,810	6	58,960	8
13.	Maharashtra	87,143	1	2,31,263	2
14.	Manipur	112	23	608	24
15.	Maghalaya	—	—	728	23
16.	Mizoram	—	—	260	26
17.	Nagaland	—	—	367	25
18.	Orissa	1,160	16	16,404	13
19.	Punjab	1,447	15	16,091	14
20.	Rajasthan	14,156	7	18,810	11
21.	Sikkim	—	—	148	30
22.	Tamil Nadu	7,282	11	57,039	9
23.	Tripura	1,152	17	1,926	20
24.	Uttar Pradesh	11,679	10	66,742	7
25.	West Bengal	81,950	2	71,977	6
26.	A & N Islands	—	—	198	29
27.	Chandigarh	419	20	1,615	21
28.	D & N Haveli	—	—	—	—
29.	Daman & Diu	—	—	248	27
30.	Delhi	7,107	12	37,137	10
31.	Lakshadweep	—	—	—	—
32.	Pondicherry	168	22	1,325	22

Sources : 1. 1970-91 : *Statistical Abstract of India*, 1975, p. 505.

2. 1995-96 : It consists of only B.Com. & M.Com. and is compiled from *Selected Educational Statistics*, 1995-96, Ministry of HRD, GOI, New Delhi, pp. 16-18.

TABLE 5

Distribution of Students Enrolled in Higher Education by Field of Studies — All India

Faculty	1975-76 Percentage	1984-85 Percentage	1995-96 Percentage
Arts	44.5	40.0	40.4
Science	19.1	19.7	19.6
Commerce	17.1	21.0	21.9
Education	3.2	2.4	2.3
Engineering & Technology	4.0	4.5	4.9
Medicine	4.3	3.8	3.4
Agriculture	1.2	1.3	1.1
Veterinary Science	0.3	0.3	0.3
Law	5.8	6.0	5.3
Others	0.5	0.6	0.8
Total	100.0	100.0	100.0

Source : *UGC-Professional Competency in Higher Education*, Centre for Professional Development in Higher Education, University of Delhi, 1996, p. 201.

PROBLEMS OF COMMERCE EDUCATION

Expansion of liberal commerce education, as a matter of fact indiscriminate expansion in its wake, has brought about certain problems too. The quantitative expansion has definitely resulted in qualitative degeneration. As a result, today a commerce graduate has little edge over his counterparts in being selected to such positions which were once considered his domain at one time.

The present courses are not adequate in preparing the students for competitive examinations either. The present system of commerce education does not equip the students either for taking up jobs requiring knowledge of general subjects or jobs that demand knowledge of a technical or specialised nature. Time has come now when a commerce graduate is not being accepted even as a qualified book-keeper. Consequently, he finds himself in a 'no man's land' neither a generalist nor a specialist.

In such a situation it is but natural that the popularity of the course declines. The process has started in many States especially in rural areas. The reasons for unpopularity/weaknesses of commerce education are :

(i) Craze for Medicine, Engineering and Management courses.

(ii) *Unpopularity of commerce at competitive examinations* : the syllabi of commerce at competitive examinations is not attracting even the meritorious commerce students.

(iii) Commerce graduates are not eligible for teacher training courses, such as B.Ed. in many States.

(iv) Lack of knowledge about commerce at school level as commerce education is not introduced at school level in many States.

(v) No preference or reservation for commerce graduate either in employment or in admissions to professional courses like C.A., C.W.A., CS, M.B.A., etc.

(vi) Poor teaching in many colleges forcing many students to go for tuitions, which means additional cost and effort.

(vii) High student and low teacher ratio.

(viii) *Lack of proper infrastructure* : it is sometimes remarked that many colleges are virtually academic slums.

(ix) Instruction in regional media and inadequate or non-availability of reading material in regional media.

(x) Inadequate teaching aids.

(xi) Untrained and ill-equipped teachers.

(xii) Lack of practical exposure both to the teacher and taught, perhaps commerce may be the only practical subject which is theoretically taught without practical exposure.

(xiii) *Defective admission policy* : in many a case students who are not able to get seats in other courses are opting for commerce. In such a case it is futile to expect wonderful results.

(xiv) *Commerce teacher is a jack of all trades* : perhaps he is the only person who is expected to teach all the subjects.

(xv) Paucity of funds for improvement.

Thus, commerce education is facing innumerable problems today. These problems have a direct bearing on the course objectives, course content and course conduct. These problems need serious attention and close scrutiny. It is high time for soul searching for an objective appraisal which will provide the basis for evolving a new strategy for giving a better deal to commerce education in the years to come. Therefore, the need for an all-out effort to re-orient and re-design the commerce education in such a way that it will be relevant for today and tomorrow. For this we have to make some sort of SWOT/TOWS ANALYSIS.

T — Identify the threats to commerce education.

O — Identify the areas of opportunities still available for commerce even after providing for CA, CWA, CS and MBAs and new opportunities into which you can enter.

W — What are your weaknesses because of which you are not preferred. (Here, deliberate efforts have to be made to overcome the weaknesses.)

S — What are your strengths, if any? It is better to concentrate and consolidate on your strengths.

MAJOR ISSUES TO BE ADDRESSED

The following are the major thrust areas (issues) which need to be properly addressed to ensure relevance to our education more particularly to commerce education :

(i) What should be the admission policy and procedures?

(ii) What should be the nomenclature of the degrees?

(iii) What skills are required to be imparted to commerce students so as to make them cater to the needs of industry and business?

(iv) Would you like them to be generalists or specialists in some skills?

(v) What should be the nature of subjects and content of the subjects?

(vi) What should be the duration of the Course?

(vii) How to ensure practical exposure?

(viii) What is the pedagogy? (*i.e.*, teaching methods and aids.)

(ix) What type of examination and evaluation system is required to ensure quality?

(x) How to ensure faculty training and development?

(xi) How to achieve and sustain University/College and industry linkage?

(xii) What are the areas of Research which need encouragement?

RE-DESIGNING OF COMMERCE EDUCATION

Having identified the domain, let us now come to the structuring/designing. While doing so level also should be kept in mind for framing the course objectives, course content and course conduct. The conventional levels are :

Level I : Pre-University or + two stage. (Two years)

Level II : Graduation (Three years)

Level III : Postgraduation (Two years)

In the changed scenario, non-conventional duration or integrated courses also may be thought of. While designing the courses the following should be adhered to, which I remember to have studied in my economics subject.

Three qualifications are essential for a "Good" before it can have value :

(i) it must possess utility (relevance),

(ii) it must be scarce,

(iii) it must be marketable.

All these three qualities are essential together. In the absence of anyone of these qualities a "Good" will have no value at all. Of course, this aptly describes our predicament.

The main branch of business education *i.e.* Commerce has gone in for quantity rather than quality, due to the pressure of demand and reached the present stage and state. The same thing is happening in case of another branch of business education *i.e.*, management education. It is time for them to learn lessons from the Commerce Education. In case of other professional streams *viz.*, CA, CWA, CS, even though entry barriers are not there, exit is not easy. Hence, they are able to maintain their status.

Any re-designing requires a systematic survey of the needs of the business and the society and a careful planning of the structure of commerce education and the numbers required. Unfortunately, there has been no systematic survey of manpower requirements in our country, nor is there any educational planning nor manpower planning. The courses are subject to shortages and surpluses from time to time. The expansion of commerce education has gone by hunches and irrational mass hysteria of demand.

It was observed that "the system of higher education was producing a prototype of manpower, where as developing economy required wider capabilities; hence for many jobs suitable persons were not available. There was a mismatch between types of capabilities demanded and the types of capabilities developed among students by the education system".[1] Further, the year 1991 witnessed major shifts in economic and social development policy in India. India opened its economy to world market by adopting a policy of economic liberalization. This in turn posed the challenges for higher education for producing competitive and suitable human resources. Hence, the need for redesigning and diversifying the undergraduate and postgraduate programmes.

Added to this, "as the economy becomes more industrialized and society becomes more complex, the knowledge and skills required to deal with the situations also change. Hence, for enabling students to acquire the desired capabilities, contents of courses and their combinations need to be revised, diversified and made more flexible".[2]

The first step in re-designing of commerce courses is that there should be a survey of requirements of business and industry, in terms of nature of courses and number of graduates. This requires a close liaison and co-operation with industry and business to find out their requirements of men and skills. If the courses are designed as per the requirements and the students are trained on those lines, then, the courses become relevant and the product saleable, instead of preparing the courses in an all-pervasive manner without any market in mind. The contents and delivery system must be tailored to meet the specific needs of the target groups for whom the courses are designed.

The various ALTERNATIVES available for re-orientation of commerce education are :

(i) *Academic-Oriented Courses* for giving liberal commerce education, for developing quality of mind, logical thinking, initiative, attitude to life and a general understanding of business.

(ii) *Self-Employment Oriented Courses* such as taxation, management accounting, financial analysis, cost accounting.

(iii) *Job-Oriented Courses* such as computer accounting, salesmanship, advertising, secretarial practice, etc.

(iv) *Management-Oriented Courses* : The Institutes of Management in the country are catering to the demands of elitist managerial personnel of industry. We need a second level of personnel to cater to the requirements of small and tiny industry.

In India, there are many small and tiny industrial units, particularly in the rural areas which need management orientation and a fair dose of management culture. We should strive to create a new class of LICENTIATE MANAGERS for them.

(v) *Professional-Oriented Courses* with complete practical bias just as engineering and medicine. They may be 5-year integrated courses with commerce laboratory/ workshop.

(vi) *Vocational Courses* : The U.G.C. has already launched some vocational courses such as B.Com. salesmanship and advertising, B.Com. Taxation, B.Com. Foreign Trade with 1/3 vocational component. Where these courses are run with rigour, they are doing well. They may be further strengthened with 2/3 vocational component instead of 1/3.

Of course, a word of caution is not to proliferate with too many degrees to avoid problems of recognition and equivalence, etc.

CONCLUSION

As you are aware, in a growing economy much of the expansion takes place in service sector (tertiary sector) which particularly requires the type of skills and knowledge that our courses offer. The much-needed practical bias also can be brought in with the developments in information technology, and with the help of a colour television, video cassettes and computers. Our market is vast and their requirements are varied. Hence, we have to provide for varied courses and not one straight jacket. The changes are very fast and our courses also must keep pace with the changes. Therefore, we have to adopt ourselves to the changing environment.

We cannot stop suddenly what is happening. But, we can plan for the future. Let the liberal and general education be there but mostly confined to open universities and correspondence courses. Let us develop micro specializations which are skill-oriented or job-oriented and introduce with new nomenclature and in selected colleges which are financially sound and have the necessary infra-structure facilities. Preferably, such colleges may be asked to have industry linkage with a Memorandum of Understanding, with industry with regard to practical training, guest lectures, teacher training, etc. The admission to such courses must be selective and restricted. Alternatively, the evaluation, system should work like the quality control laboratory of an industrial establishment.

The learned delegates may take this opportunity for an objective introspection about the commerce education — its objectives, its problems, its job potential, its quality and its relevance to the present-day needs of our county. Let it not be said that men of our generation failed to give it a timely turn towards new meaning and usefulness.

With these few words, I take leave of you, thanking the organizers of this Conference for giving me this opportunity and thanking you too for your patient hearing.

REFERENCES

1. S.K. Khanna & G.D. Sharma, "Changing Scenario of Higher Education in India", in *U.G.C. Professional Competency in Higher Education*, p. 199.
2. *Ibid.*, p. 201.

49 Impact of E-Commerce and Internet on Accounting Education, Profession and Practice

—P.B. APPA RAO

1. INTRODUCTION

Information is recognized as an important resource. A wide variety of information needs of a business are organized into what is called management information system (MIS). A management information system consists of inter-connected subsystems. They provide the information necessary to stay competitive. Accounting information system is the most important subsystem because it plays the key role of managing the flow of economic data to all parts of a business. As an information system it collects and communicates economic information about a business enterprise or other entity to a wide variety user whose decisions and actions are related to the activity. All this is made possible by the use of computers. The computer is an electronic tool that is used to collect, organise, analyse, interpret and communicate vast amounts of information with great speed. Accountants were among the earliest and most enthusiastic users of computers, and today they use microcomputers in all aspects of their work.

An accountant sitting in front of a small table opening a large bound book and writing with a fountain pen or a ballpen is an anachronism now-a-days. A modern accountant sits in a revolving chair, in front of a computer monitor and a keyboard, logs himself in and keeps himself responding to beeps is a reality. A conventional accountant has no place in the present setup is a fact. Accounts are not maintained in books but in chips, measured not in words but in bytes, written not in ink but with stylus inside the computer on motherboard, secured not by lock and key but by the use of passwords and ciphers.

The use of computers increased the pace of business, globalisation increased competition. Electronic Data Interchange (EDI) facilitated the speedy, secured and accurate transfer of documents across the globe and emergence of E-commerce blurred the boundaries of sovereign states. Increase in the pace of the business and competition both at home and abroad, a need to preserve the quality and thereby profitability is felt strongly today. Computers make possible a paperless working system. If computer of a businessman or a manufacturer is linked up with those of his customers and suppliers all the transactions can be done electronically. All these and a few other developments have brought a phenomenal change in the accounting education, profession and practice towards which accounting teachers, professionals and practitioners cannot afford to turn a blind eye and deaf ear.

2. E-commerce — Meaning

To understand better the impact of E-commerce and Internet on accounting education, profession and practice it is necessary to understand the meaning of the E-commerce and related concepts better.

Prashant Jain defined Electronic Commerce (E-commerce or EC) as "the exchange of business information using electronic formats, including Electronic Mail (e-mail), Electronic Bulletin Boards (EBBs) and Electronic Funds Transfer (EFT). E-commerce Technologies are designed to replace traditional paper based work flow with faster, more efficient and reliable communications between computers." He further stated that "E-commerce" is the process of two or more parties making business transactions via computer and some type of network, *e.g.*, a direct connection or the Internet.

This includes business-to-business transactions, online retail, and the digitalization, of the financial industry. Some experts and leading 'Netropreneurs' even argue the E-commerce includes all the steps that occur in any business cycle, such as placing ads, completing invoices, and providing customer support. The term

E-commerce, often used interchangeably with IBM's coined term E-business, covers a lot of ground and refers to all these areas.

As per the Microsoft Computer Dictionary Electronic Commerce is a "commercial activity that takes place by means of connected computers. Electronic commerce can occur between a user and a vendor through an online information service, the Internet, or a BBS, or between vendor and customer computers through electronic data interchange (EDI)". IBM has used the term E-business for E-commerce.

Electronic Data Interchange is "a set of standards for controlling the transfer of business documents, such as purchase orders and invoices, between computers. The goal of EDI is the elimination of paper work and increased response-time" (*MS Computer Dictionary*, p. 169). EDI facilitates transfer of business documents stored in structured formats — through mutually agreed messaging protocols from one computer application to another. Thus EDI is a tool for business-to-business communication. E-commerce, on the other hand, is a concept reflective of the infrastructure and technology available for conducting business using the electronic media.

Through *EDI and E-commerce*

(a) orders from the customers can be analysed and executed without any delay,

(b) orders can be raised to reflect both demand and stock availability,

(c) instructions can be sent to distributors in parallel to ensure faster deliveries,

(d) carriage by road, rail, sea or air can be booked simultaneously, and

(e) customs clearance can be obtained even before the goods arrive.

All this can be done without any paperwork.

E-mail is "the exchange of text message and computer files over a communication network such as a local area network or the Internet, usually between computers or terminals". It is also defined as "an electronic text message" (*MS Computer Dictionary*, p. 173).

Internet is "the world-wide collection of networks and gateways that use the TCP/IP suite of protocols to communicate with one another. At the heart of the Internet is a backbone of high-speed data communication lines between major modes or host computers, consisting of thousands of commercial, government, educational and other computer systems that route data and messages. One or more Interment nodes can go off line without endangering the Internet as a whole or causing communications on the Internet to stop".

3. ADVANTAGES OF E-COMMERCE

Shopping on the Internet provides with a fascinating experience. In traditional shopping a busy customer has to travel all the way to a local store to purchase things. If he is not satisfied goes to another shop and so on. In the process he will be wasting lot of time and energy. A busy person finds it difficult to go in search of a product of his liking. On the other hand a potential customer can turn to web, browse different shops and place orders for a variety of articles without wasting his precious time and energy.

E-commerce saves operating costs by eliminating human intervention in order processing.

E-commerce is profoundly influencing the structure of business supply chains. For example, Chrysler Corp., by linking to its suppliers through a Web-based network, reportedly saved more than $ 1 billion in cost of materials in 1977. By 2000, Chrysler's estimated annual average savings would amount to $ 2 billion (Subramanyam, 1998, p. 49).

One of the most exciting developments springing from E-commerce is the higher degree of personalization that is made possible. In the past, business designed a product with a mass market as a target. Now, using the reach, the information and processing power available to a business and with their customers' approval, suppliers can gain a more comprehensive knowledge of their clientele. They can use this knowledge to customize their products/services. Further, the relationship with the buyer can span a lifetime. As customization grows, suppliers will begin to differentiate their brands as much on an understanding of the customer as on price and quality.

E-commerce is a round-the-clock advantage for the customer. E-commerce allows fast and flexible execution and response to market opportunities. The Web enables a company to introduce a new product, get immediate customer reaction, refine and perfect without heavy investment and with much greater assurance of success.

Companies betting on E-commerce can learn about their customers' online buying habits.

4. DISADVANTAGES OF E-COMMERCE

Web shopping differs from traditional shopping in many ways. One of the most important differences is web shoppers' inability to browse a virtual store for merchandise. In a real store the customer can walk through the general area looking for the merchandise required by him before homing in on the exact product he wants to buy. On the other hand an online shopper turns to search tools to locate products. Ideally, he types in a word or phrase and gets back a list of products meeting his needs. The engines insist on exact and correct spelling, they cannot extrapolate from a simple phrase, and often they come up with bizarre products that are nowhere near what the customer is looking for. (Chuck Musciano, 1999, p. 11)

In personal inspection one can select or reject the merchandise several times before he finalizes the transaction and makes payment. But in online shopping he cannot do so. He cannot also look back into contents of his basket to decide whether his shopping is complete or not.

Many commerce sites do not allow order checking and cancellation. Naturally a customer would like to know whether his order has been executed or not, if not, reason for the same. In addition to that, customer may change his mind, items may get lost and cheques may bounce. A good commerce site must allow order revision and monitoring but in practice many commerce sites do not. (Chuck Musciano, 1999, p. 11)

Customers who browse the commerce/web sites do not take a fixed route. They enter in some page or the other at random and try to come out early to another product page, home page, check out page or the customer registration page. Many commerce sites are not designed to facilitate such an easy entry and exit (navigation). (Chuck Musciano, 1999, p. 11)

E-commerce may further widen the gap between the haves and have-nots. Online business transactions require a computer and an Internet connection, which have not yet come within the reach of a common man. Hence E-commerce and Internet may further marginalise the poorer population groups and countries.

In E-commerce customer relations may actually be in jeopardy. Led to believe they are transacting in real-time, they could become disillusioned and take their business to competitors or back to the offline world if their order is not fulfilled quickly. Obviously, changes must be made before the promise of E-commerce can be fulfilled.

The biggest challenge for companies involved in electronic commerce is not the technology but it is changing the corporate culture. It requires an organization to be bold.

5. INTERNET AND E-COMMERCE IN INDIA

Dewang Mehta, executive director, NASSCOM, said, EDI and E-commerce have become extremely essential for the Indian economy. According to a study undertaken by the Indian Market Research Bureau (IMRB) a mere 30 per cent of business in India which have the means to access the Internet have a Net connection at their premises. A special correspondent of *The Hindu* reports the development of Internet and E-commerce in India as follows :

(a) Net commerce came to India over the Last on year — and the impact on all sectors of business is only now becoming apparent. It is expected to become possibly the fastest growing area of IT in the coming months.

(b) For travel companies, whose clientele has a geographical spread across national borders, "going on the Net" makes sound commercial sense. Amadius, the market leader in CRS saw its terminals in India increase fifty fold in four years, to over 1,500 this year. Galileo, which began operations in India at about the same time, has about 1,200 terminals.

(c) In recent weeks, Indian Airlines jettisoned its creaky old on-line reservation system and moved to a new IBM ES-9000 based network. Air India has joined SITA to put the "Gabriel" CRS on its Unisys mainframe computer. Among the private carriers only Jet Airways subscribes to a CRS — "Sabre".

(d) Indian Internet sites like "Indiapavilion" (www.indiapavilion.com) which uses a server in North Carolina and a Chennai-based channel partner, Saigan Connections, or Indiamart (www.indiamart.com) from the Delhi-based Intermesh Systems, now offer Net-based umbrellas which shelter dozens of commercial sites — doing brisk business in a mind-bogging array of products. Indiamart boasts links to 60,000 Indian companies — manufacturers, importers and exporters, service providers and NRI operations.

(e) The high profile presence on Internet of global book-sellers like Amazon or Barnes & Noble has encouraged some India-specific book dealers to set up shop on the Net. The U.S.-based India Book House (www.indiabookhouse.com) specialized in books by Indian authors. The Mumbai based India Bookshop (www.indiabookshop.com) set up recently has quickly notched up Rs. 10,000 worth of orders in the opening week. And from Chennai, Tulika Books (www.tulikabooks.com) aims for a niche in children books in Indian languages.

(f) The "India on Internet" site from Calcutta (www.allindia.com) is another anchor for interesting commercial and information services : including the largest dealer in jute based products, Aarbur. Today one can buy fresh vegetables in Delhi by leafing through the catalogues at Baba Bazaar and pizzas in Chennai from Prizza Deli.

(g) Assisting smaller business houses, which want to graduate to "e-selling", has now emerged as a new service niche. Three engineer-entrepreneurs, Messrs. Ninad Pradhan,

M.S. Sridhar and S.K. Anand, saw an opportunity in the need for Indian language based commercial sites. They are the brains behind Domain Host India — a service which helps small businesses create, maintain and do business from Websites, at costs which could be as low as Rs. 1,500 per month. What's more they offer special font software, which enable the sites to "speak" most Indian languages. Many of their clients share their site (www.indianlanguages.com; ww.indiansites.com) but their unique URL (universal resource locator) or site name gives them "virtual sites" of their own.

(h) New players like Satyam Infoway and Manipal Control Data (MCD) focus even more sharply on the world of EDI — Electronic Data Interchange. Satyam has set up its own E-commerce backbone spanning eight Indian metros. The early clients, to use its expertise include the Cochin Chamber of Commerce, which now enables its members to exchange all import-export documents electronically.

(i) 'Delhi on the Net', a first ever comprehensive Website on the city of Delhi is now available on the Internet at http://www.ace101.com. It has been launched by Ace Internet Services, a consultancy firm. The Website contains comprehensive data of all the hospitals, discotheques, schools, markets, shops, parks, hotels, restaurants, historical places, libraries, cinema halls, etc., located in Delhi. Foreigners and other visitors planning to visit Delhi can get lots of practical tips, and other vital information from this Website. (*Information Technology*, February 1998, p. 16)

6. IMPACT ON ACCOUNTING EDUCATION, PROFESSION AND PRACTICE

Rapid strides in technology have changed the way the accounting is done. Today, PCs are an integral part of the accountant's appendage. Accountant who shuns technology has no place in the present-day business environment. Global Internet based trade practices include surfing the net, ordering by e-mail, remitting the money and generating the documents electronically, and copying and transmitting the documents through EDI.

This is an age of transition. Computers and systems concepts are not completely used by both small and big businesses. Hence accountants shall be able to maintain books of accounts both in computer-free and computer environments.

The electronic computer does not affect accounting principles because they are independent of processing methods, but the enhanced processing capabilities of the computer have improved the capability of organizations to implement advanced management information systems which were not practical using manual processing methods. Therefore, those involved in the accounting and information system of an organization should understand the capabilities of computers and the changes in data processing potential because of the computer. In organizations using the computers for data processing, the accountants shall be able to understand computer data processing methods and the organization and processing of computer files. The ability to do analysis, to provide meaningful reports and/or to prepare statements depends, to a great extent, on the existence of appropriate files and processing capabilities. The accountants shall also understand quality control for computer processing because the reliance, which should be placed on computer-based records, is dependent on the quality of files and accuracy of processing. Hence it is appropriate for any programme on accountancy to have systems course prior to accounting and auditing courses. For an accountant background in computer programming is also desirable though not essential. However, an accountant must be able to use front-end tools.

Recognizing the need some of the software development companies have released accounting packages. The students and practicing accountants have to acquire the capacity to use the accounting packages like WINGS, TALLY, FOCUS, PROFIT and E.X.NGN — the latest Business Accounting software from TCS.

Now-a-days many companies are using ERP packages like Oracle, Oracle Financial, BaaN, SAAP and People Soft. So the accountants have to be familiar with the use of one or more ERP packages.

Online trading is possible only through Internet. Hence accountants shall also acquire capabilities necessary to use the internet. Once accountants learned Dbase to make software the way they wanted it to be. But now the accountants have to learn Tcl/Tk. Tcl/Tk will do for the Internet what Dbase did for databases. With Tcl/Tk one can do whatever he wants directly. He does't require the help of professional intermediary to create Web pages on the Internet (Vijay Mukhi, Oct. 1996, p. 9).

In the second-generation E-commerce transfer of money takes the form of bytes — chains of zeros and ones. These are *Digital Value Units* (DVUs) which can be transferred easily without any loss of time from one computer to another computer at any place in the world with a few keystrokes. Only at the end of the journey it is transformed into cash or coins. Different forms of electronic money are under development. They are increasingly used in E-commerce. Accountants shall acquire the capabilities required to use electronic money of different types. Electronic money can be divided into three general forms. They are : (a) Electronic Debit and Credit Systems, (b) Smart Cards, and (c) Digital Cash.

(a) Electronic Debit and Credit Systems : Electronic debit and credit systems already exist. When a consumer uses an ATM card to pay for merchandise, funds are transferred from his or her account to the merchant's account. Credit cards are used to make payments over the Internet. Software products such as *Intuit* provide an electronic bill payment facility. Electronic debit and credit systems represent new and more convenient means of payment.

(b) Smart Cards : Smart cards are plastic credit cards with an embedded microchip. They are used over transit payment devices. They can be loaded with currency at an ATM counter. This money can then be spent over vending machines, or turnstiles equipped with appropriate devices. A smart card is simply a debit card that does not require a bank approval for each transaction. Banks and other institutions can provide value on smart cards through loans, payments for services, or products. Any immediate transfer of funds between bank accounts is not necessary;

units of value can circulate from card-to-card — and from user-to-user — without debiting or crediting third-party accounts. By reposing confidence in a creating institution, 'money' can be created on smart cards, and can circulate almost indefinitely before redemption. *Mondex* is an example for a smart card or electronic purse. It can be 'loaded' with electronic money from an *automatic teller machine* (ATM). Money is spent either by swiping the card through a retailer's terminal, or by using a card reader and a personal computer with an Internet connection. An electronic wallet allows an anonymous card-to-card transfer.

(c) **Digital Money :** Electronic money can take a truly digital form (existing as units of value in the form of bytes stored in the memory of a computer), and may or may not be backed up by reserves of real money. This 'money' can be downloaded from an account, supplied as a loan or payment, or bought with a credit card over the Internet. As long as digital cash can be authenticated, and there is confidence in its continued acceptance, it can circulate indefinitely, allowing peer-to-peer payments at will. These conditions pose big 'ifs', but they are well within the realm of the possible.

Certain advantages can be derived from using the E-cash. They are anonymity, security and divisibility. Anonymity of the transaction can be maintained. Public-key encryption technology and digital signature allow blind transactions, Identity of the payer can be kept secret. It is difficult to track the transfer of E-cash. It also offers a high security, as it is impossible to alter the value of E-cash. E-cash is almost infinitely divisible. Filters can be set in an electronic purse to screen out E-currencies that are not acceptable.

Accountants shall also be aware of computer technology and internal control principles in computer-based applications system. They shall at least know the fundamentals of data processing systems.

Twenty-first century is going to become an age of E-commerce and/or E-trade. A large number of competing E-currencies offering anonymity, security, divisibility, liquidity, convenience and swiftness will enter into the market. For a customer selection becomes difficult and for the Government control over the business becomes difficult.

All over the world the number of companies and countries using EDI and E-commerce are increasing. The E-commerce capable countries are setting deadlines for countries not equipped with similar capabilities. For example Singapore declared that it wouldn't keep trade relations with those countries that do not acquire EDI and E-commerce capabilities by July 1998. Almost 99 per cent of the Fortune 1000 companies have already implemented EDI. It is very difficult to imagine the backward thrust a company or country suffers because of delay in the implementation of EDI and E-commerce. Hence the choice is between E-trade and no trade.

REFERENCES

1. Anurag Sharma, "Policy Issues in E-Commerce", *Software Review*, January 1999, pp. 18-23.
2. A special Correspondent, "Internet Commerce - Burgeoning Opportunities", *Survey of Indian Industry 1998, The Hindu*, Madras, 1998, p. 111.
3. Balasubramaniam, T.N., E-commerce, Is it Working? *Computers Today*, January 1998, pp. 48-50.
4. Chuck Musiciano, "Are you ready for E-commerce?" *Express Computer*, February 8, 1999, p. 11.
5. *Computer Dictionary*, Microsoft Press, Washington, Third Edition, 1997.
6. George H. Bodnar and William S. Hopwood, *Accounting Information Systems*, Allyn and Bacon, Inc., Boston, 1987.
7. Pattabhi Ram, "Professional Accountant in CIRCA 2000 AD", *The Chartered Accountant*, October 1996, pp. 14-19.
8. Prashant Jain, "Doing Business on the Web", *Software Review*, January 1999, pp. 12-16.
9. Ramesh Menon, "E-Commerce — An Overview", *Software Review*, January 1999, pp. 9-11.
10. Rich Niemiec, "Getting Ready for E-Commerce", *Oracle Magazine*, November/December 1998, pp. 89-92.
11. Stephen J. Kobrin, "The End of National Markets", *Information Technology*, February 1998, pp. 65-67.
12. "The New World Order", *Information Technology*, July 1998, pp. 29-30.
13. Vijay Mukhi, "Tcklets — Internet Programming for the Common Man", *The Chartered Accountant*, October 1998, pp. 8-9.

List of Contributors

R.M. Chidambram, Professor and Head, Department of Bank Management, Alagappa University, Karaikudi-630 004 (T.N.)

H.R. Appannaiah, Principal, K.P.H.R. Institute of Management Studies, Bangalore-560 062 (Karnataka)

Parimal Vyas, Reader in Marketing Management, Department of Business Studies, Sardar Patel University, Vallabh Vidyanagar-388 120 (Gujarat)

Sandip Bhatt, Reader in Finance and Accounts, Department of Business Studies, Sardar Patel University, Vallabh Vidyanagar-388 120 (Gujarat)

Nafees Baig, Department of Commerce, Aligarh Muslim University, Aligarh (U.P.)

T. Aranganathan, Reader in Commerce, Annamalai University, Annamalainagar-608 002 (T.N.)

D. Nagayya, Former Director, National Institute of Small Industry, Extension Training, Hyderabad (A.P.)

G. Kotrappa, Professor of Commerce, University of Mysore, Mysore-570 006 (Karnataka)

S. Narasing Rao, Senior Manager, Malaprabha Grameena Bank, Head Office, Dharwad (Karnataka)

M.R. Patil, Senior Lecturer in Commerce, V.N.S. Bandekar College of Commerce, Mapusa (Goa)

T.M. Popker, Research Scholar, Department of Commerce, Goa University, Goa.

M.C. Poornima, Asstt. Professor, KLS Institute of Management Education and Research, Belgaum-590 006 (Karnataka)

H.K. Shubhangi, Lecturer, KLS Institute of Management Education and Research, Belgaum-590 006 (Karnataka)

M.R. Shollapur, Faculty Member, Department of Commerce, Karnatak University, Dharwad-580 003 (Karnataka)

A.H. Chachadi, Former Chairman and Dean, Management Faculty, Kousali Institute of Management Studies, Karnatak University, Dharwad-580 003 (Karnataka)

Z.U. Kahrioowala, Reader in Commerce, Aligarh Muslim University, Aligarh (U.P.)

Rais Ahmad Khan, Lecturer in Commerce, Institute of Agriculture, Aligarh Muslim University, Aligarh (U.P.)

M.S.M. Al-Shaikh, Research Scholar, Department of Commerce, Aligarh Muslim University, Aligarh (U.P.)

M. Manickam, Professor and Head, Department of Commerce, Bharathiar University, Coimbatore-641 046 (T.N.)

C.S. Rayudu, Reader in Commerce, S.K. University, Anantpur (A.P.)

S.B. Nageswara Rao, Reader in Management Studies, Annamalai University, Annamalainagar (T.N.)

S.S. Hugar, Professor, Chairman and Dean, Faculty of Commerce, Karnatak University, Dharwad-580 003 (Karnataka)

S.G. Hundekar, Reader in Commerce, Karnatak University, Dharwad–580 003 (Karnataka)

M.R. Chandawarkar, Principal, SRN Arts and MBS Commerce College, Bagalkot-587 101 (Karnataka)

K.K. Kuriakose, Baselius College, Kottayam (Kerala)

Shreedhar Shetty, Head, Department of Commerce, MSRS College, Shirva-Udupi (Karnataka)

Manjunath Kotian, Faculty of Commerce and Business Studies, S.B. College, Karkala-574 104 (Karnataka)

C. Kishan Rao, Senior Faculty Member, Southern India Bank Staff Training College, Bangalore (Karnataka)

P.S. Yadapadithaya, Reader in Commerce, Mangalore University, Mangalagangotri-574 199 (Karnataka)

M.P. Hrishikesh, Reader in Commerce, S.B. College, Karkala-574 104 (Karnataka)

A.B. Kalkundrikar, Professor and Research Guide, Gogte College of Commerce, Belgaum-590 006 (Karnataka)

M.R. Hegde, Department of Commerce, SPE College, Udupi-576 101 (Karnataka)

A.C. Bhawsar, M.S.G. College, Malegaon Camp, Nashik-423 105 (Maharashtra)

M.K. Rakibe, M.S.G. College, Malegaon Camp, Nashik-423 105 (Maharashtra)

B. Vijaya, Reader and Chairman, Department of Commerce, Gulbarga University, Gulbarga-585 106 (Karnataka)

Bheemanagouda, Research Scholar, Department of Commerce, Gulbarga University, Gulbarga-585 106 (Karnataka)

A.P. Kalkundri, IV Semester Student, KLS Institute of Management, Education and Research, Belgaum-590 006 (Karnataka)

A.G. Prasad, Department of Commerce, Sardar Patel P.G. Centre, Secunderabad-500 025 (A.P.)

Y. Vrushabhendrappa, Principal, Bapuji Institute of Engineering and Technology, Davangere–577 004 (Karnataka)

E.B. Brahmankar, Principal (Rtd.), KKW College, Nashik & Former Dean, Faculty of Commerce, University of Pune, Pune (Maharashtra)

Sandeep Shandilya, Research Scholar, Department of Commerce, Jamia Milia Islamia, New Delhi.

G.Y. Shitole, Faculty of Commerce, SNDT Women's University, Mumbai-400 020 (Maharashtra)

S.S. Ainapur, Research Scholar, Department of Commerce, Gulbarga University, Gulbarga (Karnataka)

C.S. Basavaraj, Reader in Commerce, Gulbarga University, Gulbarga (Karnataka)

P.N. Udayachandra, S.D.M. College, Ujire (Karnataka)

K. Swamy, Asst. Professor of Business Administration, Dr. B.R. Ambedkar Open University, Hyderabad (A.P.)

S.H. Tekkannavar, Reader in Commerce, Government First Grade College, Bilagi-587 116 (Karnataka)

V.M. Bhandari, Faculty of Commerce, S.D.M. College, Honavar (Karnataka)

S.G. Kulkarni, Gogte College of Commerce, Belgaum-590 006 (Karnataka)

G.A. Hegde, Head, Department of Commerce, Government College, Pernem-403 512 (Goa)

P.G. Dandin, Senior Lecturer in Commerce, G.V.M's College, Ponda (Goa)

R.V. Ganachari, Senior Lecturer in Commerce, S.J.R. College, Race Course Road, Bangalore-560 009.

G.L. Narayanappa, Faculty Member, Kandula School of Management, Cuddapah (A.P.)

D. Pradeep Kumar, Faculty Member, Kandula School of Management, Cuddapah (A.P.)

V. Mallikarjuna, Faculty Member, Kandula School of Management, Cuddapah (A.P.)

B.L. Pawar, Department of Commerce and Business Management, M.S.G. College, Malegaon Camp, Nashik-423 105 (Maharashtra)

J.G. Naik, Professor of Commerce, Gogte College of Commerce, Belgaum-590 006 (Karnataka)

R.L. Hyderabad, Reader, Postgraduate Department of Studies in Commerce, Karnataka University, Dharwad-580 003.

D. Obul Reddy, Department of Commerce, Osmania University, Hyderabad-500 007 (A.P.)

P.B. Appa Rao, Professor and Head, Department of Commerce, Sri Krishnadevaraya University, Anantapur-515 003 (A.P.)